Dragons & Violins

A Memoir of War and Music

DAVID A. ARMSTRONG

BookLocker.com, Inc.
2010

To my mother Georgeanne,
who taught me how to be strong in the world

How should we be able to forget those ancient myths about dragons that at the last moment turn into princesses; perhaps all the dragons of our lives are princesses who are only waiting to see us once beautiful and brave. Perhaps everything terrible is in its deepest being something helpless that wants help from us.

RAINER MARIA RILKE

Contents

Chicago, 1956

I HAVE ONLY one photograph of the occasion, yet the image shows me many things. With it and the imagination my grandfather nurtured in me, I can relive as if I were there the important evening in the sweltering summer of 1956 when he performed a violin solo at Orchestra Hall with members of the Chicago Symphony Orchestra as part of the conservatory's summer season-opening concert. His performance of Mozart's "Concerto in A Major for Violin and Orchestra" was the culmination of an intense, region-wide competition, one for which he had practiced ceaselessly for months, the kind of accomplishment he had set his heart on for four decades at least—since the time when he had been a small boy in Persia, the son of a skilled Assyrian craftsman who made tars, the long-necked Persian lutes whose sound bowls are covered with lambskin.

My grandfather was born a musician and throughout a life of huge challenge and high adventure—one in which he repeatedly struggled to survive—it was the violin and the music of Mozart, Beethoven, Brahms, and Mendelssohn that fascinated him, moved him, and to which he brought his colossal persistence and dedication. Born near the salt-encrusted shore of Lake Urmia in far northwestern Persia—a place that today is part of Iran— my grandfather traveled with his family on foot and by train to Russia to escape the slaughter of Assyrian, Armenian and Pontic Greek Christians by marauding Kurds and Turks, endured the famine that presaged the Russian revolution, saved his mother from rape at the hands of a tsarist soldier, then, miraculously, escaped with her to teeming Constantinople, now Istanbul, where they awaited visas that eventually would allow them to sail to the United States.

Born Sargis Georges Yadgar, my grandfather arrived at Ellis Island on July 4th, 1921, and he long since had become a citizen with the Americanized name of George Edgar—as well as an aspiring Olympic gymnast and aeronautical engineer—when he and his fellow combat

1

engineers came ashore at Normandy's Utah Beach four days after D-Day, then fought all the way to the outskirts of Berlin. He had become a captain and been awarded a Bronze Star for bravery by the time he returned home to Chicago where his wife Ann and a daughter he had yet to meet—my mother—eagerly awaited him. He would live seven decades longer, immensely productive years during which he would father a son, help design and develop the microwave oven, infrared scopes for the military, as well as a host of other technological advances, co-establish the Santa Barbara Symphony Orchestra and play in its violin section for thirty years—and became the person in all the world to whom I foremost turned for friendship, adventure, solace, support, and, most importantly, love.

Yet it was his treasure trove of stories from the first extraordinary decades of his life to which I clung. The stories from those years were the tales I longed to hear again and again as a boy, tales into which I could escape from my own troubled childhood.

*

After everything he survived, it was far from Poppy's most violent account, nor was it his most heroic, but the story of the evening when he performed a violin solo with members of the Chicago Symphony was his favorite tale. He had set out to prove to himself and to others that he was a musician of the very first rank, and had practiced far into every night in order to be ready for the competition he ultimately won. Even decades later, I would be soothed into sleep by the sounds of my grandfather practicing his violin until 1:00 or 2:00 in the morning, the pleasure he took from the music and the striving for perfection distracting him from bed.

In the photograph I keep on my desk at home, my grandfather is dressed in black tuxedo trousers, a white dinner jacket, and a black bow tie. His dark hair is cropped short on the sides, and his 1950s-era glasses frame his expressive eyes. I wasn't with him that evening, of course, and my twelve-year-old mother and my grandmother were seated high in the mezzanine, each of them nervously waiting for the concert to begin. But it's certain that Poppy wasn't anxious as he waited offstage. Somehow, in the difficult and adventurous life that led up to that moment, he had learned how to vanquish fear and replace it with steady-handed resolve and the strictest sort of discipline.

I can see in my mind's eye the steely focus his face must have conveyed when the orchestra's conductor brought him on stage, and I can watch him walk into the spotlights of the great concert hall with the same athletic stride he still exhibited as his years waned half a lifetime later in California. He had survived extraordinary trials in nearly a dozen countries in reaching that Chicago stage. This impoverished and largely abandoned son of an Assyrian lute maker had proven himself a remarkable man along the way and was about to prove to himself in the moments to come that he was indeed a violinist.

*

With my grandfather's support and guidance, I grew up to be a successful director and cinematographer working in Hollywood while he remained in nearby Santa Barbara. I was wise enough over the years to bring a camera along on many of my regular visits, and, over time, I amassed dozens of hours of videotape of him describing his life and adventures, something he did with the clarity of memory and precision of expression that he brought to every other endeavor.

What follows on these pages is the story of my grandfather's early life, as he told it—and in his voice. Although he is gone now, I'm renewed each time I hear him describe his first decades, years in which he was intimately linked to some of the twentieth century's most monumental events, a life that began quite precariously inside a barn, his mother and a cow in a nearby stall both laboring and giving birth at precisely the same moment, while gunfire flashed all around them in a harsh land torn apart by war.

Chapter 1

A Faraway Place

I WAS BORN at a violent time in a faraway place you can hardly imagine. No one, not even my mother, remembered precisely when I came into the world, but it was springtime, of that much she was certain—she knew the trees were budding and that early flowers had begun to bloom. People in our distant corner of Persia paid little attention to record keeping in those days, and saw no need to make lists of the births, marriages, and the deaths that were rather commonplace, after all. I might have been born two or three years earlier, but my mother's best recollection was that I arrived in the spring of 1912, at a time when the winter snows had receded enough to allow Kurdish tribesmen to cross the mountains on horseback and descend on the village called Sheinabad where my parents lived at the time, the Kurds stealing everything they could—food, wine, tools, money, rifles, sometimes even terrified children snatched from their mothers' arms.

The story I heard from the time I was very small was that on a day when my father and other men from the village were crowded into a small parapet on the roof of the barn, firing at the Kurds to keep them safely at bay, my mother, whose name was Khatoon, or Katherine, lay in the interior of the barn below, far into labor and ready to give birth. A high wall made of mud bricks stood near the thin mat on which she reclined; the wall leaned precariously, and it worried Khatoon as she lay twisting in pain, trying with all her strength to push me into the world. Somehow, she got to her feet and staggered away just seconds before the wall collapsed to the ground where she had lain. A milk cow in the barn was deep into labor as well, and its slippery, half-liquid calf came first, accompanied by a bellowing moan of relief from its mother. A moment later, I arrived, and a woman assisting my mother slapped air into me and suddenly I was alive and screaming. As soon as she had attended to me and secured me to my mother's breast, the woman carried the news up to the roof to my father, yelling at him amidst the gunfire, "Georges, you've got a new son!"

According to the story I heard so often I began to think I remembered the day myself, my father shouted back that any boy who chose to be born at a moment like that would surely grow up to be a bum, and his lifetime of subsequent insults makes me believe those almost certainly were the first words he directed toward me. For some reason, from that very first moment, he needed to hate me—not so much for what I'd done, but evidently simply because I existed. And, beginning at that moment, I did exist—a tiny little thing with a wobbly legged calf for a nurse-mate, a heavily burdened mother who had too many kids already, and a father who wanted nothing whatsoever to do with me, surrounded by Kurds who would have been rather gleeful if they could kill us all.

*

When I was two, my family moved from Sheinabad to a place they hoped would be a bit safer—a town called Alwach whose residents were long-persecuted Christian Armenians as well as Assyrians like us, Aramaic-speaking Christians who were the original inhabitants of Mesopotamia and inheritors of the culture of ancient Assyria. Early in the twentieth century, the Armenian and Assyrian homelands were a place of perpetual conflict, and we lived in constant fear of the Muslim Arabs, Persians, Kurds, and Turks who encircled us on every side.

Violence was as commonplace as daylight in that corner of the world, but the beautiful plain of Urmia to the west of the saltwater lake was etched with small rivers that fed lush gardens, vineyards, orchards, melon, tobacco, and even rice fields. Lake Urmia itself was enormous—ninety miles long and fifty miles wide, it's glassy and heavily brackish water punctuated by more than a hundred islands where migrating birds would briefly rest as they traveled north and south.

Like most families in Alwach, we raised sweet and delicious grapes, most of which we sold to the local vintners each autumn, our vines planted behind a wall of linked houses to protect them from the Kurds. The exterior walls of the rows of houses were built of mud-and-straw bricks, the flat roofs of timbers and stout planks that allowed people to sleep on them when the weather was hot and even the slightest breeze was welcome. Inside our house, everyone slept on woven mats on the packed-earth floor, but the focal point was the canuda, an adobe-walled pit inside of which a fire for cooking constantly smoldered. My mother would bank the fire as she began to prepare each meal, and I remember that all of us would sit around as if it were a table, careful to keep our feet from the hot coals.

*

By all accounts, the man who sired me, but who had tired of the rewards and responsibilities of raising children by the time I entered the family, was a superb woodworker. In addition to the beautiful tars that local musicians would travel dozens of miles to purchase from him, he could fashion virtually anything from wood. And like many other men in Alwach and nearby villages, he often left home to find work in distant cities, sometimes traveling as far as Russia, where he would join building crews or work in factories making furniture or wooden molds for casting steel. He would be gone for months at a time, then return with paper money—something our household otherwise seldom had—staying home until, inevitably, my mother was pregnant again and the money was spent, leaving the family without a father and husband once more.

Soon after I was born—and I was the youngest child—my brother Polous, eighteen years my senior, left home as well, traveling to the city of Urmia where he attended an American mission school that was operated by Christians and tolerated by the Persians because they respected its teachers and musicians. That left my sister Nanajan, intelligent like Polous and quite beautiful; Sophia, whose temper was as fierce as a gale; Maria, second from the youngest, and me at home with our mother. I was still very young during the brief time I lived in that house, but I remember being innocently happy there, buoyed by the meals we shared and the warmth that spread out from the canuda to embrace us all, my sisters and I safe and secure every night, my mother constantly tending to our meals, my father absentmindedly playing the tar, one of the dozens he'd made, its familiar but haunting sound filling the small house as the light of the lanterns seemed to flicker in time to his strumming.

My playmates during each day were the animals we kept—cows and sheep and the two horses that patiently endured my playing at their feet—and in those early years I know I learned something important from those creatures about being steadfast and loyal and something too about what it meant to care for them. Love for those animals poured out of me, and I thought they cared for me equally in return, and I learned that I could count on animals in ways I couldn't always depend on people, even the people, such as my father, to whom I might have been closest.

My mother loved me without reservation, of that I was always certain. But she had a mountain of work to accomplish each day, and her long evenings kept her at the canuda until our often-meager supper was done. Then, she would mend clothes and attend to a dozen other tasks before she finally stole a bit of time to read the Bible. There were no other books in the house, certainly none meant for children, and sometimes at my insistence, she would read biblical passages aloud to me, and I loved the curious stories about people

7

with strange and exotic names. The Bible, it seemed to me, was full of stories about war, and I began to imagine that life itself was very much shaped by war when the Kurds and Turks returned with more bloodshed very much on their minds.

With the outbreak of World War I and the international chaos it wrought, the Kurds were emboldened to attempt to take total control of far northwestern Persia. First, they attached and plundered the regions of Tergawar and Mergawar, many of the Assyrian and Armenian residents fleeing to presumed safety in Urmia, where Russian troops had been stationed for some time, keeping an uneasy peace. Then, in October 1914, the Kurds sacked and burned Alwach and the nearby town of Anhar as they advanced toward a massive assault on Urmia.

In a dozen towns and villages like ours, the "Mishelmani," as my mother called them, rode out from their redoubts in the surrounding hills, killing everyone they could find. Sometimes, a sole rider would gallop into a village and announce that on the following day he would return with a hundred men. The villagers lives would be spared, the rider would declare, but *only* if the villagers left their children behind and fled. And, as impossible as it is for me to remember, many young children—including my own aunt's—*were* tied to trees and left for the Kurds, in the desperate hope that some of the family might be spared. In our case, the marauders leveled our home to the ground, but, miraculously, none of us was captured or even injured, and my mother and my father—who happened to be at home at the time—saw no choice but to attempt escape, and the sole place they believed might be a safe haven was far southern Russia, immediately north of Ottoman Armenia.

We reached Urmia on foot, our beloved horses and other animals left behind to fend for themselves, and there we discovered that Polous, too, was safe. The Turks were at war with the Russians by now, and in early December, when Turkish soldiers succeeded in

destroying a railway line that led north to the Russian city of Tiflis—
now known as Tbilisi in independent Georgia—the tsarist
government was alarmed enough that it made immediate plans to
withdraw every Russian soldier from northwestern Persia to go join
the battle against the Turks.

The city of Urmia and the flood of Assyrian and Armenian
villagers who had crowded into its streets soon would be defenseless
against the Kurds and their new allies—the Turks. By Christmastime,
the situation seemed dire. As soon as the Russian withdrawal was
complete on January 2, 1915, the Kurdish and Turkish armies
blocked every road out of the city, trapping us in the bitterly cold
confines of Urmia, where my father and mother were certain we
would die.

Yet the rail lines had been repaired, at least temporarily, and,
somehow, thousands of Assyrians and Armenians were able to climb
onto long trains of flat-cars that rumbled north out of Urmia in the
first frozen days of the new and terrible year. I must have been about
four, and I remember how strange it seemed that we had to crowd
like bees in a hive on those rail cars. Why was everyone so frightened
and why were we riding open-air cars in the dead of winter? It was a
dreadful journey; we had no water, no place to relieve ourselves, and
except for those people crushed in the center of the flat-car deck, no
one was safe. Parents desperately held their children's hands, but
sometimes the car would lurch and a child would fall to the cinders
that sloped away from the tracks, his parents shrieking in horror,
screaming for someone to help, but every time someone fell off, the
train simply rumbled on, bound for the mountains of Armenia, and,
we, hoped, for freedom.

*

From left to right, Nanajan, Georges, Polous, Maria (seated), Sargis (George), Khatoon and Sophia, Urmia Persia, circa 1913

Assyrian Woman's Volunteer group of St. Mary's Orthodox Church of the East, Urmia, Persia 1912

Students of the Orthodox Church of the East in Urmia, Persia 1905. Polous Georges Yadgar (Paul Edgar) is #17 between boy #5 and #6

David A. Armstrong

An Assyrian priest, left, and Bishop Nisan of the Orthodox Church of the East, Urmia, Persia 1912

Market place butcher, Urmia, Persia 1912

We spent many long weeks in Ottoman Armenia, my father trying to arrange entrance visas for the six of us that would allow us to enter Russia. In Yerevan, and later in Gyumri, we were lost amidst the sea of the many thousands whose lives had been upended by the fighting, and who were fleeing—somewhere, anywhere—in hopes of encountering a place where they were safe from slaughter and where they might begin their lives again. I remember little more of those weeks than the masses of people, scurrying, running, shouting at family members to hurry along, everyone sensing, I suppose, that with movement came a bit of hope. Like everyone, we lived in daily terror, and Russia was only an imagined refuge that remained very far away.

Then, at last, my father secured the documentation we needed, and we boarded a train for Tiflis, just fifty miles or so across the Russian border. In earlier times, my father had spent several sojourns working in the Russian city and felt comfortable there. We found two small, dirt-floored rooms in the basement of an apartment building, rooms that became our home in a quarter of the city that teemed with refugees like us, people from other places, people with nothing except their desperation.

I was too young to understand why, but not long after we'd settled in Tiflis, my father left us once more, this time traveling to a faraway place called America to see if he could find work. Because those of us who remained behind spoke decent Russian—in addition to Assyrian, Farsi, Armenian, and some Turkish—it was relatively easy for my two older sisters to get work as servants in the homes of Russian Army officers—cleaning, cooking, washing clothes, taking care of the officers' children—and they regularly found ways to bring a bit of food home for us. Sometimes, too, we would wait for long hours outside the kitchens of the palatial houses where my sisters spent their days, and Sophia and Nanajan would appear suddenly with leftovers from the Russians' tables, then quickly run back inside.

But a couple of years after our arrival, my father had returned with news that Nanajan and Sophia were wanted elsewhere. Two cousins—who were related to us on my father's side of the family and who had known both girls back in Alwach—had safely emigrated to America, and, according to letters that somehow reached us in Tiflis, they were doing well in a place called Bristol, Connecticut, but now were in need of wives. One, named Sargis, formally offered to marry Sophia, and the other, Absalom Marshall, asked for Nanajan's hand. The two prospective couples knew each other only a little, but that wasn't unusual in those days, and in the tumult of 1916 the offer seemed to arrive as an opportunity sent to us by God, or at least that's the way my father saw it.

He knew and respected the two young men who were offering to pay the girls' travel expenses, then husband them throughout their lives; the children they would raise would help keep Assyrian culture alive, even in the United States, and when these two new Americans cousins offered to pay for my father's passage to the United States as well, the deal was done. Never mind that my father would be leaving his wife and three of his five children in a war-torn Russian city overwhelmed with refugees; never mind that our very survival would remain in doubt as they traveled. My father would send for the rest of us, he promised as he, Sophia, and Nanajan packed three small bags and walked out of the tiny room and out of our lives, the man who was certain I'd always be a bum, too eager to be underway, I suppose, to take a moment to tell me goodbye.

We wouldn't know the stories from their journey for many years, but actually reaching America was not such a simple matter for them. Because Assyrian Christians continued to be hunted and murdered, even inside Russia, my father and sisters pretended to be Russians themselves, traveling under the name Edgaroff as they crossed the breadths of Russia, Finland, and Norway before finally boarding a ship in Kristiania, now known as Oslo, and sailing across the Atlantic. It was an arduous and exhausting trip from Tiflis to faraway Connecticut, but the three of them had arrived at last, we knew, when a letter arrived assuring my mother that as soon as he had earned enough money, my father would send for us as well.

Six months after my father's letter arrived, my twenty-three-year-old brother Polous left Tiflis too—not for America and its many delights but for the Russian city of Sartov, where he would enroll in medical school, something the missionaries and teachers at his school in Urmia had made possible. It was Polous whom we knew was capable of great things, Polous whom everyone in the family looked to for support and counsel more than we did to my father, and my mother was thrilled to think that a son of hers one day would be a physician—it was wonderful just to imagine it—but Polous's departure left her with a thirteen-year-old daughter and a five-year-old son to care for alone, and who knew how we would eat and pay the rent on our damp, dirt-floored basement rooms?

*

The Russian people had grown weary of the world war by 1916. Two million soldiers had been killed in battle; two million more were prisoners of war, and a million army regulars had deserted. People in every part of the huge country hated the autocratic rule of Tsar Nicholas II, and in Tiflis their passions were equally intense. The Caucasus, in fact, was a hotbed of Bolshevik partisanship, and when the revolution began in the fall of 1917, thousands of the tsar's soldiers boldly strode through the streets of the city each day in a heavy-handed show of strength the government hoped would keep the revolutionaries at bay.

But the revolution and the civil war that followed were still young when their terrible violence descended on Tiflis. We felt the wall-shaking and always terrifying percussion of bombs during the long nights and sometimes watched in astonishment as buildings near ours burst into flames and burned to the ground. Mortar fire shrieked across the night sky; the bullets from machine-gun sliced through shadowy midday streets and alleys, and the fighting—and the killing—were things to which I quickly became accustomed. I can't remember why we were out in the streets, but one day my mother and I were with my friend Alexander, who I loved like a brother. He was fourteen and very grown up and worldly, it seemed to me. I was still no more than five or so and very proud to be in his company, and Alexander was clutching my hand to be sure I kept up as we crossed a busy street. Suddenly, we heard rapid machine gun fire and saw everyone around us, even the soldiers, begin to run. As we fled, too, Alexander fell to the pavement, and, as he let go of my hand, I felt a hot stinging sensation on my back, as if I'd been jabbed with the point of a fireplace poker. Then, I felt the sting a second time, but I was afraid for Alexander, and I rushed back to him and shouted, "Come on, Alexander, get up, get up!"

Alexander didn't move, however, and it was a moment before my eyes focused on the pool of blood that was spreading away from his head and the terrible wound that now marked his temple. I tried to lift him, but before I could, my mother grabbed me and whisked me off the street and into a nearby alcove. "Alexander fell! Alexander fell!" I kept shouting at her, but she begged me to keep quiet. "Alexander is dead," she whispered. "He's dead." It was only then that she saw that the back of my jacket was stained with blood. She gasped, lifted me in her arms, and as the gunfire subsided, we made our way back to our basement rooms.

By the time we got home, the pain from the bullets that had entered my back was intense. My mother laid me on a sleeping mat, stripped off my jacket and shirt, then left me for a moment while she gathered a shaving razor my father had left behind, a few clean rags, and a bottle of vodka. Small and strong and afraid of nothing, my mother took a long drink from the bottle, then poured some of the vodka on each wound, as well as on the razor. She used her own weight to hold me still, then dug into me to try to find the bullets. The pain was terrible, and I fought to escape it, but my mother was strong enough to hold me, and soon she held one of the bullets in her hand for me to see. She searched the second wound, and the pain made me scream in agony, but no matter how deep she dared push the razor, she never could feel it hit the hard metal of the bullet. When she gave up her search and ended the makeshift surgery, she cleaned my wounds with vodka again and bandaged me with strips of cloth. She offered me a sip of vodka to help ease my pain, but I didn't like the taste, and fell asleep in terrible pain, the images in my mind focused on my dear and trusted friend Alexander lying motionless in the street, his head surrounded by blood. I was too young to understand, I suppose, that my mother had saved my life. Nor could I have imagined that soon I would do what I could to return her favor.

*

Before he had marched off to America, my father had left his pistol and a few bullets with us, thinking, I'm sure, that they might help keep my mother, Maria, and me safe in his absence. I hadn't told my mother, but a distant cousin named Benjamin, who also had found his way to Tiflis from Urmia, showed me how to use the pistol, and I was quickly a decent shot with it as we practiced in the alleys.

One day, I was playing games in the street with my friend Abrahaim, and we noticed a group of the tsar's soldiers enter the large building where we both lived. After a while, I heard screams from inside, and, somehow, I knew they were the cries of my mother. I ran inside and down the stairs to the basement, terrified by what I might find. The door to our rooms was open, and inside I could see that a Russian Dragoon soldier had pinned my mother against the mattress and pallet we slept on, which were stored against a wall. She was fighting desperately to escape the soldier's grasp, shrieking in horror, and pleading with him to spare her. I *had* to help and was wise enough not to rush up to the soldier and try to tear him away. Instead, I slipped into the room where we kept the pistol, found it, and made sure it was loaded with bullets.

When, seconds later, I returned to the sleeping room, the soldier had his pants down, and he turned toward me with a look of disdain when I pointed the pistol at him and shouted at him to stop. "Get out!" I screamed in Russian, but he simply cursed at me and threatened that I would be next. As forcefully as I could, I announced that I would kill him if he didn't stop, and even with his pants at his ankles, the brute awkwardly tried to move toward me and snatch the pistol from my grip. As he lunged at me, I pulled the trigger and the bullet I fired tore his face apart. He fell instantly to the packed-earth floor and was dead, his blood and tissue heavily splattering my mother, the mattress, and the walls.

She and I stood silently for a time, shocked and disbelieving. How was it possible that one of the tsar's soldiers had marched into a residential building and attempted to rape her? And after that odious business, did he intend to kill her? How had a seven-year old with a pistol in his hand managed to stop him? For a single moment, I imagined my father being very proud of me, but then I realized that, more likely, he would be angry because I had allowed the soldier to enter our rooms in the first place. That was my father's way; nothing I did ever pleased him, and I suddenly was very afraid that he would blame the attack on me when, inevitably, he heard about it in a letter from my mother.

Before either of us finally was able to speak, my cousin Benjamin burst into the room. He had heard the shots in the basement and now he was astonished by what he saw: the grizzly remains of a uniformed soldier, my mother still dazed and afraid, and little Sargis holding the weapon whose loud report he had heard seconds before.

"What did you do, Sargis?" he asked in disbelief.

"I killed him," I told him calmly.

"But you'll be . . . he's a soldier and you'll—"

"Forget it," my mother interrupted, finally able to talk. "He saved me from being raped by this scum. He did a good thing. Sargis was brave."

I almost never heard words of praise from her, and those she offered me now seemed to fill me up and make me into a man. I had saved her, and she understood that I had, and at last I amounted to something, I now was sure. When my mother said, "Now we must get rid of the body," I was eager to help and to further prove both my valor and my worth.

But Benjamin was reluctant, still afraid that we all would be killed for killing the tsar's soldier, asking, "Where can we take him?"

"Close the door and help us," my mother scolded, and Benjamin did as she said. "They say the tsar's soldiers desert more and more every day. Who will think that this one didn't do the same?"

"But where will we put him?" Benjamin asked again.

"Can you get a cart? In the dead of the night we'll dump him in the incinerator."

Benjamin looked frightened, yet he nodded his head. Yes, he could find a cart. I echoed my mother's words, as if to affirm them. "We can burn him. No one will know."

"All right," Benjamin said after he considered the plan for a moment longer. "I'll find a cart. But I'm not sure I can get a horse. We may have to pull it ourselves." Then he instructed me to take the soldier's money, his identification, and his weapons, and telling my mother to find something to wrap his body in."

"I know what to do," she reproached and hurried him toward the door, telling him to return late in the evening, warning him not to breathe a word of this to anyone.

*

The soldier had no more than a few rubles in his pocket, but I took what seemed to me to be a whole cache of weapons from him—a rifle, the bayonet that was attached to it, a pistol, a knife, and what I imagined was mountains of ammunition. I would have to hide them away from our rooms, we agreed, in case someone came looking for the soldier, and I knew just the place. My mother, my sister Maria—now home from her job as a maid—and I worked into the evening, cleaning the blood from the walls and floors and wrapping the dead man in burlap sacks that we secured with rope.

Then we simply waited, and I thought it would take forever for the night to descend and the streets to empty. But at last Benjamin knocked on the door. His younger brother was with him, and the two men came into the room, looked the bundle over, and pronounced it acceptably wrapped. We worked together—all five of us—to get the body out to the hallway, up the stairs, out to the cobblestone street, and into the horseless cart that awaited us there. Then, we pulled the dead soldier through the silent Tiflis streets, telling ourselves we would explain that we were en route to the cemetery with a son and brother who had died of consumption if a policeman or soldier should ask us to explain our errand. But no one stopped us in the few blocks between our house and the public incinerator, and when we reached it, we dumped the body over the high metal lip of the smoldering furnace, simply dispensing with the tsar's soldier without a prayer or even a word of good riddance.

Before it grew light, I made two trips to the hiding place I had determined was perfect for the weapons, ferrying the rifle first, then returning a second time with the pistol, knife, and ammunition. Someone my sister Nanajan had known before she left for America operated a grocery store not far from where we lived; he had befriended me and had offered to pay me a token if I would look after the pigeons he kept in coops on the roof of his store, and I had quickly agreed.

I loved animals of every kind and was much more drawn to them than I was to people, perhaps because they never were cruel, as far as I could ascertain, and they always filled me with both pleasure and a sense of peace and the rightness of things. I spent long hours feeding those pigeons, and cleaning their cages, and I was always happy there, where it was quiet and safe above the din of the streets, a place from which I had a broad view of the city, including the great house where friends of the tsar lived, or so people said.

There was a crawl space under the eaves of an adjoining roof that I'd already made my secret spot; no one in the world knew of it, I was sure, and that was where I hid the rifles and knives. They would be safe there, and if anyone came round asking us about missing soldiers or their weapons, we simply would say we knew nothing. I couldn't have imagined during that long night that I would use those weapons repeatedly, or that that devil soldier would not be the only man this refugee boy would ever kill.

The smoke from the incinerator carried with it a terrible smell as it wafted into the air above our neighborhood, a hideous stink that lasted more than a week, no matter how hot the fire burned or how much new trash the people of the city heaped upon it. Yet none of us ever spoke of the smell or what we suspected must be its cause, and unfortunately, it would not be the last time I would smell the stench of burning corpses.

Santa Barbara, 1962

SOON AFTER HIS *first and only solo performance with the Chicago Conservatory Orchestra in the summer of 1956, my grandfather moved with his family from Chicago to Santa Barbara, California when Raytheon, the large technology company for which he worked, relocated its Chicago plant. The small city nestled in the green hills between the rugged Santa Ynez Mountains and the Pacific Ocean was an idyllic place to raise children in those days, and despite my grandmother's chronic kidney disease, my grandparents were able to create a life for their family that seemed to mirror the California dream.*

My mother continued to play the piano, just as she had in Chicago, but she was also a true tomboy, and in the summer of 1961 she met a fellow surfer from nearby Ventura and the two became surfing buddies and close friends. Harry Armstrong was handsome and a smooth talker and my grandparents encouraged what they thought was only a friendship—at least until the following spring, when my mother announced that she was pregnant. A wedding was quickly arranged and the two teenagers did their best to become sudden adults, but neither of them were ready for domestic life, and Harry, it turned out, had a dramatically dark side that only began to be evidenced following my birth in December 1962.

My mother tells me that my grandfather was immediately smitten by me and couldn't spend enough time in my company, but for Harry, I was simply the thing that now chained him to a life he didn't want. He began to unpredictably disappear, and when he was at home he was often both verbally and physically abusive to my mother. By the time I was three, she'd had enough of Harry's fists and had moved with me back to her parents' home, and my first true memory of my father was on the night he held us hostage in their living room.

My grandparents were out for dinner, and a friend of my mother's named Tibby was visiting when Harry stormed into the unlocked house, grabbed one of my grandfather's hunting rifles, loaded it and began to bellow incoherently at us. My mother protectively tried to stuff me under the piano in the living room but Harry brandished the rifle and demanded that she leave me and move to the opposite side of the room.

I began to cry, then scream, but Harry wouldn't let my mother come to me and comfort me. Things were going to happen his way, he shouted, although it was never clear to her what he wanted. Somehow, Tibby convinced Harry to let her leave, and when she did, she immediately called my grandparents and the police, and for hours Harry continued to hold us hostage while the police waited tensely outside, hoping that time might help diffuse some of Harry's rage.

At last, my grandfather convinced the police to let him go inside and try to reason with Harry, and something in Poppy's demeanor and in the soft but commanding words he spoke eventually did allow Harry to relax enough that my grandfather was able to take the rifle from him. The police stormed in and took Harry away, but they chose not to detain him—terrifying your wife and infant son with a loaded rifle apparently didn't qualify as much of a crime in those days.

My mother was giving me a bath to calm me down a bit later when she heard Poppy shout, "Harry's back!" And in an instant, she pulled me from the tub, wrapped a towel around me, and ran out the back door. And that's the flash of memory I still retain—my mother's sudden fear and her panicked movements, a glimpse of a tall and angry man, and my mother holding me tightly in her arms as we rushed out into the night.

Chapter 2

A Thief & A Dragon

ALTHOUGH I HADN'T been alive for even a decade yet, I was certain that saving my mother from the soldier earned me not only the title but also the rewards and responsibilities of being the man of the house, such as it was. I made certain that my father's pistol was loaded with bullets and was easy to reach if I should need it again, and, without asking my mother for permission, I simply began to play the tar my father had made but left behind. I'd carefully watched him and my brother play it over the years, and with a determination that I later became renowned for, soon the tar was making wonderfully alluring sounds as I sat in the thin light of a candle for hours every night, clumsily strumming its strings with my small fingers.

I imagined myself a bona fide man when I climbed to the roof of the grocery store as well, knowing I had a small arsenal hidden away there if I needed it, and positive, too, that from that high place I could see everything that was important to see in the teeming city of Tiflis—all the squalor, all the violence, and all of chaos that the revolution spread through the teeming streets like a terrible wind. I could see it all, and I felt as if I mattered as I tended to the pigeons and looked out over a world in disarray.

People everywhere in Russia were going hungry. Food was scarce, often rotten, and people stole whatever scraps they could find. My mother had begun to travel outside the city each day to pick tobacco, but the few rubles she brought home hardly helped us because money had become almost worthless. A single loaf of bread cost ten-thousand rubles or more—if you could find a bakery with bread for sale. People literally stuffed paper money into the cracks in their walls to keep the cold out; they burned it in little fires they built in gutters to keep themselves warm, and I remember sometimes seeing whole baskets of crumpled bills in open doorways that passersby simply ignored. I could have taken all the money I wanted, but, even as young as I was, I knew the only real help it could offer my mother, my sister, or me would be in lining our threadbare coats.

Our fortunes began to change, however, on the day I pulled my little rickety wagon up the hill to the neighborhood of steeply terraced streets where the wealthy people lived. I knew my brother's friend Freydun and his wife Anna lived among them, although I didn't know where. They were Assyrians, like us, but they had lived in Russia for many years, and the tall and angular Freydun long had been a close friend of my brother Polous. In the years before Polous went away to medical school, I remembered him talking often about how brilliant his friend Freydun was, and how he spoke perfect Russian and Persian, too, and how wealthy his great mind and linguistic skills had made him, although at the times I had met this so-called remarkable fellow, he seemed much like any other man to me.

By a fine stroke of luck, Freydun's wife Anna saw me pulling my little cart through the street that day; she recognized me and opened her door and called my name. And almost as if she knew why I had traveled so far from home, she said, "Bring your wagon, here. I have some food for you to put in it and to take home to your mother." I remember that days often would pass during which we had absolutely nothing to eat, and so I was thrilled when Anna offered me a muslin bag filled with bread and dried meat and sausages and potatoes.

She told me I was welcome to return again, and I obeyed her, of course, visiting her again several times. I remember wondering whether I should carry my father's pistol with me as I made my way home on those repeated days, pulling a wagon whose contents desperate people might have killed for, but for some reason I never opted to bring it with me.

One day, when I reached the small street where Freydun and Anna's palatial house stood high above the river, I saw saddled horses standing near the gate, attended by a soldier. I was afraid for an instant that somehow news had reached the tsar in faraway Moscow that I had been receiving free food, and that the tsar had sent his army to arrest me. I wished I had brought my pistol with me, but it quickly dawned on me that the waiting horses and their attendants probably simply meant that important army officers had come to visit Freydun. So, I gathered my courage and walked past the soldiers and rang the bell.

Freydun himself answered the door. I saw a hint of recognition in his eyes—he knew who I was—but he scowled just as quickly, asking me what in the world I wanted. His wife had told me to come for food, I explained, I was just following her instructions, and his scowl deepened, but he opened the door a bit wider and told me to come in.

Inside, the house was more extraordinary than I could believe—purple and red velvet drapes covered the high walls; beautiful dark mahogany furniture filled the rooms; tall candles were lit everywhere, and, in the dining room, an enormous polished-wood table was laid with china and crystal and lavished with magnificent food. My jaw dropped and my eyes were as big as saucers, I'm sure, but Freydun clearly wanted me on my way again. He asked the army officers who had come to dinner to excuse him for a moment, then marched me to kitchen and ordered a cook to fill my bag. "I don't want you to come here ever again," he instructed. "Do you understand? Is that clear?" I told him it was very clear and he followed me to the front door. I put the food from Freydun's kitchen

26

into my wagon and made my way home, certain that I had just entered the home of the richest man in the world.

*

My mother, my sister Maria, and I had become rather accustomed to eating every day; we liked it enough, in fact, that I found it impossible to obey Freydun's strict instruction. I decided that if I were careful to go near the house only during the work day, Freydun would be away and it would be safe for me to wait in the street until Anna saw me and invited me into her kitchen. But on the day when I was finally brave enough to walk up the hill again, I was surprised to encounter a woman wearing expensive clothes lying in the narrow street in front of Freydun and Anna's house. One of her eyes was swollen shut; her face was smeared with blood, and I could also see blood through the tear in the high collar of her dress.

The woman looked at me — just a kid, of course — as if I might be the only hope she had, and I asked her what had happened. She cried and took a long time to tell me her husband had come home, screamed that she was having an affair with another man and then attacked her with a fireplace poker. She was seriously enough injured that she couldn't lift herself up off the cobblestones, and I told her I would go to Anna and Freydun's house to get her some help. But before I could leave her, a short, powerfully built man with lurid green eyes and a head the size of a watermelon stormed out of the house across from Freydun's. "What do you think you're doing?" he demanded of me. I told him I was on my way to Freydun's to get the woman some help, and added she was hurt very badly.

"It's none of your business," he shouted. "I'm not going to let you or Freydun or anyone else interfere with me, see?" Then, he marched toward me, and I backed up toward the low terrace wall at the edge of the steep street until I was trapped against it. The man still had the poker in his hand, and he lunged at me, swinging it wildly. I ducked out of the way of the blow, but as the stocky man swung hard, he slipped on a smooth cobblestone; his right leg flew into the air, and, for an instant, I could see terrible fear spread across his face as he tumbled over the stucco wall. He made a sound like a muffled scream when he hit the tiled and sloping roof of the house below the terrace, and I watched him slide down that roof, then fall again onto a third roof still farther below. I ran to a place where I could see, and in seconds he had fallen over a succession of steeply pitched roofs and all the way down to the Kura River. From above, I saw his body splash into the filthy brown water of the wide river, which, to me, looked as vast and ominous as the sea, and that was the last I ever saw of the short, watermelon-headed man.

His wife had seen nothing more than his sudden disappearance over the wall, and she was in too much pain to ask me more. I ran to Anna and Freydun's house and knocked loudly, and I was afraid when Freydun himself answered the door. But he could see his neighbor in the street and immediately turned his attention to her, forgetting for a moment that I had returned to his street against his demand. "Her husband, the short man, beat her with a poker," I told him between my hurried breaths. "He beat her, and she tried to get away, and then he came out to the street and told me not to help her and that she wasn't my business or your business, and then he tried to hit me, there, by the wall, and he slipped and fell over and he hit all the roofs sliding down to the water."

"Where?" Freydun, asked me, and I took him to the spot where we could see all the way down, and he said, "My, God, he must be dead. Did you see him after he hit the water?"

I shook my head, no, then Freydun said he should send for the police, and he must have instantly understood that his words frightened me. He put his hand on my shoulder and told me it was okay and that I hadn't been responsible for the man's death. Then he added, "Because you have your little wagon with you, let's see if we have some food for you and your mother and sister."

Freydun's wife Anna and two of their servants helped the neighbor woman into their house; the cook filled a sack for me, and Freydun told me everything was okay once more, then encouraged me to go home. I meant to obey him this time—just as I'd meant to before—but, as I was leaving, I saw him go out his front door and circle behind his house, and I can't explain why, but somehow I was compelled to follow him. I left my wagon hidden on the side of the house, and at the back I could see Freydun disappearing into the huge pines that densely covered the hillside. I stayed back, but I was able to follow him through the trees in the early evening light. When he reached a gigantic tree that grew up against the base of an outcropping of rocks, the most amazing thing occurred.

Freydun looked around as if to make sure no one was watching him, then he opened a kind of trap door at the base of the tree that was disguised by its thick bark, then disappeared inside. The door remained open, and the opening grew bright when Freydun lit a lantern. I don't know how, but I was brave enough to make my way to the door and peer inside.

The opening in the tree led to a cave in the rocks, one filled with stockpiles of enough food, it seemed to me, to feed everyone in Tiflis. I didn't dare go in; I wasn't *that* brave, but I made careful note of the route Freydun had taken to reach the tree, and the next day I returned to discover its treasures.

*

I doubt Freydun, my brother's rich and brilliant and conniving friend, ever did contact the police about the death of the man whose name I learned was Benno. He and Benno had become bitter enemies when Benno attempted to blackmail him, Freydun's wife later told me, and I don't think he wanted the police or soldiers anywhere near his house or his cave unless he had invited them there to specifically curry their favor. What *was* certain the cave appeared to prove, was that Freydun had become a major black marketer of the single commodity that was in shortest supply in those days—food—and no doubt he could demand whatever price he chose from people who were wealthy enough to pay him in whatever form he demanded. And, as I discovered, the size of his storehouse inside the cave was astounding.

I didn't have trouble finding it the following day, and I was able to open the door just as Freydun had done. Sunlight streamed far enough inside that I could see a lantern on a small table. I lit it, and with its light I could see much better than before just how much food Freydun had stored inside the cool and secret cavern. There were dozens of hams and dried meats, skinned chickens and pheasants and rabbits, mountains of turnips and potatoes and beets and vegetables I'd never seen before, great bins of flour and salt, even sugar. The sight of it dizzied me; how could anyone ever have gathered that much food in a single place? And how did Freydun get it out of the cave and to his buyers without being found out?

I was very afraid that Freydun or one of the men who surely assisted him would find me inside the cave, so I worked quickly. I filled my wagon with as much food of as many kinds as I could stuff into it, then I covered my load with a filthy piece of canvas I found, secured it with rope, turned out the light, closed the door in the tree, and hurried out of the woods and back into the chaotic city.

I carried out this same procedure repeatedly over the following weeks, each time being as careful as I could be not to get caught inside the cave, making my way back into the city as casually as I could each time. I began to lay sticks on top of the canvas so anyone who noticed would think I had gone to the forest for firewood, but even so, my heart always jumped into my throat until I was safely home with the food.

My mother was scared to death that I would be caught, and even more afraid of what might happen to me if I were, despite the fact that Freydun was a friend of our family. Yet we were eating enough to sustain us for the first time since we had left our village in Persia; my mother even passed food along to others who were as desperate to eat as we had been and trade it for clothes, bars of soap, and candles. She seemed proud of me, but she made me promise each time I ventured up the hill that I would take no unnecessary risks and that I would return to her safely.

On one of my trips to the forest on a rainy morning, by chance I encountered Freydun's men ferrying food to the cave. A boat was docked at the edge of the river, and they had engineered a lift out of steel chains, cables, and pulleys in order to hoist a big wooden box up from the boat to the heights above Freydun's house. At the top of the lift, a group of men hurried to empty the box and cart its contents into the cave before the box descended back down to the boat to be filled again. None of the men saw me, I felt sure, nor did I see Freydun, but he must have seen me, I was certain a few days later.

It wasn't smart of me, but I walked right down the middle of Freydun's street on that occasion, ignoring the fact that he hadn't rescinded his order for me to stay away. I didn't plan to stop at his door—I wasn't in need of food from his kitchen, after all—but just as I passed his house, he opened the door and called out to me. "Sargis, you're back again," he said brightly, as if he were glad to see me. He spoke in Assyrian and walked toward me with a wide smile on his face, and it worried me; Freydun may have loved my brother dearly but he had never been particularly friendly with me before, and I could see something behind his smile that chilled me. He put his arm on my shoulder when he reached me, and said, "You look well, my boy. You look like you've been getting plenty to eat. Who has been feeding you so well?"

And with that, my fear seemed to stick in my throat. I blurted out something about my mother, about how she often came home with a bit of food for us from the tobacco fields. Freydun nodded, and asked nothing more about my belly or the food it received, but he kept his hand on my shoulder, and now he held it too tightly. "Do you know they never found Benno?" he asked. "The police said they could not find his body. It either floated away or the fishes ate it or something." Then, Freydun steered me to the place where Benno had slipped and plummeted over the wall, and it was obvious that he clutched my shoulder so tightly to ensure that I couldn't pull away.

"Show me," he said when we reached the terrace wall. "Show me exactly what happened with Benno. The police asked me, but I didn't precisely know. You didn't show me that day when we were trying to help his poor wife." I stood stiffly and simply responded, "He slipped as he tried to hit me with his poker, and he twisted around and went over the wall. That's all."

Freydun pressed us closer to the wall and asked if I could show him where Benno landed on the roof that was closest below. As he spoke, he pushed me out over the wall, and now it was utterly clear that he meant to send me to a death like Benno's. I was only a fraction the size of tall and slender Freydun, and I sunk and twisted and fought to escape his hold. I was free for a second, but then he grabbed me again, and I lunged low for his foot and clutched it and pulled as hard as I could. Freydun's shoe came away in my hand, and, as it did, he fell backward onto the wall. For an instant, it appeared he would catch his balance, but too much of his weight already was over the wall, and—impossibly, just like Benno—Freydun, too, fell from the wall onto steep roof after roof and into the Kura River. I couldn't believe it; it couldn't have happened again, but it *had*. I had watched for myself as wealthy and brilliant Freydun tumbled into the water far below.

I turned away from watching the water at last, and there stood Freydun's wife Anna in the open door of her house. I couldn't think what to say, and I just looked at her, and she looked back at me without any sort of expression on her face. Finally, I spit out, "I'm sorry. He tried to push me over and — "

"I saw that," she said, as calmly as could be. "I saw what happened, and it was an accident, but now you've got to help me get out of the country."

"How can I do that?" I asked her. "I'm just a boy."

"And you're a very clever boy," she said. "Smarter than you know, and you know about many things, don't you?" I didn't answer her before she added, "What you can do is reach your brother in Saratov and tell him he must help me. Tell him I'll give him all the money he needs, but he must get the papers I need and get me safely on a train. I cannot stay here now. It's impossible." She didn't cry, didn't even get tearful; her husband's death was just something that had happened that afternoon, it seemed. She was beautiful, and she was wealthy, and now all she cared about was how she would escape from Russia and the war.

*

That night, my mother wrote to my brother as Anna requested, and he succeeded before many more weeks were out in helping her leave Tiflis. I never knew where she went or if she survived in her new home and I was very surprised years later when Polous made a reference to poor Freydun being arrested by the tsar's soldiers and hung as a spy in the early years of the revolution. That curious explanation of his demise could only have come from Anna—it certainly didn't come from my mother, or Maria, or me.

I don't know what became of Freydun and Anna's great house high on the hill, but I do know that the secret cave continued to be filled with food, because in the weeks after Freydun's death I kept visiting it regularly and taking some of its stores home to my mother and sister. It's hard for me to imagine that after a couple of brushes with death I still was willing to climb that hill; I might have learned an indelible lesson that a poor Assyrian kid like me had no business venturing into the city's heights, but somehow I did not. I kept returning to the cave, although for reasons I cannot explain, I now took smaller amounts of food than before and was careful to make it appear that nothing had been disturbed, and the cave remained a horn of plenty for us. Rounds of cheese, bologna, legs of pork, strings of sausages: they all were there for the taking, and the cave's cool temperature kept them fresh.

Yet finally, my thievery—my redistribution of wealth on behalf of the revolution—came to an end. But it wasn't over until I got caught inside the cave on an early morning by one of Freydun's partners, a man with a pistol in his hand that he seemed all-too-willing to fire at me. When he asked what in the hell I thought I was doing, I told him I was starving—my mother and sister were starving too—and that I was only taking very little. I told him I had known Freydun, and he said he was Freydun's partner and that Freydun had disappeared—strung up by filthy Reds, no doubt.

I guessed this bearded man owned the boat that brought the food into the city. He said I was lucky he had found me and not one of the others with whom he worked. "They would have killed you the second they saw you and buried you in the woods where no one would find you," he said. "Me? I don't know. You're just a boy and there is plenty of killing these days."

The man told me he and his men were going to empty the cave of all its food, but even so, he wanted me to know that if I ever returned, he wouldn't spare me a second time. Then, he barked at me to go and told me once more that I was lucky to still be in my skin.

I tried my best to stay away from the cave and the food that had been so important to our survival, but sometime later—when my mother, my sister, and I had become very hungry again—I made a final trip to the tree that guarded the cave's entrance, but I couldn't get the trap door to open. Behind the tree, I found a spot where I tunneled my way inside by moving away some rocks. I lit a match, and in its brief light I could see that there was plenty of food there still, but it was rotten and would never be eaten either by Russia's wealthy or her terribly poor. Stinking liquids seeped from the piles of food onto the rocky floor, and after just a minute or two of picking through the muck to find something edible, I was sick to my stomach. I rushed out of the cave and vomited, took some deep breaths to settle myself, then made my way home, never returning to Freydun's cave again.

*

My brother Polous traveled south to Tiflis to visit us during the Christmas holidays of 1920, despite the fact that the civil war now raged and travel was often dangerous. And it was while he was with us that he, my cousin Babajan Pera, and my mother hatched a plan they hoped would eventually help all of us get to America.

Short but strong and incredibly big-hearted, Babajan was just two years younger than Polous; the two of them always had been very close and neither could imagine living for long on separate continents. Polous planned to return to Saratov Medical University, finish his medical training, then join my father and the rest of us in America in a couple of years. And because he wouldn't be with us as we traveled, it seemed logical enough that Babajan could take his place, traveling as my mother's son. With my father already in the U.S., it would be far easier for us to obtain visas than it would be for Babajan, who had no family there. As they imagined it, the four of us—my mother, Maria, Babajan, and I—would travel by train across the Caucasus Mountains to the port of Batoum, nowadays called Batumi, then cross the length of the Black Sea by ship to Constantinople, where, Polous and Babajan were certain, we could secure the visas that would allow us to book passage on an immigrant ship to New York.

In the first days of February, my mother received $400 that my father had sent via the New York-based Near East Relief Society—an organization that worked tirelessly to help displaced Assyrians and Armenians—which she hoped would be enough money for the four of us to book passage to America. And on February 8, 1921 we received the visas that would allow us to begin our journey to Constantinople where we hoped to book passage to America as soon as possible.

We had just a couple of days to pack the few belongings my mother believed we simply could not leave behind, but she was adamant that I could *not* bring with me the pistol, rifle, and bayonet that once had belonged to the Russian soldier. When I protested that we might need them for protection as we traveled, Babajan sided with her, telling me that we likely would be searched along the way, and having hidden weapons could get us arrested.

We arrived at the Tiflis train station with suitcases and satchels, trunks, and the beautiful tar that now seemed to belong to me as much as my father, and somehow, in the rush to load them into the baggage cars and get ourselves into the boxcars in which we would have to ride like packed sardines, I got separated from the others. I was barely eight years old, but I was as worldly as any twenty-year-old, I believed, yet I was terrified when I realized that, except for the small and beloved kitten named Mooshy I had cradled inside my coat, I was utterly alone in a sea of strangers. I knew which train my mother and the others planned to board, so I simply climbed into one of the cars as the departure whistle sounded, then burrowed myself into a tiny space near one of the corners, and my kitten and I whimpered for hours as the train chugged its way west to the shore of the Black Sea.

Along the way, a friendly old man with a big gray beard befriended me in the dark and miserable boxcar. I was cold, and he did his best to help me keep warm. He said that he, too, was leaving Russia forever and that he was a rabbi—a kind of Jewish priest, he explained. When we reached the train station in Batoum hours later, the rabbi hoisted me and my kitten onto his shoulders and walked up and down the station platform with us until, at last, I spotted my mother. She was thrilled to see me and furious in the same moment, but—for once—I didn't know what I might have done wrong. I hadn't run off or disobeyed in any way, and it seemed that they had been as much at fault for losing me as I was for losing them. Babajan offered the rabbi some rubles for his help, but he refused them, telling us we could buy him a glass of vodka in America one day instead.

Batoum was a horrible place, I remember—a filthy oil-importing and refining city, where slick black oil seemed to cover every street like a sheet, but we were there only a few days before we were able to board a passenger ferry for the overnight sail to Constantinople. I loved being on the water, and I stood at the rail of the ferry's deck for long hours, trying to imagine why this was the *Black* Sea, when, in fact, it was much more the color of cabbage soup. We slept in chairs and on benches, or tried to, and I remember thinking how very tired we all would be if this was the kind of ship that would carry us to America as well.

Babajan had hoped that our stay in Constantinople would be as short as our time in Batoum, but after waiting in line all day for medical examinations at the American immigration office, those hopes were suddenly dashed when a doctor announced that my mother's chronic eye infection would bar us from admission into the United States. We weren't at all certain what to do now, but we did find a little room for my mother, Maria, not too far from the American embassy; Babajan found lodging elsewhere, and we settled in, our trip to America underway yet stalled for an indeterminate stretch of time.

*

Constantinople was a wondrous place. There were cheese shops full of cheese, shoe shops filled with shoes, and the center of the city was densely packed with every kind of store you could imagine. You could travel from place to place on trolleys; even in winter the weather was easy to endure, and, best of all, no war was underway — no bombs, no machine gun fire, no snipers with high-powered rifles shooting your friends in the street. I spoke not a word of Turkish in the beginning, but it was easy enough to find people who spoke a bit of Russian. Language was seldom a barrier and it was always a thrill to be out in the streets of the great city where, people said, Europe and Asia met — a concept that, admittedly, I didn't quite understand.

My mother's eye infection was the thing that kept us in Constantinople, but it was the fact that she was an excellent cook that eventually allowed us to sail for America. Our good fortune began on a day when my mother prepared bushala, a simple soup that had long been a staple in our home, one made with spinach, cabbage, yogurt, and spices. If you stopped stirring bushala, it would curdle, and I remember the dozens of times my mother would call me to come stir a heavy pot, admonishing me not to quit until she returned from some errand or another. That particular day, I had taken some bushala with me in a tin box as I went out for the day, and, at my mother's request, Babajan and I stopped at the American embassy to inquire about when she would be eligible to be checked by a physician again, because her eye infection had improved.

At the embassy, a man asked me what I had in my box that smelled so good, and, with Babajan's help — who spoke some Turkish and even a bit of English—I explained that it was my mother's bushala, and I even offered him some, thinking it never hurt to be polite to an American. He liked it—he like it a *lot*, in fact—and asked me if my mother would cook for him and his co-workers because they needed to replace the cook who had left the day before, but neither Babajan nor I were entirely sure what he meant. We did understand enough to know that the man was serious: he would like to speak with my mother about cooking for the Americans, and I went home to tell her.

"Oh, dear God!" she exclaimed when I explained that the Americans wanted to see her. "What have we done now?" She was terrified that she would be told we had to return to Russia, but she went to the embassy with us anyway, and we were all amazed to discover from someone who spoke Russian that the Americans wanted nothing more than for her to move to their palace and do their cooking for them. The embassy was housed in the grand and ornate Palazzo Corpi, by far the most imposing building I had ever entered, with its gated and gas-lit formal entrance, an American eagle crest embossed in stone high above an imposing entrance, and dazzling interior frescoes that adorned virtually every wall. I'm sure our mouths were all agape when, escorted by the embassy man who had smelled the bushala, we reached the large kitchen where my mother and Maria would work—complete with running water and sparkling appliances—then saw the comfortable room where the three of us would live and he also offered my mother more money to cook for them than she could imagine. She said yes immediately, of course, and so we moved out of our tiny, back alley room and into a Constantinople palace.

The Americans loved my mother's Assyrian cooking and she learned how to prepare their favorite American dishes as well; we liked them and liked our new home, and I remember my mother telling Maria and me that God had richly blessed us on that day she had made bushala. Living among the Americans and working for them meant that one day before too long we would be able to go to America, she assured us.

But I wasn't in a particular hurry to leave. I was intrigued by the idea of seeing my father again; I hoped that once he discovered how grown-up I was, he could begin to love and respect me like he obviously did my brother Polous, but I remained wary of him nonetheless. And I didn't know why everyone evidently believed America was such a wondrous country in the first place, particularly when Constantinople offered far more pleasures than tiny Alwach, Urmia, or war-ravaged Tiflis or stinking Batoum had, and it was hard to believe that New York or a city with the long and exotic name of Bristol, Connecticut could offer more.

My kitten had run away, and I was heartsick—the animals to whom I poured out my love always left me, it seemed—but then, by some magic, I acquired my dragon and my horse, and now I was certain that Constantinople was the only place I ever wanted to be.

*

I was making my way through the dark and narrow streets of the ancient Eminönü district one day when I heard a great commotion through the open door of the pet shop where I was a regular visitor. I went inside and saw the shopkeeper standing on his counter with broom in his hand, and he was striking a reddish gray lizard that was as big as a dog with the heaviest blows he could manage. In the best Turkish I could muster, I asked the shopkeeper what he was doing, and he shouted, "God, damn it, Sargis, I'm trying to get rid of this animal!" I asked him if I could have the lizard if I got him out of his shop, and he instantly agreed. He bent down and handed me a dog leash and said I could have it, too, and as the man stopped beating the lizard for a moment, I slipped the leash over his head and off the two of us went. As the lizard and I made our way back to the embassy, I was more convinced than ever that my mother was right—we *were* richly blessed.

When my lizard and I arrived home, one of the young Russian-speaking secretaries with whom I had made friends showed me a book she called an encyclopedia and inside it a photograph of a lizard that looked like mine and which was called a Nile dragon, a creature that had come from a chain of islands in the Far East. "Let's call him Drago," she suggested. I liked the name, and she helped me assemble a pen in the alley behind the embassy where I could keep him—sure as I was that my mother and the embassy people would not agree to let him live indoors with us.

Drago *was* big, and I remember my mother dismissing me as a *khmaa-raa*, a jack-ass, when I proudly took her out to the alley to see him. I explained the details of the acquisition, and pointed out, too, that she could pet him any time she wanted; he was quite gentle. He did have dozens of razor-sharp teeth, but he didn't appear particularly eager to use them. Probably only because my mother had so much to attend to in her kitchen, she acquiesced to my keeping him in the alley pen, perhaps only to keep me distracted and busy, and for weeks to come, I occupied my time with the feeding and walking of my dragon. He would quickly devour anything I brought him from the kitchen—vegetables, meat, fish, bread. Out in the streets, he never tried to escape his leash and I was careful to keep him close at hand. We walked everywhere—up to the mosques that sat atop each of the city's seven hills, along the beautiful Bosporus waterfront, sometimes even through the dark and labyrinthine Grand Bazaar, where shopkeepers would scold me for bringing such a menacing creature into a place of commerce.

One day, Drago and I walked near a horse farm at the edge of the city, where we encountered a trainer with a string of horses. As we drew near them and the horses spotted the dragon, they began to snort and stamp nervously, and a mangy and sway-backed horse reared and tried to run away. "Hey, what are you doing here with this crazy thing?" the irritated trainer asked me. I told him the dragon was very tame and didn't hurt anyone, horses included, and I offered to show the beat-up old horse that he didn't need to fear Drago, if the man would let me. I loved horses, and had been around them since I was very small, and before we left Alwach, I had learned how to ride.

But the horse, so skinny his ribs showed and as black as coal, remained very skittish, and even with the help of a rope and halter, the man had a hard time quieting him. "I let a friend sell me this worthless creature," the man explained. "What was I thinking when I said yes?"

"How much for him, then?" I asked, even though I didn't have a single Turkish lira in my pocket.

"He's a damn nuisance," the trainer replied. "You really want him? You can have him." He gestured with his hand as if to push the colt out of his sight, then went to a tack room and picked up a weather-beaten saddle blanket from the dirt floor. "You'd better take this, too," he added, "if you ever hope to stay on his back."

Of course, I wanted the horse, I said. He was worn-out and not much to look at, but he was prize to my eyes, and I thanked the man for him and the blanket as well. After he had placed the blanket on the nervous horse's back, he lifted me up. The horse wasn't happy to have me there, but I stayed on and finally was able to calm him, and the trainer said I was a fine horseman, which made me proud. Drago's leash wasn't long enough for me to hold it while I was on the colt's back, and I worried whether the colt was strong enough yet to carry my weight, so I jumped off and led both the horse and the dragon back down into the heart of the city.

This time, the friendly Americans at the embassy said, "Good heavens, Sargis, what are we going to do with you?" They weren't at all sure that the two animals were a good match, and they laughed when I said I planned to keep them both in the same pen in the alley. But, in the end, it worked perfectly. The colt, who I named Da-ba-sha, bumblebee—because, it seemed to me, he could move so fast even though no else thought so—decided Drago was his pal, and Drago became the colt's guardian, hissing at anyone other than me who tried to go near him. And the three of us made quite a scene on the days we would go out—a boy leading an odd looking little horse in one hand and a dragon in the other, the three of us walking through the bustling streets as proud as you please. There was no location I didn't take my pair of companions, no place where they weren't always eager to accompany me as we roamed the remarkable city.

*

I don't know precisely what it was about the city of Constantinople, but somehow people there seemed inclined to offer me creatures they had no use for, and my remarkable run of luck continued when an Assyrian man named Brikha who I'd become friendly with offered me the use of his barge out of the blue one day. I'd gotten to know him because I loved to spend time at the docks along the Bosporus, watching boats and ships of every shape and size come and go in the narrow waterway. I'd heard Brikha speaking Aramaic, our language, and I greeted him like the compatriot he was. I told him how I'd come to be in Constantinople, and told him, too, of course, about my colt and my dragon, and Brikha, in turn, seemed to think I was pleasant to have around. His barge wasn't much of a boat; it was old and small and good for little more than ferrying a couple of pallets of flour or salt or coal from one part of the city to another. But I was always welcome to come aboard when Brikha spotted me and waved for me to join him.

I would often bring my tar, and Brikha seemed to be enraptured by the Assyrian folk songs I had taught myself how to play, songs that dependably brought tears to his eyes. I, in turn, loved touring the waterfront as he made his rounds. He taught me how to steer with the rudder, how to cut the smoke-belching engine as we approached the dock, even how to start the diesel engine that always shook to life as if it suffered a terrible cold.

Then, one day Brikha announced as we chugged our way through the city that he would be gone for a few weeks—he had to travel to Athens, he explained—but I was welcome to use the barge. I was thrilled, and I studied him carefully to see if I could tell whether he was teasing. "No, you can use it," he said again. "Just tie it up right where I always do, and I'll find it when I come back, even if you've left for America by then." He told me he would tell the men who pumped diesel near the big bridge to fill the barge's tank when it needed fuel. He would pay when he returned, he explained, and all I needed to do was to check with a broom handle to see how much fuel I had, the way he had shown me. I couldn't believe my good fortune or Brikha's largesse, and I did my best to assure him that his barge would be safe with me. He tousled my hair and told me he knew it would, and that was the last I ever saw of him.

Something bad may have happened to him in Athens, or he may have had to stay there longer than he expected, I never knew, but the barge became mine to do with as I chose, and what I loved to do—you won't be surprised to hear—was to lead Da-ba-sha onto the barge's flat wooden deck and tie him to the rail, then bring Drago on board. The three of us would travel by water where we pleased or simply stay tied to the wooden pier where the men who worked the docks would stop and marvel at what a site we made, telling me I was a hell of a clever kid in ways that filled me with pride and made me wonder why their opinions of me and my father's differed so dramatically.

*

We didn't know how long it might be before the doctors declared that my mother's eyes were healthy enough for her to go to America, but the people at the embassy assured us that although they would hate to do without my mother's cooking, they would see to it that we could continue our journey soon.

I took the news rather badly—I didn't want to leave the city where so many people had been kind and generous to me and to us—and I even talked with one of the secretaries about whether I could continue to stay in our room, even if my mother was no longer the embassy's cook. She laughed, telling me there were plenty of horses, and surely even Nile dragons in America—if that was what I was concerned about. I told her I planned to take Drago and Da-ba-sha with me, if I had to go, and she laughed again, telling me that was impossible.

My mother was angry with me again when I tried to get her to take my side. "If you can't go to America with a swollen eye, do you think they let you get on a ship with a horse and a huge lizard?" she asked. "You *cannot* take them with you, and you must find them a home before we leave. Do you understand me, Sargis?"

I sulked, and said I understood, but the truth was more complex. Yet, I did begin to try to find my pets a home. For the past few months, I had been collecting old clothes wherever I could find them, bringing back to our neighborhood on the barge, then selling them for a few liras. Each day I would display my goods for the dockworkers for a few hours, then move them under the portico of an empty building near the embassy where shoppers would find me. As people stopped to look at a shirt or a pair of trousers, I began to ask whether they might be interested as well in buying a swayback horse or a most remarkable dragon, animals I cherished and was sure many others could as well. But no one took me up on the offer—no one seemed remotely interested, in fact—and finally I began to ask both the shoppers and the men at the docks whether anyone knew somebody who might take them from me, free of charge. In response to that question, at last a dockworker offered me a great idea. Why didn't I inquire at Constantinople's zoo?

I'd never been to a zoo, but I'd heard of them, of course, and he explained to me where the city's zoo was located, and the next day Da-ba-sha and Drago and I set out to see if we could secure them a new home. When I finally encountered the right person to speak with at the zoo—a man who admired my pets even before we spoke and who clearly loved animals, I could tell—I explained that I was about to leave for America with my family, and that I couldn't take my pets with me. I asked if the zoo would give them both a home, and the man said, yes, it would. They would be happy to take my animals and so I simply handed him Drago's leash and Da-ba-sha's lead-rope and turned away.

I didn't want to say goodbye, and I'm sure the man understood. But as I started to walk away, I looked over my shoulder at my two companions, and they were looking back at me, wondering where I was going without them. Too often in my young life, I'd lost family members and friends and animals I loved. So many people and animals had abandoned me, or simply disappeared, and I couldn't imagine doing the same. Yet here I was, consciously turning my back on my beloved dragon and horse.

I was heartsick as I made the long walk back to the embassy. I was nine years-old and far too grown up to cry, but I just couldn't help myself. Four times on the long walk back to the embassy, I stopped and sat on a curb with my head in my hands, sobbing uncontrollably, blaming my father for making me go to America and taking from me the creatures I loved most in all the world, creatures that had loved me steadfastly in return.

Many of the women at the embassy were similarly tearful on the day we departed. Everyone gave us big, enveloping hugs and wished us great luck in our new lives. Babajan had joined us again, and his English was far better than ours, my mother asked him to tell the Americans how grateful we were, and that, without them, we never could have reached this day. The young secretaries promised to go to the zoo regularly to visit Drago and Da-ba-sha and they insisted on paying for a taxi to carry us and all our belongings to the pier where our ship waited, and, to this day, I still can see them standing in the street and waving as we drove away.

At the docks, we had to pass through another check of our papers and have a final medical inspection. The doctors paid close attention to my mother's eyes, then examined each of us all over again, listening to our hearts with stethoscopes, looking in our ears and mouths, and checking our hands and feet. Each of us passed the exam; each was officially healthy enough to become an American, it seemed, and a last we boarded. As the afternoon grew hot, the huge ship slipped away from the pier and through the narrow Bosporus and on toward a destiny a boy like me could not imagine.

Santa Barbara, 1968

SANTA BARBARA IN the 1960s was a far cry from the exotic delights of Constantinople, but there were plenty of people who were convinced that it was a kind of American Eden nonetheless, and my grandfather was certainly one of them, throwing himself into the life of the little city with the kind of energy that always had been his hallmark. He and a small group of other musicians formed the Santa Barbara Symphony Orchestra, which was led early on by conductor and film composer Ernest Gold. My grandmother became the symphony's office manager, and for many years Poppy was a stalwart in its violin section. His lifelong love of athletics continued in California, where he became an avid golfer and bowler and a dedicated member of the YMCA, visiting the gym virtually daily to swim, run, and continue the gymnastics training he had begun in 1923. He loved to scuba-dive in the waters off the Channel Islands, and he went deer hunting a number of times, but it was the camaraderie and the stalking he loved, and I remember him confessing to me that although he'd often had a deer in his rifle's sights, he had never been able to bring himself to pull the trigger. His work at Raytheon fascinated him, and he was proud of what he did and I was proud of him, too. Although I didn't know any details, I knew Poppy invented things—appliances everyone used and weapons he couldn't talk about—which only added to his mystique.

Harry Armstrong was admitted to Camarillo State Mental Hospital soon after his divorce from my mother, then was drafted and sent to Vietnam. He eventually returned to California with a Silver Star in exchange for the machine-gun blast that had left him with a hundred percent disability. He couldn't have sex, his right leg was useless, and his spirit was so terribly broken that he did little but drink and take Methadone for the decade that followed, never getting to know me, never letting me get even a glimpse of him.

My mother married again, this time to an abalone diver named John Hoffman—also an alcoholic, also a wife-beater—who apparently hated me as much as I did him. He would come home roaring drunk after a long day of fishing and drinking, march into the room where I was sleeping, pick me up, throw me against the opposite wall, then leave. He loved to taunt me and play the tough guy, refusing to let a six-year-old call his mother "Mommy." My mother and John had a daughter, Jennifer, and my mother did her best to make a life for herself and to offer some stability to my sister and me, but our home was a place in which I was constantly afraid.

Yet always by my side in my early years was Poppy. The small house he shared with my grandmother was the sole safe place I knew. I connived to be there every moment of the day I could be, and I spent hundreds of nights on a bed beside his, my chronically ill grandmother asleep on the living room sofa where she chose to spend most nights.

I found acceptance at Poppy and Mimi's; I learned how to give love and receive it, and I grew up wanting to be just like the man whom everyone in Santa Barbara, it seemed, admired, respected, and wanted to be near. In any restaurant we entered, it was certain that it would take us ten minutes to reach our table, Poppy necessarily stopping repeatedly en route to greet his legion of friends. Despite the constancy of the fear and the pain I experienced at home, I never longed to have a loving father. I had Poppy, and what more could I have wanted?

Chapter 3

To America

ON JUNE 10, 1921, we sailed out of Constantinople on the *King Alexander*, a steamship that was bigger than any boat could possibly be, it seemed to me. Watching from the rail on the deck where steerage passengers were allowed, I was fascinated as we slowly moved out of the Bosporus and into the Sea of Marmara, and although I hated to leave the enchanting city of Constantinople, where I had thrived in so many ways, it was clearly going to be an adventure worth pursuing to cross the Aegean, the Mediterranean, and the Atlantic as we traveled a third of the way round the world.

Although I was transfixed by the view from the rail, my sister Maria was so afraid of the water—just as she had been on our passage across the Black Sea a year before—that she refused to go on deck or even to glance out of a porthole, and my mother wasn't much braver. Babajan and I, on the other hand, loved to gaze for hours at a time at the gray-green expanse of sea spreading to the horizon in every direction. We had entered a world made entirely of water and I marveled at how far I already had traveled from a village in the far corner of Persia that Assyrians had called their home for thousands of years.

We had watched helplessly as Alwach and Urmia were destroyed by the Turks, the Kurds, and their Persian allies almost seven years before. And my mother had often spoken of the horrors that followed after we escaped from Urmia. We knew of the New Year's Massacres in which the soldiers of the Young Turk regime systemically assassinated hundreds of priests, bishops, and archbishops of the Syriac Orthodox, Chaldean Catholic, and Church of the East churches, and of the slaughter of many hundreds of thousands of people in our Assyrian homeland. In Tiflis, rumors reached us almost daily of new atrocities, but we did not know until much later that the Turks had, in fact, perpetrated a horror that could only be labeled genocide.

The Young Turk nationalists who controlled the Ottoman Empire hoped to create a pan-Turkish state that stretched from the Bosporus to the frontier of China, and the Armenian, Pontic Greek, and Assyrian nations—each of them Christian since early in the first millennium—stood in their way. In the international chaos of World War I, the Turkish government began its assault on the Assyrians by singling out the able-bodied men who would be most likely to resist their conquest—forcing them into labor battalions, marching them into preplanned attacks by Kurdish tribesmen, and often simply taking them to secluded spots and murdering them alone or in small groups.

Next came the plundering and destruction by fire of more than 750 Assyrian towns and villages. Hundreds of thousands of people fled northward into Russia, as my family had done, but those who did not were doomed. Like the religious figures before them, political and military leaders were sought out and executed in a successful attempt to block the formation of a resistance movement, and thousands of peasants and townspeople were forced to abandon their homes and march for hundreds of miles without provisions. Many died en route to concentration camps in the Persian desert, thousands more died in the camps themselves, and by 1919, when the Ottoman Empire was dissolved, more than 750,000 Assyrians had been slaughtered, in addition to the deaths of an estimated 1.5 million Armenians and a million Pontic Greeks—deaths the governments of nations throughout Europe and the Americas all but ignored.

During our years in Tiflis and Constantinople, my mother had determinedly kept her religious faith. Forced to make something of a life for her family largely without my father's help, she still found time to read the Bible for hours every evening, and to attend mass as often as she could. She reminded Maria and me often that we were part of an ancient and singular race. We were Semitic kin to the Jews who gave birth to Jesus, and we were the last people on earth still speaking Aramaic, the language Jesus spoke.

In 33 A.D., Assyria had become the first nation to accept Christianity, at the end of a golden age during which Assyrians had ruled all of Mesopotamia. By 750, the Assyrian Empire encompassed all of the Middle East, and in the thirteenth century, the Assyrian Church—larger than the Greek Orthodox and Roman Catholic churches combined—spanned the Asian continent, from Syria to Mongolia, Korea, China, Japan, and the Philippines. When Arabs and Islam began to sweep through the Middle East in 630 A.D., they encountered centuries of Assyrian Christian heritage, with a highly developed culture and advanced learning and technologies—a civilization that was the foundation of the Arab florescence that followed.

But inevitably, the Islamic and Christian traditions began to clash; their conflicts grew bloody, and as Islamic power grew, the Assyrians increasingly were persecuted. The Islamic Ottoman Empire gained dominance over the region long controlled by Assyria, and, at its end, the empire ruled by the Young Turks did its best to destroy not only a nation, but an entire people.

By 1921, you could no longer find Assyria on a map, and the Assyrians still living had fled their homelands in a Diaspora, one of which my family and I were a very small part. Assyria remained alive only in those of us who had escaped, and although my mother remained a devout Christian possessed of a centuries-old hatred of the Turks, I was part of a different, twentieth-century generation. I had already seen unspeakable violence early in my life, but it was violence perpetrated by both Arabs and Christians; and in Constantinople, for centuries the capital of the Ottoman Empire, I had felt strangely at home and at peace.

In that great city, no one had singled me out as a hated Christian or a vile Assyrian. Islamic Turks had given me an exotic dragon and a wonderful horse; they had cheerfully purchased my wares and listened to my songs, and I'd been at ease among them. I was proud to be an Assyrian, but already I knew that I was about to begin to define myself in other ways. As soon as the *King Alexander* crossed the wide Atlantic, I would become an American, in fact—a nine-year-old with a new name on a new continent, with all of the twentieth century in front of him for the taking.

*

If the views from the deck of *King Alexander* gave me the sense that I was the freest boy in all the world, the dark and densely packed quarters deep in the bowels of the ship where we slept in bunk beds lined up in endless rows made me feel trapped like one of the pigeons on the roof of the grocery in Tiflis. Each family was assigned a bunk or bunks—we were allotted two for the four of us—and a specific toilet, one we shared with dozens of other passengers. Crews regularly cleaned them but the toilets were always foul nonetheless, and the huge long room that housed us all stunk of feet, and farts, and the chronic absence of soap.

We ate our meals in a similarly massive and dingy dining room, a cacophonous place where we had to stand in line to take seats at long tables, and where stewards brought big plates of food that, to me at least, always tasted good, although the adults constantly complained. Everything was regimented and carefully controlled—life in steerage was more than a little like living in a sea-going prison, in fact—but everyone knew that in order to reach

America, the journey had to be suffered, and people tried to endure their days at sea without too much complaint or conflict.

For kids like me, to tell the truth, the *King Alexander* could often be lots of fun. Except for those times when we *had* to be in our bunks or at the table, we had endless free time. We raced here and there in packs of a dozen or more; we dared each other to do any number of acts that might have tossed us overboard and into the roiling water, and we fought each other whenever a sudden disagreement forced a fight—boys furiously trading shouts and the harsh blows from fists until an adult brave enough to enter the fray pulled us apart and warned us in one of the dozens of languages spoken aboard the ship to stop acting like monkeys and get along.

I was fascinated by the bustling port of Piraeus, near Athens, as the ship briefly docked there to take on more passengers, and it was always fun to rush to the rails when someone spotted land on the otherwise watery horizon—the southern tip of Sicily, Cap Bon in Tunisia, poking like a big thumb into the placid waters of Mediterranean, the Straits of Gibraltar where Africa and Europe almost met, and where a terrible storm forced the captain to weigh the ship's anchor and simply wait for what seemed like days. Morning after morning, I remember, I would rush to the deck certain that we at last had reached the Atlantic, but there the rock always stood close at hand on the ship's starboard side, taunting us, it seemed, making it clear that America would have to wait for at least another day.

But the skies finally cleared and the weather grew beautiful; the ship's engines shuddered to life and at last we sailed out of sight of the rock and on toward the new lives none of us could quite fathom. Every kid in steerage on the *King Alexander*, I can vouch, was delighted to be sailing again. Life onboard had begun to be more than a little monotonous; there were only so many games we could devise for our mutual entertainment, so many quarrels about surpassingly important subjects, so much racing and hiding and daring each other to be brave or foolhardy or both.

I missed my animals terribly by now, and just thinking for a moment about Drago or Da-ba-sha or my kitten Mooshy, who had run away as soon as we reached Constantinople could make me very melancholy. When I remembered each of them and the wonderful companions they were, I often sobbed, particularly if no one was near who might make fun of me. I felt alone in the world without them, even though I spent each night crowded onto a bunk with Babajan, with my mother and Maria just inches away and the snores and grunts of hundreds of others filling the darkness around me. No person—not even my mother—could make me feel loved like my animals could, and I cried into my pillow on those nights when I couldn't sleep, no longer excited about the ship or America or what might become of me and only deeply sad.

*

But everything about the journey changed rather remarkably for me on the day a man walked past as I sat playing my tar in the steady breeze and soft morning light on a catwalk just outside our dormitory. He stopped, listened to me for a long time, then tried to say something nice to me in several languages before at last he spoke in Russian. It was a language we discovered we shared, and he explained that because he was both a Russian and a Jew—and that because both those facts defined him—he and his family would be far safer in America, he believed, than anywhere else in the world. His name was Alexei, he said, and he shook my hand, explaining that he and his family had boarded the ship in Piraeus, then asking if he might hold the instrument for a moment. I told him my father had made it as I passed it to him, and he marveled at how beautifully it was constructed.

I'm sure I looked more than a little astonished when this thin and angular man who was older than Babajan but not by much quickly made music with my tar, then he explained that it was because he was a violinist. I knew what a violin was, of course—I was a *worldly* kid by now, remember—but I'm not sure I'd ever heard in any language the word for a person who plays a violin. He was a *violiniste*, he told me again, this time in French, and I was enchanted by the sound and the wonderful idea it sparked in my brain. I knew in that moment on the *King Alexander* in the middle of the enormous Atlantic that I, too, wanted to be a violinist—even though I'd never held a violin in my hand or tried to make one sing.

Because I knew plenty of Russian from our years in Tiflis, Alexei and I could converse without problems, and he suggested that, if I had time, he would go to his sleeping quarters and bring his violin back for me to see. I was thrilled, and I assured him I wouldn't move, and before long he returned with his violin in a hard leather case. When he opened the case and held the violin up for me to see, it looked far more delicate than I thought it might. Its neck was narrow and crowned with a dramatic scroll, and the wood of its body was quite dark and polished to a beautiful sheen, except for the spot near the tailpiece where the pressure of his chin had worn the bright finish away.

He encouraged me to hold it, and I was very careful as I did, and was amazed when it seemed to weigh nothing at all. "Give it a try," Alexei said as he handed me the bow, but I could make nothing more than a screeching sound as I timidly drew the bow across the strings. He smiled and asked whether I'd like to learn to play it, and I could hardly say yes fast enough. I had taught myself how to play the tar, I told him, so perhaps I could learn a bit about the violin, too, and he said he was sure I could learn in no time. There were twelve more days of sailing ahead of us before we reached New York, and there was plenty of time to teach me, he assured me, and we agreed that we would meet for an hour each morning and afternoon in a rather dreary salon below deck where his violin would be better protected from the salt that hung in the humid air and where I would be allowed to enter.

I shouldn't have been surprised when my mother was angry with me the moment I told her about meeting Alexei and how he planned to teach me to play his violin. "Sargis, what have you told this man that he agreed to this?" she shouted at me. "I have no money to pay this Russian for violin teaching."

I explained that Alexei hadn't asked me for money; we had only begun to talk because he admired my father's tar—and the moment I mentioned the tar she was afraid I had bartered it for violin lessons. "Your father's own tar," she moaned, "how could you?" When I was finally able to make her believe that Alexei had offered me lessons at no charge and only because he was kind, her anger at me abated, but she remained suspicious, and she insisted that Babajan join me for my lessons the following day to ensure that "this Hungarian," as she repeatedly called Alexei, did not have an ulterior motive.

*

For twelve days, I did my best to do just as Alexei instructed me—pressing the strings tight against the fingerboard with the tips of my fingers, finding the notes I sought with only the subtlest movements up and down the strings, holding the bow lightly at the frog and drawing it rhythmically across the strings, allowing the bridge and the hidden sound post to vibrate in the way Alexei explained they must for the sound to be rich and strong and satisfying. Before too many days were done, I could passably play the scales, and even play a little Hungarian folk song; I played it well enough, in fact, that once a few other Hungarians onboard the ship who heard it stopped for a moment to sing along. I hoped Alexei would take up the tar, in turn, but he was content just to be my instructor. I had real talent, he repeatedly assured me, and he seemed to take as much pleasure in teaching me as he did when he sometimes took the violin himself and played a bit of Mozart or Chopin or Liszt so wondrously that the people who gathered around responded with strong and grateful applause.

It was hard to imagine that I had so clearly learned what I wanted from life in the middle of the Atlantic Ocean, but I had. I wanted to be able to play the violin as well as Alexei did—more than anything. I wanted to bring tears to people's eyes just as he could, to offer them beauty and the kind of emotion that only music could express so sublimely. I wanted to be a *violinist* one day, and I remember my desperate hope as the ship ventured west that you could find violins in America and that even poor boys like me could learn how to play them. And it was in the middle of a lesson one afternoon, as I stood playing for Alexei, that three Armenian boys rushed through the salon with the extraordinary news that land had appeared on the horizon—America was only barely out of our reach and we were steaming in her direction.

Alexei was as excited by the news as I was, I could tell, and we forgot the lesson and quickly put his violin in its case and raced to the nearest deck where, *yes*, we could see the low hills at the mouth of New York's harbor and the thin ribbon of water that separated them and allowed passage inside. It seemed everyone in steerage class had joined us now—people from many faraway worlds eager to see this new one, this *America*, and rumors rushed through the crowd that once inside the narrows we would see the tall buildings of Manhattan Island in the distance, and then the statue of a lady that, they swore, the Americans had placed in the harbor simply to welcome immigrants like us.

The great ship's steam engines continued to growl at full speed as we sailed toward the mouth of the harbor, but inside the narrows the captain cut them back and we seemed only to inch forward now, a pace that everyone on the deck soon began to complain about; why in the world should we slow to crawl when we were this close to our destination?

I could glimpse New York's high buildings in the far distance whenever someone shifted his spot at the rail, but I couldn't spot this lady people said we would see until at last she stood very near at hand on the port side. And she *was* huge, this lady, and made of green clay, it appeared. She wore something that looked like the bed sheets the Greeks and Romans wore and carried both a torch and a tablet, and crowning her head were the rays of the sun, or some such thing. It was hard for me to imagine why she was so famous—even among people who had never ventured to America before—but I was glad to see her nonetheless, and so was Alexei, who lifted me onto his shoulders so I could get a better view despite the fact that he wasn't a particularly well-muscled fellow.

A few of the men on the deck who had been to America before pointed out the block of buildings on what was called Ellis Island where, they said, we would have to endure still more examinations before we were free to go where we chose, yet the ship did not stop there. Instead, it sailed still farther into the harbor, then made a long and dramatic starboard turn before docking at a pier on Manhattan Island, not far from a collection of more enormous buildings than I thought could possibly exist in all of the cities of the world.

As we watched men on the pier wrestle with the huge ropes they used to secure the gigantic ship, crew members onboard began shouting in several languages into bullhorns, telling those of us in third class that we would not be leaving the ship for perhaps a couple of days. It was hard to believe that we had reached America yet would remain stuck onboard a ship we had grown awfully tired of, but apparently a number of vessels had reached New York's harbor at the same time and their thousands of passengers as well as those of us in steerage on the *King Alexander* would have to take our turns at passing through Ellis Island.

But there was better news for those who had traveled the Atlantic on the *King Alexander*'s upper decks—the people in first and second class. I had lost track of Alexei in all the excitement and commotion as the ship docked, and I sadly presumed that he was among those who were welcome to disembark directly into the heart of the city at their leisure. If people like the violinist and his family could afford the cost of those pricey tickets, it appeared, no one was worried about the condition of their eyes, their lungs, or their pocketbooks. America was the land of equal opportunity, I'd heard a hundred times as we sailed in her direction, but it appeared that your opportunities were decidedly more equal if had some coin in your trouser pocket.

*

S.S. King Alexander (previous to 1920, she was named the S.S. Cleveland)

George's visa photo taken at the U.S. Consulate, Tiflis, Caucasus, February 8, 1921. His mother is center with sister Maria on the right. Note: The large upside-down letters read, "-SEEN- DEPARTMENT STATE OF NEW YORK"

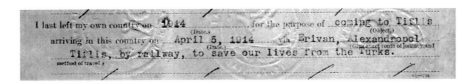

A section of the visa that was filled out when the family was applying to come to America. It read, "I last left my own country on 1914 for the purpose of coming to Tiflis arriving in this country on April 5, 1914 via Erivan, Alexandropol, Tiflis, by railway, to save our lives from the Turks."

I was beside myself. The weather was blistering hot and the bowels of the ship where we slept smelled far worse than they had at the beginning of our journey three weeks before. The food I had wolfed down in the beginning now no longer interested me, and neither did the kids with whom I'd played for so many days seem worth my while any longer. I'd never see Alexei again, I was sure, so there would be no more learning the violin, and there seemed to be nothing else for me to do but stand at the rail and try to imagine America from a part of New York City that evidently was called "Pier 72."

Yet as dusk approached on that first afternoon in New York, I was amazed when Alexei walked to the rail beside me and, still speaking in Russian, said, "When would you like your first violin lesson in America?" I couldn't believe someone like him hadn't walked off the *King Alexander* a free man hours before. Was it possible that he had crossed the Atlantic in steerage, too, and that a remarkable musician like Alexei was as poor as we were, and also subject to the interminable wait and inspections of Ellis Island? "We don't have anything better to do," he added, "and a steward told me it could be a couple of days before it's our turn to be processed."

I told Alexei I was ready to return to the violin the moment that he was, and the following morning the two of us felt rather kingly as we entered an upper-deck salon we would have been tossed out of just thirty-six hours before. The place was deserted except for a steward or two who walked through in the midst of my lesson, and I played better than I ever had before—and maybe I had New York City to thank for that—then I asked my friend if he would play an entire piece for me. "Sure," he said and he asked, "How about Paganini?"—assuring me this Italian who'd lived long ago was the greatest violinist who ever lived before he dazzled me with a piece so intricate, so complicated—and so wild—that I couldn't imagine how a boy like me could ever dream of playing with such mastery.

Alexei and I met for a lesson again in the afternoon, not long after the good news had reached us that tomorrow we would be ferried to Ellis Island for processing and, we hoped, the freedom to enter America at last. That night—a beautiful evening when the heat of the day had given way to cool breezes, and people had escaped the confines of the dormitory to talk, laugh, and make music in the open air—we sat in broad white lounge chairs on an upper deck as I told my mother, Maria, and Babajan for the third or fourth time how wonderfully Alexei had played in a private concert simply for me. Then, out of the darkness of the summer night, the sudden and seemingly impossible sounds of explosions rocked the *King Alexander*. It was cannon fire, we instantly knew—we had grown all too familiar with the ear-pounding blasts of cannons during our years in Tiflis—and the deafening booms rattled the steel walls of the ship.

Instinctively, we jumped from the big wooden chairs and hid behind them, as did dozens more people who, like us, had become bitterly acquainted with war before we'd arrived in New York. In only seconds, the blasts were followed by great bursts of fire that lit up the sky in flashes of red and orange. I saw on my mother's face that look of terror I hadn't seen since we escaped the revolution in southern Russia, and I think her expression frightened me more than the blasts themselves. "My God, it can't be," she cried, and her plea was echoed by the shouts of the people surrounding us.

Soon, the night sky was bombarded by fire. Shells seemed to explode every second, the fire raining down in terrifying fountains of color, and this time my mother shouted, "Save us from more killing!" There were wild cries from every direction; some people were desperate to get off the open deck and find some safety; others were paralyzed with fear and did not move, and a few tried to convince those around them that there wasn't a cause for alarm.

My mother shrieked at me to stay by her side, but I couldn't help but follow Babajan to spot where people had gathered. There, we could see the open water as well as the city, and it was clear that the war had spread to the town someone called Hoboken that lay on the opposite shore. In Hoboken, like New York, shells exploded above the rooftops in terrifying shapes, and it was hard to believe that we had been in America for most of two days without hearing that this country, too, was wracked by killing, just as our Assyrian homeland had been, and Russia as well, and all of the world that had gone to war just a few years before.

When we returned to my mother and Maria, we found them huddled together behind a chair, and my mother shouted at us to protect ourselves as well. I looked at her again, and saw by her face that she was as broken-hearted as she was afraid, but just as I got down to join her, two Greek stewards who seemed exasperated by the steerage passengers' reactions to the firebombing and the commotion it caused stopped to assure us that everything was okay.

I couldn't really understand them, but it was clear from their demeanor that, as far as they were concerned, these "fireworks" were rather different from revolution, and that there was nothing to be afraid of in the spectacular explosions that filled the sky. A fellow who spoke some Greek got the stewards to explain that fireworks, in fact, were a kind of celebration—today was America's birthday, they claimed—and that information quickly made its way into a half dozen languages and, as it did, people began to get up from behind their chairs.

One of the stewards took me by the shoulder and walked with me to the rail, where he pointed to the sky and made a big motion with his hands. "Boom," he said in broken Russian. "Boom is good. Not bad. Everything fine. Everything happy."

And I made sure my mother understood, too, that all was well, but not before I stood for a bit and simply watched the fantastic shapes and colors that lit the night over New York and Hoboken and all of America perhaps, and I marveled that these Americans had such money to spend on a birthday.

*

Early the following morning, half a dozen cabin stewards made their rounds with news that by eight o'clock sharp we were to have our bags packed and be standing ready at our bunks, at which time they would begin to call us in groups to make our way to a boat that would ferry us to Ellis Island. Everyone was nervous now and people were largely silent as we waited. Despite the sweltering early July heat and the humidity in the steerage dormitory that ran the length of the ship, we wore our overcoats to free our hands and arms for our luggage, and I remember sweating miserably while we waited. Then, at last it was our turn to make our way off the ship and onto a barge, where we stood packed together like fish in a net while the boat churned its way across the harbor.

When it docked and we stepped onto the island, I raised my hands and shouted, "Hey, I'm standing on America!," but my mother scolded me to keep quiet. She was afraid once more, I could tell—afraid about her eyes, of course, and whether they would pose a problem for us again; afraid that she would make some mistake that would cause the Americans to send us back across the ocean; afraid, perhaps, of what it would be like to join my father again if we were, in fact, set free.

The weather only continued to grow hotter as we stood in interminable lines throughout that day—first waiting to check our baggage, a requirement that immediately worried hundreds of people whose whole lives were contained in their tattered cases, and then waited again for our turn to speak with immigration officials who, in our case, already possessed copies of the documents executed by the American embassy in Tiflis and the steamship company.

The visas prepared in Tiflis had identified my mother as "Mrs. Khatoon Keorgich Aziz"—"Keorgich" had been a gross misspelling of my father's first name, "Georges," by someone at the American consulate in Tiflis. On the ship's manifest, which would become the official Ellis Island document, a similar mistake had been made, but this time my father's name was spelled "Georghiz." The name "Aziz" didn't appear on the documents because my father wasn't traveling with us. He had been born "Georges Yadgar Aziz," and in the Assyrian tradition, I was named "Sargis Georges Yadgar"—his first and middle name becoming my middle and last name.

The Ellis Island clerk with whom we first met saw no need to ask whether the manifest entry was correct, and with a few scribbles on his part, the papers correctly listed her age as 48 and incorrectly identified her ethnicity as "Syrian" rather than Assyrian. They ominously explained as well that her reason for immigrating was "to save our lives from the Turks," a statement that had been tragically true when the flight for her family's lives had begun back in Alwach six and a half years before.

When the clerk turned his attention to the three dependents with whom my mother was traveling, he listed Babajan, her 25-year old "son," as "Polous"—just as we had planned—and Maria remained "Maria." Someone at the American embassy in Tiflis had used the Armenian spelling of my name—"Sarkis"—instead of Assyrian "Sargis," and, like my mother and sisters, my new surname would at least temporarily be "Georghiz," and that was entirely fine with me. The plain truth was that if it meant leaving war and famine behind, someone could have named us "Yankee" or "Pluto" or "King Alexander," and we simply would have nodded our heads in gratitude. Like everyone else in our weathered shoes, we were desperate not to be put back on the ship as deportees.

Each of us breathed a great sigh of relief as the clerk officiously stamped the papers and hurried us out of his sight, then other officials barking orders ensured that we moved immediately to the broad and high staircase that led to the Great Hall. As we climbed the stairs, men who were dressed in uniforms and military caps watched us carefully, looking for signs, I later learned, of problems with legs or lungs or a host of other conditions—maladies that might preclude us from entry into the United States. I'm not sure why these men were dressed more like soldiers than the physicians they actually were, but occasionally one of them would interrupt the flow of people up the stairs to write in chalk on someone's coat or shirt—the letters E, H, L, SC, and X alerting, we suspected, officials we were about to encounter to medical suspicions they didn't bother to explain.

In the Great Hall, there were seas of tables and dozens more doctors in uniform stationed beside them, examining every one of us with a quick flurry of attention. The fellow who attended to me gave a perfunctory listen to my chest with a stethoscope, pulled back my eyelids with something that looked like a button hook, then asked me in English how old I was. I didn't understand until he held up his fingers, then I, in turn, held up ten fingers of my own—a response that proved I wasn't mentally deficient, although he must have wondered whether I was.

We collectively held our breaths when this doctor turned his attention to my mother. She had escaped being marked with an E as she climbed the stairs, but still she was gravely concerned that the eye infection that had kept us in Constantinople for those months now might block our progress again. But even after he poked at her eyes with his button hook, the doctor appeared unconcerned, and rather quickly our biggest hurdle was behind us; neither my mother, Maria, or me, or the cousin who pretended to be my brother worried these men whose jobs were to keep America healthy, and soon our medical papers were stamped and we faced only one more interrogation—this one a series of questions about where we planned to settle, and whether anyone was waiting for us, and how we planned to travel from New York to our destinations, questions that we had ready answers for and that once more satisfied the weary people who asked them.

*

We were all but free now, and our spirits were light, and even my mother's face seemed to lose the fear that had frozen it since our arrival in the harbor. All that remained to do before we stood in a final line to board the ferry that would take us back to Manhattan was to collect our baggage, and I was thrilled as we waited when Alexei the violinist came to retrieve his and his parents' luggage as well.

They, too, had passed all their tests, Alexei explained, but he was worried nonetheless. He had been forced to leave his violin and the case that held it with the baggage clerks as the process began, and he wouldn't be at ease, he said, until the instrument was safely in his hands again. I let him move ahead of us in line, which the people behind us complained about in a language I didn't understand. Alexei presented his ticket, and waited, then watched helplessly as the clerk returned with his case and, in the crush of people at the counter, presented it to someone else. A look of terror suddenly flooded Alexei's face, and he shouted at the clerk and the man who now held his violin. The case belonged to him, he frantically tried to explain, and as he did, the man—dark-haired and no older than

Alexei was—tried his best to make the clerk understand that the case didn't, in fact, belong to him.

It took only a second or two for everyone to understand, and the man who now held the case smiled broadly as he handed it to Alexei, aware perhaps of the precious contents a case of that shape probably contained. The two men struggled to find a way to communicate, but they couldn't find a language they commonly knew, so they contented themselves with broad smiles and a hand on each other's shoulder.

I watched as Alexei continued to try to express his thanks to this dark-eyed fellow who had such a friendly demeanor, but all he could think to do was to continue to smile, bow a little, and press his palm to his chest as he pronounced his own name. "Alexei," he said second time, tapping his chest twice more.

The fellow's eyes brightened at that, and he, in turn, he patted his chest as he offered his own name. "Giuseppe," he proudly announced, "Giuseppe." Then, still smiling broadly, he turned to me to make the same introduction. "Giuseppe," he said, and I was glad to meet him, and I patted myself with my palm, and I was Sargis, I told him.

"Sargis," Giuseppe repeated.

"Sargis," I said once more as my mother called to me to hurry and join them and I smiled and waved goodbye to him. It always had been easy for me to meet people till now—whether in Tiflis, or Constantinople, or on a lumbering train or an immigrant ship. And although I was sad to be leaving Alexei—and who knew if I'd ever play the violin again?—I was glad to get the sense that even without knowing a word of English, I could keep making friends in America. I picked up my bag and joined my mother, Maria, and Babajan as we made our way out of the Great Hall and toward the ferry—free, all of us, and at home, a very long way from home.

Yalapa, 1972

I WAS TEN-YEARS-old, my sister Jennifer was six, and my mother, still only twenty-eight, was itching for some adventure. Three years earlier, we had visited Mexico with my mother's second husband, and she had fallen in love with the country's remote and beautiful Jalisco coast. So, when she finally had had enough of John Hoffman and left him in 1972, off we went—just the three of us—to an Indian village called Yalapa that had no electricity or running water and was accessible only via an hour-long boat ride from Puerto Vallarta.

We rented a large palapa surrounded by jungle and overlooking the bay, and my mother was quickly happier than I'd ever seen her, free at last from abusive husbands and enchanted by the simplicity of life in the Mexican tropics. I loved to wander into the jungle to watch for and listen to birds; I rode donkeys and horses and was fascinated to watch men butcher cattle and goats, then sell their meat to the village families. My only daily task—one I'm sure I decided was mine—was to make the short walk to the tiny adobe post office, where the few pieces of mail for the day were simply placed on an open window sill. I would sift through the letters desperately hoping I'd find one from Poppy, but I was disappointed almost every day. He wasn't much of a letter writer, and back in Santa Barbara his life remained as busy as always, but I fiercely missed him and longed to be in touch.

Occasionally, we would make the trip into Puerto Vallarta and endure the hours-long wait at the Larga Distancia telephone office. As we waited, I would imagine that teams of Mexican workers must be hurriedly laying telephone cable across the mountains and deserts to reach the United States, but then finally our call would be ready, we would enter a tiny booth, and I could talk to Poppy for just a few minutes—and those brief conversations were all that I needed. His voice comforted me, and assured me of something I couldn't describe then and still cannot.

I'm not sure how long my mother had hoped to stay in Yalapa—it might have been forever—but when we ran completely out of money we had no choice but to go home. We boarded a train and settled in for a long trip, sharing crackers, tortillas, and cheese as we wound our way north. At the station in Culiacán, I got off the train to wander around a bit and was shocked to see and hear the train begin to move again. From an open window, my mother screamed at me to get on, but I froze. I didn't know what to do, and my mother was absolutely panicked until a conductor jumped off, swooped me up in his arms, then bounded onto the train again. My mother cried as she hugged me tightly, asking if I didn't remember the story about how Poppy—in much the same way—had almost lost his family as they traveled by train out of Russia. But I hadn't been attempting my own sort of great adventure, I assured her, and I knew, too, that even at my age, Poppy would have known how to jump aboard a rolling train.

Chapter 4

A Violinist

THE FERRY RIDE to Manhattan was very different from the kind of travel by boat we were accustomed to by now—in largest part because we were no longer stateless. We weren't American citizens yet—and who knew whether we ever would be?—but unlike our strange and uneasy status in Russia, and then in Turkey, as we departed Ellis Island and traveled across New York's harbor, we were no longer refugees.

We were *welcome* in the United States; we were free to stay as long as we chose—forever if we took to the place—and although my mother never openly smiled as the moist breeze reddened her cheeks and the city's unimaginably tall buildings approached, I could see a deeply calming kind of relief spread across her face now that we had passed every test and proven our worth. We had been told that yes, we could proceed to Connecticut.

It was late in the day by the time we made our way by clattering streetcar from the ferry terminal to immense and crowded Grand Central Station, where we boarded a train—and although none of us said so out loud, I think each of us was relieved that the loud and frenzied city, whose streets were teaming with more people than I could imagine, was not our final American destination. For all we knew, the city called Bristol to which we were bound was every bit as big and chaotic as well, but at least in Bristol we would find family members who had made homes there, homes where we would be welcome.

I remember being sad once more about the loss of my animals as the train tunneled its way out of the city, then emerged in the gloaming light of the summer evening, and no doubt I sniffled along the way, leaning against my mother, who wore her coat despite the heat, her scarf she tied tightly under her chin. I dozed at last, then awoke in the darkness to news that we had reached the town of Berlin, where my sister Sophie and her husband Sargis stood on a platform to greet us as we stepped off the train, our bags in our hands at the end of a journey that had begun three weeks before in Constantinople.

My mother cried when she saw Sophie, hugging her again after five years of separation, and Sophie cried, and Maria cried, and Sophie's husband Sargis—a huge and immediately friendly man—embraced Babajan like an old friend, although he'd never met him, then lifted me in his arms and asked me in Assyrian how I liked America, telling me it was the best place in the world to be and assuring me that I would like it just fine before I had spoken a word.

Sargis found a way to get all of our baggage into the trunk of the car that belonged to Cousin Babasi, who was waiting behind the wheel, and when we all were squeezed onboard, I realized that this cousin I'd never met before was surely the *owner* of the car and therefore a wealthy man. I wanted to ask him if he was rich, in fact, but I was in the backseat and everyone was talking nonstop, and I fell asleep not long after we'd left the station.

*

Sargis must have carried me inside and put me down for the night, because the next thing I remember is waking up the following morning in a real bed—the kind with a mattress made with wires that felt like I was lying on a cloud—with two kids standing beside me and staring me in the face to try to ascertain something about this sleepy stranger.

"Who are you?" I asked them in Assyrian.

"I'm Julia," a girl about five- or six-years old announced—and I later learned she was Sophie and Sargis's daughter. She introduced her brother Albert, and I asked whose bed it was that I was sleeping in. When Julia said it was hers, I quickly began to get up, but she said it was okay; she had slept with her mother and father. Albert didn't say much at all, but Julia was full of information, and soon the two of them began to show me the house—a palace of a place with a roller piano in the parlor and bedrooms everywhere, it seemed, and a roomy kitchen in which a huge dog lay on the floor. His name was Pal, Julia said, and he was quite gentle, and I immediately made friends with him and knew that I'd be fine in a house with a dog like him.

Nine of us lived in close quarters during those first days, but that was nothing about which I bore any complaint. The house had electricity in *every* room, an icebox and a big wood burning cook-stove in the kitchen, and these were plainly the most impressive circumstances in which I had ever found myself, the embassy in Constantinople included. I marveled at the bathroom, where *hot* water ran from the faucet as well as cold, and I loved when it was my turn to take a shower. I'd stand in the center of the big tub, and deliciously warm water would rain down on me from above, and I'd hold a fat bar of soap in my hand and think, no wonder so many people love this America.

My niece and nephew—just a few years younger than I was—showed me the backyard, filled with grape vines and fruit trees and the garage that Sargis had built, and when I asked if he was as rich as they were, they laughed, and Julia said, "I don't think so." Her father was a house painter, she explained, and as far as she knew, house painters were very important, but they weren't wealthy. Then we walked out to the street in front of the house, and Julia wanted me to know that many children lived nearby, most of them Polish. I didn't know what sort of child a Polish child was, so Julia explained that the

Polish had a different language and a different church, but, otherwise, they were the same as us.

We walked to a park with big, broad canopy of trees and deep green, rolling lawns, then made our way down the hill, across a short bridge, and soon we stood at the shore of a beautiful little lake. There was a playground at its shore, with slides and swings and rings suspended by chains. I watched boys who hung from the rings by their hands arc out over the water and drop into it with a dramatic splash, and I was amazed to see people who appeared to be wearing their bedclothes lounging on the grass that sloped down to the water's edge, and I thought that everything must be easy and fun in America, if this was how every hot summer day got underway.

But the truth was that as the following days unfolded, I found that I wasn't really comfortable around my young niece and nephew, who were so proud and eager that first morning to show me their house and their town. I loved spending time with Babajan and people who were older than me, but till now, I'd never really played with other children—my sister Maria included—and I quickly discovered that I didn't like it. For me, nothing felt better than to explore—whether forests or docklands or boisterous city streets— and exploration was an enterprise that seemed best undertaken on my own, certainly not in the company of two younger kids who clung to me like damp clothes wherever I tried to go.

It wasn't that the two of them were unkind to me; it was just the opposite, in fact. They seemed to look up to me in a way I couldn't understand, particularly because *they* could speak English, and speak it as well as any other American child, something that was very much beyond my skills at the moment. Neither Julia or Albert seemed to mind in the least that Maria and I had invaded the house in which they had been the only children, nor had they been concerned, I supposed, when newborn Bobby and his mother—my sister Nanajan —had moved in soon after Nanajan's husband

Absalom had died of infection after having his tonsils removed. I presumed I simply would have to learn how to accept the attentions of the three younger children—or find better ways to ditch them when I ventured out to pick the blueberries that grew in profusion or walk the shore of the lake—until my mother announced one day that we were about to move on, this time to my father's house in nearby New Britain.

*

*Sophie's Daughter Julia, left, Nanajan's son Robert, "Bobby," center and
Sophie's son, Albert, right, with George standing in rear.
New Britain, Connecticut 1921*

My father, by that point was someone I barely remembered, although his presence always had loomed large in our lives, whether he was physically with us or not. Somehow, he had made his patriarchal presence felt at Sophie and Sargis's house as well as several days passed before he telephoned to announce that he now was ready for us to join him. New Britain was no more than ten miles away from Bristol, but his work and his many commitments had consumed him during those days, and he hadn't managed to visit the wife and two children he hadn't seen for five years. Yet at last he was ready for us—whatever that meant. Perhaps he'd been busy repairing and painting the apartment, but he'd known for months that we were on our way. Perhaps he had a tryst of some kind to put to a close before we properly joined his household, yet I knew from the way Sophie, Sargis, and Nanajan spoke of him that he remained highly esteemed in New Britain's Assyrian community and at the local Assyrian Church of the East and that he even delivered sermons at mass from time to time when the priest was ill and his voice was gone.

Whatever the reason for the delay, at last it was time to encounter the man whom Sophie and Nanajan now were eager to caution me about. "Be sure to behave yourself in front of Father," Sophie suggested as we piled into the car for the short drive. "He's grumpy most of the time. Do exactly as he says and you won't be into trouble."

Yet Father didn't seem bad-tempered so much as formal when we pulled up to the large house on Lafayette Street where he lived in a third floor apartment. He met us downstairs, and I remember him shaking my mother's hand as if he was pleased to meet her. She took his hand easily enough but was careful to do nothing more—not a hug or even a quick kiss on the cheek at the end of their long separation. But he did hug Maria and ask her if she'd come to America to find a boyfriend; Maria blushed and dropped her eyes to the ground and said simply, "No." Then he turned to

Babajan, gave him a rather formal embrace, and thanked him for looking out for us as we traveled.

Prior to my reintroduction to my father, my mother had rewarded me with my first pair of proper trousers. I was thrilled to be out of short pants and to wear men's clothes at last—complete with a belt and a shiny buckle that made me particularly proud. But I must not have appeared too grown-up because, when it was my turn to greet him and I held out my hand, Father hugged me as well and even kissed my cheek.

"Are you a good boy?" he wanted to know.

"Yes, I'm a good boy," I responded without a moment's consideration, but he wasn't persuaded.

"Well, we shall see," he said, and that was that.

I did my best to follow my older sisters' advice as we carried our baggage up the stairway to the third floor, and I was astonished when my father opened a door inside the big apartment and said, "This is your room, Sargis." I was completely bowled over by his announcement; I would have a room to myself in my father's house in New Britain, Connecticut, U.S. of America, and my feelings toward this man whom I didn't really know improved markedly in that moment.

As we settled into our new home on Lafayette Street, I was careful to keep my room clean and orderly. Father had announced as we ate our first supper together that the one thing he couldn't abide in our new lives together would be coming home after an arduous day's work to a messy or dirty apartment, and I took his words deeply to heart. In addition to making a virtual showplace of my bedroom, I began to take off my shoes each time I entered the front door, careful never to track dirt or mud inside. I did everything I could to help keep the bathroom clean and to lend my mother a hand in the kitchen, and I was successful enough keeping the floors swept that one day my father went so far as to pat me on the head and say, "You *are* a good boy. You're not going to be a bum after all." And bums, it turned out, were the worst kind of creatures my father could imagine. "You know what ought to happen to bums?" he wanted to know, and I shook my head. "Every useless bum," he continued gravely, "ought to be rounded up and taken out into the middle of the ocean and dumped." I paid attention—in part because I couldn't yet swim, but also because it seemed that perhaps things would be permanently different in America. My father would *like* me rather than hate me, it began to appear, and I wanted to do everything I could to exhibit no sign of bumness.

If everyone in our household—my mother included, of course—tried hard never to upset my father, it appeared that his colleagues and friends at work and at church had nothing but abiding respect for him and that none of them had any reason to fear him. My father Georges Aziz, now 55-years old, had been processed at Ellis Island as "Georg Edgaroff"—the surname he and my two oldest sisters had used to help hide the fact that they were Assyrian Christians as they traveled through Russia en route to Norway and the ship that would carry them across the Atlantic. "Edgaroff" was a derivative of "Yadgar," of course, but to simplify things, he changed the family's surname to "Edgar" soon after his arrival. Yet if George Edgaroff now was his American name, he remained Georges Aziz among the Assyrians in New Britain. In fact, he was *Usta* Georges Aziz, we discovered—an Assyrian honorific a bit like "master" or "sir," one that was applied only to men who seemed to richly deserve it.

Father would rise at dawn six days a week, eat the breakfast my mother unfailingly had ready for him once he was shaved and dressed, then walk the ten blocks to the Willington Pulp Company where he built wooden patterns for iron and steel castings. It was the same highly skilled work he had done during the times he sojourned

in Russia when our family still lived in Persia, and in New Britain—
an industrial town people often called the "Detroit of the East" for
reasons I didn't entirely understand—it was work for which my
father was highly paid. He earned remarkable money for an
immigrant who still struggled to speak English, and enough that he
was able to provide for his large family in ways that made us seem
unimaginably prosperous, particularly in comparison with the years
in Tiflis when we often had to scavenge to eat.

Our third story home had indoor plumbing, steam heat,
running water that was heated by the kitchen's cook-stove, and
Persian rugs, my memory insists, covered almost every floor in the
house and many of its walls. On the walls as well hung the
instruments Father made—beautiful tars and balalaikas, many of
them inlaid with mother of pearl and rubies and each with a sound
as rich and pure as any made in Persia or Russia, instruments he
proudly displayed and sometimes played, the one instance in which
that very private man would let something of his inner self shine
through.

Soon after we settled into our new house in America, Father
bought my mother—the wife he remained reluctant to kiss or even
touch in his children's presence—a *ghalyan*, an elaborate water pipe
with a long, flexible stem that sometimes is called a hookah, this one
made of brass, glass, silk, and inlaid stones. It was a gift my mother
treasured, and I remember her smoking it almost every night after
the dinner and dishes were done, while we sat in the parlor and
played backgammon or cards or listened as my father played
mournful songs on his tar, or simply sipped the liqueur he made
from raisins. And I was the recipient of his largesse as well. He was
careful not to make a big show of its presentation to me, but I was
bowled over when he gave me a beautiful red and green bicycle, a
remarkable machine I rode every day thereafter, thinking I was the
luckiest and perhaps the richest boy in the world, and which I

learned to ride only after I discovered that the faster I pedaled the easier it was to stay balanced.

Then, out of the blue one day, I saw him walking up the sidewalk with a box under his arm as he returned home from work. "Come upstairs with me," he gruffly announced, then we climbed the stairs together. Inside the kitchen, he stiffly added, "This is for you," as he handed me the box. Inside were a pair of knee high, lace-up boots, the kind of boots every boy dreamed of owning in those days—*manly* boots that fit me perfectly and that I wore almost constantly and of which I was extremely proud.

This man who kept so much of himself safely secured inside him did occasionally converse with me as well—something fathers often do with sons, but which, in my case, was a rare enough experience that I still remember him inviting me to sit on his lap one day a few months after our arrival. He asked me to tell him about my school and the things I was learning there. "I want you to study hard and get good marks," he told me, "because if you're going to get along in this world, you've got to have an education."

I promised him I would study hard, but he wanted to say more. "I'm doing well in America," he explained, "but I would do much better if I had an education. I never went to school like you are."

I didn't quite understand how an education could be of value to someone as talented as he was, and said, "But Father, if you did have an education, your hands would still work the same way. You could still make things as beautifully as you do." He agreed that an education wouldn't rob him of the gift of his hands, but there was much more that it could give him, he assured me, adding that the more education you had, the more money you made. It was a fact, as far as he was concerned, and something I'd never considered till then, and before I got down from his knee, I solemnly promised that I would learn everything I could about—everything.

Despite those assurances, I was eager to work with my hands as well, to develop the skills I admired so much in him, and Father was always willing to let me watch him use his woodworking tools, so long as I remained utterly quiet. I learned that every tool had to be kept razor sharp—whether a knife or chisel or saw—and I quietly noted which tools were best for particular tasks, and before long I secretly began to construct a sailboat, just twelve inches long or so, but complete with a wooden hull, masts, rudder, and stabilizers, and sails made from scraps of fabric my mother said she could spare. I hid it carefully away, and worked on it a little each day. When it was complete, I varnished it just as I had seen him finish wood many times, and at last I was brave enough to show him what I had made.

I took it out of my closet and held it up for him and he said, "You made this?" with a note of surprise in his voice. I assured him I had and he pronounced it "very nice," then said now he would show me how to make a platform for it, so we could display the boat on a bookshelf. I was thrilled. My sailboat was worthy of being exhibited, just as his instruments were, and I think more than at any other moment during the short time I lived with and knew him, I felt truly accepted by him. I wasn't a bum but rather someone who could make something of value with his hands and maybe even play the tar acceptably well. In other words, I believed I was someone like him as he praised and admired my sailboat, and that was something I wanted entirely to believe.

*

But if my father occasionally was kind to me and offered his attention and even his praise, the truth was that those times were exceedingly rare. Georges Aziz had been a fighter for much of his life—he had been shot at dozens of times, and had fired at and killed a number of marauding Turks and Kurds—and he found it difficult to trust men, even boys, or to truly like them.

Aloof as he regularly was with everyone, I often observed him interacting with my older sisters or Maria or my mother in ways that were far less guarded, less insular, less self-protective than the ways in which he approached me, or even the men with whom he worked or the priests at the church who held him in such high regard. I suppose it's likely that he grew close to Sophie and Nanajan as they arduously made their way across Russia to Norway, then on to the U.S., and that they remained close during the years they lived in Connecticut prior to our arrival. Although Maria was terribly shy—or perhaps because she was—he would patiently draw her words from her, and even her emotions, in ways I wished he would do with me, and occasionally I would see him studying my mother's face with great interest and affection as she mended clothes or did other kinds of needlework in the hours after supper.

But except for the gifts of the bicycle and boots, except for the time he cautioned me that I would very much need an education, except for that wonderful occasion when he openly admired my sailboat, my father was as cold and severe with me as he was toward strangers he passed on the street, as disdainful of me as he was of the "bums" who vexed him so terribly.

As I look back, it's clear in very long hindsight that my father was deeply troubled the day he learned that I had killed the soldier who attacked my mother, and from then on, his opinion of me dramatically changed. "It was your duty as a foreigner not to interfere with a soldier of the tsar," he pronounced, and when my mother heard him say this, she was outraged.

"Sargis saved me from that pig," she said, spitting her words at him. "I could have been killed, who knows? But Sargis put an end to it. He was very brave and you're wrong to condemn him."

I had never heard her tell him he was mistaken about *anything* before, certainly not about something pertaining to life and death, and my father leveled an icy glare at her that seemed to wilt her, and she said nothing more.

Then, he turned to me, his cheeks flushed with rage. "You were just a little boy with no business holding a pistol in your hand. No business trying to be a big man. You're not a man. You're a bum, like I was afraid you would be."

I hadn't heard the word "bum," for a month or more, and the word—coming from him—cut into me like a knife. I was crushed to think that he believed I was a bum, crushed to think I might actually be one if this man so many people admired believed I was. I didn't want him to see me cry, yet I could feel the tears begin to well up in my eyes, and I simply turned and walked toward my bedroom, Father shouting out, "Shall we dump you at sea with all the other bums?" as I retreated.

It was hard to imagine that my father was deeply angry with me for saving my mother, but he clearly was. She couldn't dissuade him from it, and certainly neither could I, and from that day forward my father treated me dismissively every time he encountered me, except on those occasions when his venom accumulated and he shouted at me in a fury. No amount of doing what I could to keep the house clean, no errand-running on his behalf, nothing I made or said or acquiesced seemed to make the slightest difference. I had killed a Russian soldier as he was trying to rape my mother, and for reasons I could not understand, it was an act for which this man could not forgive me.

My mother was aware of the change in him, and surely everyone else in house—Maria and Nanajan and even her infant son Bobby—must have sensed the bile that hung in the air, but no one ever said anything. No one explained Father's reaction to me, or excused it, or even tried to comfort me. And all I could do was to remind myself that nothing really had changed. My father had pronounced me a bum on the day I was born, then had dismissed me as a bum a dozen times before he left Tiflis for America, and it really wasn't a surprise, I decided, that I remained a bum in his eyes in New Britain, where he was free, and employed, and proud of the respect with which he was honored by so many, a place where his son simply didn't measure up.

As the weeks passed, I did my best to give him a very wide berth—that was the one self-protective thing I could do. I had to sit with him at the dinner table, of course, but otherwise I largely succeeded at keeping as much of Connecticut as I could between him and me. And it was fine with me soon thereafter when Father announced that I was no longer welcome to eat with him and the rest of the family. I could eat outside, he said, or in my bedroom, and that was fine with me, and no one dared to try to dissuade him.

During good weather, my father liked to sit for hours on the wide porch that ran the length of our third-story home, and while once I had enjoyed spending time near the place where he sat, working on whatever wood project he was captivated by at the moment, now I stayed away. Yet one day, on the way home from school, my mother met me a half a block from the house, where I was lingering with boys from my class before we parted for the day. Father was ill and had stayed home from work, yet he was well enough to sit on the porch, and he had seen me with my friends, she explained, and didn't like it, and wanted me home immediately. "I have to take you to him," she explained as we briskly made our way back to the house. "He'll yell at you, but don't let it bother you," she urged. "He doesn't mean anything by it. He's impatient, is all."

She escorted me out to the porch after we'd climbed the stairs, and she was right: he launched into me with particular passion because I hadn't come home as fast as I possibly could. "I was just talking to my friends," I timidly tried to explain, but my attempt to explain myself enraged him, and he reached for the ancient sword with a rubber tip that he used as a cane and swung it at me, striking me first on the rump, then twice more on the shoulder before my mother bravely wrestled it out of his hands, screaming at him to stop. I climbed over the porch railing and onto the second story roof and got away before he could curse me or hit me again, and that was that. He never said anything more about my grave misdeed, nor did my mother by way of defending me or explaining his bizarre reaction, and I remember crying in bed sometimes in the aftermath of that day, filled with sorrow about the fact that my father wanted to dump me in the sea.

The proof of his desire to be done with me arrived not long thereafter, on a Sunday morning as we strolled home from church — everyone in our house and perhaps a dozen other Assyrians who lived nearby — all of us enjoying the break from the summer heat and a day of play and leisure. A boy whom I knew and liked suggested we run ahead, and as we squeezed our way between the sea of adults, I heard the man my father was talking with say I was a good-looking boy.

"I could kill him," he announced. "He's not worth a thing. I'd love to be rid of the bum."

His words might have been meant to evidence a bit of hyperbole, but to me in that moment, they seemed like a virtual death sentence. He was a man who had killed before, of course, and I had, too, and we both had seen more death and barbarity than anyone ever would want to, and I couldn't help but hear my father's statement as solid evidence that I wouldn't live long, if he had anything to do with the matter.

*

In the late summer of 1922, Babajan moved to Yonkers, New York to join other family members and Father grew gravely ill. He had become jaundiced, then had grown very weak, and by now he was bedridden, and I know my mother believed that, at just 56 years of age, his life was about to end. One day after I returned home from my daily adventures, my mother invited me into their bedroom, where he lay motionless on the bed. I wasn't sure whether he still was alive as she lifted his hand and turned his palm up, then placed my much-smaller hand inside his. But there was obviously both life and malice left in him when he turned his head and stared into my eyes for a moment, then threw my hand out of his, as if to make crystal clear to me that the possibility of his demise wasn't enough to change his opinion of me. He didn't want to hold my hand, didn't want me in the room, so I turned and left them alone, and that was the last time I saw him alive.

When, at my mother's request, I entered the bedroom again the following day, my father looked much as he had before his death, except that now coins covered his eyes and he was dressed in the suit he wore on Sundays.

My mother—her eyes bright and clear and tearless—sat in a chair beside him, and she reached her hand out to me when she saw me. "He died peacefully," she said, speaking Assyrian, of course, "and now he is with Christ, the King." Then she instructed me to kiss Father's forehead, but I refused.

"I don't want to kiss him, and I don't want to stay in this room," I said, as my tears returned.

My sisters immediately wrote to Polous in Russia, telling him about our father's death and asking him to come to America as soon as he could because his help was now sorely needed. And the next day, dozens of people came to the house on Grove Street for my father's wake, most of them Assyrians with whom we attended St.

Thomas's Assyrian Church of the East, as well as some of the men beside which he had worked. Stiff and awkward in their suits, the men drank strong tea and stood outside, smoking and talking only occasionally, while the women seated themselves in parlor, where my father's body now lay in a coffin, wailing and crying as their custom demanded and as if a terrible tragedy had occurred. When the men came inside, my mother began to sing as much as to wail, her song of mourning one she created as she sang, the lyrics in praise of my father's many talents, the ways in which he provided for us, his love of God, and his reward in heaven. It was a kind of mournful singing I'd never heard before, probably because we hadn't lived in a close-knit Assyrian community since I had been very small. The strange singing and crying made me tearful, and I missed my father like everyone else did, and I forgot amidst the tears and the singing that he had wanted me dead.

After the funeral the following day, we walked to the cemetery where he would be buried, and I remember my fascination with the amount of soil that had come out of the hole that would be his grave—the enormous mound almost entirely covered in flowers. Everyone returned to the house to eat afterward, and people's moods were lighter now, even festive, and many strangers as well as people I knew came up to me and told me what I fine young man I was and how my father must have been very proud of me. I understood that this was not an occasion on which to contradict them, so I simply nodded, and I'm sure they believed that, like him, I was a person of limited words.

Life got back to normal soon thereafter—at least as normal as it could be without my father's huge presence to shape our days and the ways in which we went about them—all of us aware that we would have to live far more frugally than before, and that Nanajan likely would have to find a job and let my mother look after her children.

My sister soon did find work doing alterations at a nearby laundry, and before long I began to bring home a few dollars each week, as well as all the milk we could drink, when an American dairy farmer named Clinton Dickson began to let me help him make his deliveries. On Saturdays and Sundays, he would pick me up at four in the morning, his big wagon pulled by a pair of handsome roan draft horses. A dog named Blackie who lived next door liked to join us, and Blackie and I would climb to the top of a big stack of metal five-gallon milk cans, a vantage point from which I loved to watch the dawn come up as we made the rounds of the markets. I loved being around horses again, and although the draft horses were each about double the size of my beloved Da-ba-sha, and I thought of him—and missed him terribly—each time I saw them. Blackie was one of those dogs that are at least as smart as most people, and I loved him from the moment I'd first rubbed in his ears; Clinton was fine with letting him join us on our early morning rounds, and I remember those times as always filled with a kind of joy. The milk cans were heavy when they were full, and I was hurt a time or two when they shifted while we rode, or when one would roll onto my ankle as I helped unload them, but it was work I cherished, and Clinton was as warm and kind as my father had been cold, and he often told me what a great help I was and how he wished he had a son like me.

But however much I might have liked to become Clinton's de facto son, and to work with him as often as I could, it was a job that didn't last long because money grew very tight, and five months after my father's death we were forced to move to a house on Glen Street. It was another building split into three homes—one family per floor—a place that was older and smaller than the house on Grove Street, and the monthly rent for our second floor space was a substantially smaller burden.

Perhaps because people of so many ethnic backgrounds lived in the neighborhood, Glen Street had a reputation as the toughest street in town, maybe in all of New England. Although I didn't have much with which to compare it, I do know that living on Glen Street meant that my nose was bloodied a lot, and that I came home with scraped hands and torn trousers often enough that my mother was afraid I was becoming a thug. But the truth was that I was simply fighting for a bit of respect among the legions of Greek, Polish, Russian, Armenian, and Irish boys in that part of town.

I hadn't enjoyed spending time with other children when I arrived in New Britain, and I still preferred to be alone—or to spend time with an adult I admired—but the streets in that part of town teemed with children who were roughly my age, and they were impossible to ignore. I made true friends with a number of boys, and although I was small, I was tough as hell. Sometimes, I know, I'd end up in a fight simply because I didn't understand the words someone spoke to me in English, or I'd unwittingly say yes to a fight, thinking I was acquiescing to a far more peaceful plan. I'd come home bloody and battered, my confidence battered a bit, but my mother would remind me that I'd defended myself through a revolution already, then encourage me to return to the streets the next day and really show those toughs who I was.

Few of them dared to test me again once a fellow named Eddie Pettijohn, who ran a boxing gym he had converted out of an abandoned dance hall, taught me how to throw punches and move on my feet. And when gangs from other neighborhoods would sometimes amble down Glen Street—provoking us by entering our turf without an explicit invitation—I was always one of the first to greet them and explain that they could go home healthy or go home hurt, whichever condition they chose.

Those were the years of prohibition in the U.S., a tumultuous time in which it was illegal to sell or purchase alcohol, meaning that in towns like New Britain, hundreds, if not thousands of otherwise law-abiding men broke the law virtually every day, and on street corners and in alleys the air hung thick not so much with menace, but with the constant threat of trouble. My buddies and I were too young to try to find booze—although we certainly never spurned it when it miraculously came our way—but if many of the men we admired were, in fact, hoodlums of a sort, then we wanted to be hoodlums as well. We seldom got into real trouble, but I still remember the time a grocery store was robbed and my buddies and I were wrongfully suspected of the crime. The cops came to my house to talk to me, and my mother was horrified to think that I might have been involved in such a significant crime—and afraid, I suspect, that we still could be sent back to Turkey.

When she told my brother Polous, who had recently arrived in New York, what had happened, he threatened to shave my head and hang a sign around my neck that read, "I AM A THIEF," but in the end I was able to convince the police that I'd had nothing to do with the break in. Yet I did have a few shortcomings, I occasionally had to admit. I had a hot temper that often was eager to flare, and I loved to play jokes on people—the kind that tickled me but that they found less than funny. And one time, even I came to deeply regret a stunt I pulled that seemed nothing less than brilliant at the time.

When Betsy, the wife and mother of the family who lived on the floor beneath us on Glen Street, died, her family asked the mortuary people to bring her body back to the house after it had been prepared for burial so Betsy herself could be on hand for the wake that the Irish people of New Britain seemed to view as a vital part of sending a loved one on her way. My friend Ivy was sad about his mother's death, but she'd been ill for many years, and he and I could share the experience of reacting to a parent's death with something less than a sense of tragedy. Ivy invited me to the wake because he wanted to have someone there to have some fun with.

Betsy's coffin had been placed near the window in the house's front parlor; its lid was wide open, and her body was propped up so she was easy for everyone to see. The coffin was elegant—beautiful dark wood on the outside and mounds of padded white silk on the inside, even on the lid, which supported in its open position by a stand the mortuary men had brought. At one point in the long evening, a Polish kid named Marek—a tough-guy I sometimes tangled with and the kind of fellow who liked to brag that he was afraid of nothing—said, when he was sure his parents were out of earshot, that he knew for a fact he could sleep all night on the open coffin lid. He could spend the dark night just inches from Betsy's body and not be bothered a bit, he swore. I challenged him on his boast, and I set the bet at twenty-five cents, and neither Ivy nor I could wait until everyone finally went home so we could see just how brave this Polish kid really was.

It was fine with Marek's parents for him to spend the night with Ivy, and I lived a floor above, of course, so at about three in the morning, I snuck downstairs and, sure enough, there was Marek sound asleep on the coffin lid, still wearing his fancy clothes from the wake. I wasn't about to lose twenty-five cents, so I tip-toed into the laundry room and found a dozen or so clothespins, and, as quietly as I could, I carefully pinned Marek's trousers and shirt-sleeves and collar to the plush silk of the coffin lid. He didn't stir once as I went about my business, then I left to go start my early milk-delivery rounds with Clinton.

When I returned at about 7:00, no one appeared to be out of bed yet in Ivy's house, so I opened the front door and went inside again. There in the parlor, right next to the dearly departed Betsy, was Marek, still sound asleep. I wanted to get some sleep, too, but I wasn't going to miss a show I'd so carefully produced, so I closed the front door loudly enough to wake him up. At first, he only shifted his body, then his eyes opened and he tried to get up. He only stirred at first, then he opened his eyes, saw me, and tried to get up. When he couldn't, he panicked, and suddenly he screamed at the top of his lungs, "She's got me! She's got me! Let me go! Let me go!"

The clothespins couldn't hold him long and he quickly escaped his bonds, but once on his feet, Marek still was terrified. He looked at me, and his face was as white as snow, and I tried to explain that I had pinned him to the silk but he wouldn't listen and raced past me and ran out into the street. I got the hell out of there, too, because I wasn't eager to explain anything to anyone about what had happened, and I followed Marek as closely as I could, but I couldn't keep up with him. He raced down alleys and across the big park and finally a cop on a motorcycle stopped and asked me if the kid who was racing so fast had done something he shouldn't have. I explained to the policeman that I had just played a trick on him, but I'd scared him to death and he was running to save himself from a ghost. That explanation satisfied the cop—and it was the truth—but by now my trick didn't seem worth Marek's reaction.

I didn't see him for weeks—a stretch of days during which I increasingly felt lousy about what I'd done. Luckily, the clothespins hadn't torn the silk fabric of the coffin lid, and Ivy, my good buddy, stayed mum about my part in the morning's chaos, but when I learned that Marek had hopped a freight train and ridden it all the way to New Haven, I knew I'd gone too far. I paid him the twenty-five cents I owed him when we finally crossed paths again because, after all, he *had* slept beside Betsy all night long.

*

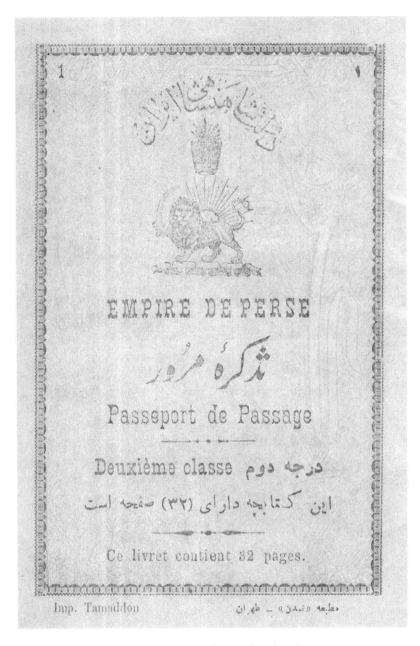

The Cover of Polous Edgar's Persian Passport

David A. Armstrong

Polous Edgar's, wife Eugenie Ruppell, and son George Edgar (named after my grandfather) as they came to America, 1925

Nanajan, Sophie and George. June, 1926

*From left to right; Nanajan, Polous, Bobby, George, Sophie, Nana Khatoon
and Maria. New Britain Connecticut, 1925*

If I was sometimes a smartass—and I *was* every so often—I was also a musician, or at least an aspiring one. With my mother's approval, I had used some of the money I'd earned delivering milk to buy an inexpensive violin at the New Haven Institute of Music in New Britain, where I'd also begun to take lessons—an hour's group lesson each week for which I paid twenty-five cents. It was an expense that wasn't essential, of course, but virtually nothing mattered more to me, and I suspect my mother was proud that, even in my father's absence, we hadn't been forced to abandon the musical tradition that he had begun and nurtured in our lives.

The man who owned the house in which we lived—a bear of a man named Jan Kaminski who also worked in his family's butcher shop alongside his brothers—had heard me practicing my violin on the occasions when he had come to collect our rent. One evening in the middle of the month during those prohibition years, he knocked on the door and my mother answered. I was sitting on the floor nearby, and I could sense her confusion, followed by the fear that welled up in her whenever something unexpected occurred. She had paid Mr. Kaminski the whole month's rent just two weeks before, and surely he couldn't want more.

What he wanted, as it turned out, was to ask a big favor of me. I got to my feet and shook his hand when he extended it, then my mother motioned for us to sit. With his hands folded in his lap, Mr. Kaminski explained in English that he had heard me play my violin and thought I had real talent. I translated his words for my mother. "Thank you," she responded in English before she realized those words would more properly come from me, and the three of us laughed a little.

Then he explained in English that wasn't even as good as mine had become that he'd come to ask whether I would consider loaning him my violin. His violin was being repaired and remained in the shop, but he was expected to play in two days at a mass at the

Polish National Catholic church on Concord Street. He would need to borrow it only on Sunday morning, he explained, then would return it later that day. I told him, of course, he could borrow it. I wasn't sure if it was an instrument of the quality he was accustomed to, but he said he knew from my playing that it would serve him very well.

I went to my bedroom to get it and I could see that my mother was proud that I hadn't hesitated to offer it to him. I asked if I could go to the mass to hear him play, assuring him that I knew where the Polish church was, and he said he would be honored to have me in attendance.

"Honored" was a word no one had ever used in relation to me—in any language—and when I translated what he said for my mother, her face flushed and she gave Mr. Kaminski a little bow. "But I hope," he said, "that a violinist such as yourself will forgive the mistakes I make."

I tried to make sure that he knew I often missed notes myself as I handed him my violin, secure in its hard black case. As he said goodnight and we closed the door, my mother put her hand on my shoulder in a way she seldom did and told me I'd done a very good thing. And I knew I had, but I knew, too, that the loan was only a little thing. What was huge, on the other hand—and so remarkable that I sleeplessly considered it throughout most of that night—was that he had called me a violinist.

I was a *violinist*, at least according to the butcher Mr. Kaminski I was, and I wasn't a bum, and I hoped my father rested in peace.

Santa Barbara, 1972

AGAIN AND AGAIN, I pressed Poppy to tell me about his early years. I related to those stories best, I understand now, because he was often unparented as he struggled to grow up, and that, of course, was something we shared. His father had callously withheld his love from his youngest son, and mine had been too defeated even to try. As a small boy, I hadn't marched across the ancient terrain that bridged the Black and Caspian seas, hadn't been forced to hide, steal—even kill—simply to stay alive, hadn't secreted my way to safety as one of the twentieth century's great revolutions chaotically swirled around me. Yet Poppy's earliest experiences were accessible to me because, in my own minor way, I already knew that growing from birth to manhood wasn't always a journey of joy and delight.

If Poppy had been an immigrant kid who had a particular knack for fitting in wherever he was, it seemed all too clear once we returned from Mexico that I didn't even belong in the very place in which I'd always lived. I didn't have any real friends in Santa Barbara and was very much a loner. I hadn't learned much in the way of social skills at home or how to interact with other people. I couldn't figure out why growing up seemed so easy for other kids, nor could I understand why relationships between fathers and sons necessarily seemed so complicated.

Although Poppy had connected with me from the moment I arrived on the scene, and although he stood steadfastly at my mother's side as she faced her highs and lows, he could not create the kind of relationship with his son Paul that I knew he truly wanted to have. The two of them loved each other—that much was clear—but it didn't seem to me that they liked each other all that much, and despite everything Paul did to impress his father, Poppy always seemed to find a way to criticize him or suggest that he do better.

I know he didn't mean for his comments to be critical—it was just the only way he knew how to parent Paul. My grandfather was a very *external person—athletic, physical, gregarious. My uncle Paul, on the other hand, was a more internal and private man, someone who was very creative and entirely devoted to his mother, my grandmother Mimi. Pop's upbringing required him to be big in all his actions if he were to survive, and Paul approached the world in ways Pop simply couldn't understand. He grieved that he couldn't be closer to Paul, and it was a subject he discussed with me from the time I was a young man until his final days.*

I know Paul was deeply hurt by all the attention Poppy showered on me, but I didn't know what I could do about it, and of course I didn't want to risk the sole relationship that held my life together.

Chapter 5

A Boy in New York

EVERY YEAR ON the Fourth of July, the thousands of us in New Britain who had come from foreign lands celebrated our lives in America with a particular kind of immigrant gusto. Something about the day seemed to be *our* holiday, in fact. We knew—even as children like me—what it had been like in other nations to be terribly impoverished, beaten down by tyrants, or at risk of losing our lives in bloody rebellions, and many of us had experienced all three circumstances with brutal intimacy. But now we lived in a place where anyone willing to work hard could find a decent job and where the people themselves elected their leaders, and America's birthday was a holiday we made the most of in every way.

Assyrians, Armenians, Greeks, Russians, and Poles gathered together as a single people on that summer day—as Americans—and it was a day of parades and races and baseball games, picnics and concerts and speeches, and each Fourth of July was crowned with a fireworks show, not as grand perhaps as the one that had terrified us onboard the *King Alexander* in New York's harbor, but nonetheless loud and beautiful and spectacular in its own way. I loved to watch the showers of fire in the black sky, the cascade of light raining down on our happy town, and I remember how curious it seemed to me that immigrant men would gather at the corner of Grove and Lafayette streets in the gloaming light and, as the first Howitzer blasts signaled the start of the fireworks, collectively fire a noisy barrage of blank bullets into the air to join in the tumult and celebratory emotion.

I liked guns well enough, and was comfortable around them, but I'd been in too many situations already in my young life in which the ammunition was live and the rifles and pistols in men's hands were aimed not at the sky but at each other. How strange, I thought, to celebrate living in place where there were no revolutions or wars by shooting off the weapons that were so emblematic of those conflicts.

*

Conflict—call it street fighting in plainer language—did remain a rather fundamental part of my life in New Britain. Maybe it was because I was so independent, and I'd become even more solitary and fiercely assured of myself in the time since my father's death. Or maybe it was because I was small and fellows from other neighborhoods who didn't know me often made the poor decision to call me out for a fight, thinking that they could make quick work of me, but discovering that I was a pit bull. But whatever reason or reasons, I grew up with my hands curled into fists much of the time, and I often had to look out of the corner of my eye to be sure I wouldn't be sucker-punched by some guy out to get me in retaliation for the beating I'd put on him a few days before.

Had I been a bit smarter, I might have realized that the last thing a violinist wants to risk is his hands, but I doubt I could have kept myself out of many of my fights—even if I had wanted to—by suggesting that my opponent and I talk things through, or by asking someone else to help us mediate our issues and reach common ground. Since I'd been a small boy, the world I'd observed was one in which people quite readily tore each other apart, and the street world I knew in New Britain wasn't materially different. Like dogs, people just had to fight from time to time, I came to believe, and although I only fought when I thought my cause was just, I was a true fighter nonetheless.

*

For most of my years in New Britain, my bona fides as a fighter didn't in any way interest the girls—and I had become interested in *them* long before the other boys in my classes at school did, specifically because I was older. Although my mother truly didn't know precisely how old I was, she had made a point to claim I was three years younger than I probably was—as a way for me to begin school in the first grade because I'd had no formal education till then. The fact that I wasn't very tall for my age helped with the ruse, and by the time I entered in junior high, puberty was something with which I'd long since become acquainted and girls held my fascination like nothing else I knew, including the violin.

There was an aspect about me that has always been shy, despite my bravado. I remember that soon after we arrived in Connecticut, I hated the fact that my mother continued to think she needed to help me bathe. I would stand with my back to her in the shower, and staunchly refuse to turn around.

"It's fine, Sargis," she would assure me repeatedly. "I am your mother. It's fine for me to see you. It's not a sin for you or for me." But I wasn't persuaded, and I was delighted when, at about the time my father died, my mother decided I had reached an age at which I could bathe alone.

My shyness hadn't been lessened much by my years at school. I'd become "George Edgar" back when my mother enrolled me; "Sargis Georges Yadgar" didn't seem to her to be the best moniker for a boy starting out in the American public school system. But despite my Americanized name, the acne that overnight seemed to take command of my face in junior high school now filled me with shame. I hated to look at myself in a mirror, and knew, positively, that *everyone* believed I was utterly repellent, and not simply the girls whose attention I increasingly longed for. But somehow, an

American girl named Eva Gagner with pretty, dark eyes, a little freckled nose, and auburn hair took a liking to me, and I was thrilled. We sat together in class, walked between classes holding hands, and we were so such much in love that I rather seriously took her home to meet my mother one day.

When I introduced them, I said, "This is my girlfriend, Eva," and my mother stepped back with a start, as if I'd just said something very wrong.

"My son marries Assyrian," she announced in her poor English. "No American girl."

I was horrified and Eva was embarrassed, and my mother must have been embarrassed, too, by the emphatic force of her words. She gave Eva an awkward little hug, as if to say, "Nothing personal, sweetheart."

Neither Eva nor I had ever remotely considered getting married, of course, but we were young enough that we simply accepted in that moment the certainty that we never would. I walked Eva home in silence, and my mother's outburst—which might have appeared to be proof that our love was as star-crossed as Romeo and Juliet's—instead simply seemed to announce that our romance had ended. There were no tearful goodbyes, no bittersweet words of farewell. Eva simply walked in the front door of her house, and when I saw her at school the next day, everything was forever different.

I was working at a butcher's shop the next time I fell in love, making home deliveries in a little wagon I pulled behind me, one that reminded me of the battered wagon I had used in Tiflis to bring food into town from the secret cave. I liked the butcher, and he liked me, trusting me to make the deliveries accurately and promptly, and one day he told me he had a big order for me to deliver to the Page house on Trumbull Avenue in Plainville, about a mile away from where I worked.

I couldn't believe my good luck, and I felt my heart in my throat when I tried to tell him, yeah, sure, I knew the house. As far as I was concerned, *everyone* knew the house on Trumbull Avenue, because it was the place where the divine Katherine Page lived, a palatial kind of house because Katherine's father was an executive at the Hutchinson Lockers, a large New Britain manufacturer that employed many people. I'd never set foot in the house because although I was sure I loved Katherine more than I could ever love anyone else, Katherine *hated* me.

The two of us had been in the same classes in school since I had moved to town, yet, like most boys, I hadn't really begun to appreciate the truly angelic nature of Katherine until my voice had begun to change and I'd started growing hair in places where formerly I'd had none. I liked to sit as near Katherine as I could, but often she would move to another seat as soon as I'd drawn near. One of our teachers even intervened on Katherine's part one time, asking me to stop for a moment after class and exhorting me, please, not to try to sit near Katherine any more. "She doesn't like it when you do," explained Mrs. Robertson, a woman who wore her hair pinned tightly to her head and whose waist was as wide as her shoulders. "Katherine has threatened to transfer to another school because you sit so close, and we'd hate to lose her, wouldn't we?"

I couldn't believe it, and I was crushed. Katherine would move to another school just to get away from me? I virtually never spoke to her, and I didn't smell or wear dirty clothes or—oh, at last I did understand. She didn't want me near her because of the red pimples that covered my face like a field of poppies. She was afraid my pimples were contagious, I guessed, or, at the least, their presence so near her simply spoiled the otherwise lovely day she hoped to have. I told Mrs. Robertson I would be careful not to ruin

Katherine Page's view any more, and although my feelings were hurt, I wasn't angry, and somehow I still retained the hope that one day Katherine would see beyond my pimples and recognize that we—the two of us—were a heavenly match.

I hoped that today might be that day as I eagerly pulled the wagon loaded with wrapped meats to the Page's house, and I was momentarily speechless when Katherine herself opened the door. I smiled as winningly as I knew how, and simply said, "Hi, Katherine," in that breezy way I knew American kids liked to talk, but she didn't say hello in response. And neither did she smile. She simply twisted her neck and shouted in a voice that was at once loud and expressive of her utter disinterest, "Mother, somebody's here to see you," then she turned and disappeared.

Mrs. Page quickly came to the door, and apparently my pimples didn't scare her as much as they did her daughter. She asked me to carry the cardboard boxes full of meat into the kitchen, then wanted to show me the brand new electric refrigerator with a freezer compartment built in where she would store it. "In fact," she said, "why don't you see if you can carefully fill the freezer for me, and if you do a good job, I'll have you fill it every time you deliver." She wanted me to separate the beef cuts from the pork and chicken, and to separate roasts and chops and steaks, and I must have done a good job because she asked when I was finished if I was good at other chores, too.

I told her I was darn good at anything I set my mind on, and she said, "I bet you are." She went to get her husband, and he sat at the kitchen table in his shirt-sleeves and said he had lots of jobs around the house and the yard that he could use a hand with. "Worst of all," he said, "I've got to get rid of all the mice in the basement."

I told Mr. Page I knew exactly how to rid his house of mice, but explained that we would have to wait until the weather warmed up a bit for my plan to work at its best. Mr. Page said sure, and I shook his hand, and as I walked back to the butcher shop, I imagined Katherine Page's parents asking her at dinner that night if she didn't agree that the butcher's delivery boy was a fine specimen of a young man, the kind of fellow they hoped she'd have for a husband one day, or at least a boyfriend they could invite over for ice cream on hot summer Sunday afternoons.

*

A few days later, Katherine utterly ignored me again as a large group of us sat in the bleachers of the school's gymnasium, where we were allowed to eat our lunches. Some of my pals were there, and so was a filthy rich Greek kid named Papadokas, whose father owned the Palace Theatre, where everybody in town went to see movies. Papadokas always came to school wearing a starched collar and a beautiful suit; he was tall and had wavy hair and if all the girls thought he was a dream, Katherine was foremost among them.

I was minding my own business and eating my lunch on the gymnasium bleachers when, for a stunt, Papadokas came up beside me and plopped himself down in a seat, and started to pull at my sweater. "Is this all you have to wear, pimple face? You wear this every day, for God's sake." I told him it was none of his business, but I worked after school so I couldn't wear good clothes like he did. He called me pimple face a second time, and I tried to brush his hand away, but he grabbed the sweater tighter and pulled it as hard as he could, ripping it and almost pulling it off me, and I was enraged.

Maybe it was because I hated his rich kid attitude, or perhaps it was because I knew Katherine was watching, but whatever my motivation was, I simply stood, took hold of him by his necktie and his belt and shoved him down the bleachers and onto the hardwood floor.

I was the first kid to race down the stairs to reach him, but I didn't want to help him or see if he was okay. I wanted to him to *pay*, and I pounded him in the face until Mr. Brewster, the physical education teacher, finally pulled me off him. "George, stop," Mr. Brewster shouted at me, "You're going to hurt him."

"Hurt him? I want to *kill* him," I raged until at last Mr. Brewster wrapped his arms around me so tightly I couldn't move.

Papadokas was severely injured enough after his ignominious fall from the bleachers and his face's encounters with my fists that an ambulance had to be called to get him to the hospital. I was in huge trouble, I knew, but I didn't care because Papadokas had started it and had gotten what he deserved. His father, the rich theatre owner, demanded of Mr. French, the school principal, that I be expelled and sent off to a prison school, but Mr. French thought the best thing to do was to hold a hearing.

So many people were in attendance on the day my fate was to be decided that the hearing scheduled for the principal's office had to be held in the gym. My mother and sisters were there, of course, and so were many Assyrians who wanted to make a strong show of support. The butcher was there to put in a good word for me, and so—I couldn't believe it—were Katherine Page and her parents. Papadokas was there, all bandaged up, and his father stood up and made a big show about how I nearly crippled his son and how I ought to be in jail because I couldn't be trusted not to do something vicious again.

Then Mr. Brewster, who'd always liked me and who had seen in me the potential to become a good athlete, spoke next, suggesting that I explain why I'd attacked Papadokas. Mr. French nodded his head, and Mr. Brewster waved me to come stand beside him.

I was nervous, and I knew I'd better speak better English than I'd ever spoken before, and I began by saying that I'd lived in Persia where we were hunted by Turks, and I'd lived in Russia where there was a great revolution, but I'd never seen anywhere else the terrible discrimination I'd seen here in New Britain. I said I'd never been called the names I was called constantly in Connecticut, never been ridiculed like I was here. I told everyone who was listening that Papadokas had made fun of my clothes and ripped my sweater in two, and made fun of my complexion. "I lost my temper, but I couldn't help it. He talks like that to me all the time, and this time I wanted to kill him."

You could hear people murmur throughout the gym, and I could see the looks of shock on the faces of many of my teachers, but I pressed on, taking my report card out of my pocket and holding it up. "These are good grades," I wanted everyone to know. "If I deserved to be discriminated against I wouldn't be a decent student. I don't call people names; I don't tear up their clothes, and if they do it to me, from now on they are going to pay."

When Mr. French asked if any other students who were in the bleachers that day could corroborate my claim that Papadokas had repeatedly harassed me, I saw Katherine Page's parents' encouraging her to raise her hand. At last, she did, and Mr. French asked her to explain what she'd witnessed, and I doubted that she would come to my defense, given the fact that always before she'd shunned me as if I were a leper. But this time, in a voice that was soft and timid, Katherine came to my aid, telling the principal that events occurred on the bleachers just as I'd said they had. "George didn't grab him until he had ripped his sweater and said too many bad things," she added.

In the end, and with Katherine's help, I was exonerated. I wasn't sent to prison school, wasn't expelled, and both Mr. French and Mr. Brewster told me privately they were sorry that I and other students like me often had been taunted, and that they would do what they could to change things. Papadokas, on the other hand, never returned to school; his parents were so outraged that I wasn't placed in front of a firing squad that they pulled their son out of school and enrolled him in a private school somewhere.

Despite Katherine's good deed, her belief that I was repulsive didn't seem to change. At a school dance soon thereafter, I buoyed up my courage and asked her if she would dance with me, but she declined, and I decided I'd have to wait a very long time for her to come around. I continued to deliver meat from the butcher's shop to her mother, however, and do odd jobs for her father, and I even successfully rid her home of the mice that had plagued it for some time to Mr. Page's great delight.

I captured a gopher snake near a little pond at the edge of town, fitted a wooden box with a screen to let in daylight and a mouse-size hole in the side against a small basement window, then let the snake loose inside the basement and simply waited for dozens of mice to flee into the box in terror. It was a trick I'd seen a fellow do in Constantinople a few years before, and it worked like a charm. Mr. Page was grinning from ear to ear as he paid me the princely sum of fifty cents and told me I was clever as hell, and for the rest of that day I also thought *I* was rich—rich enough that even Katherine might change her opinion of me if only I was patient.

*

I didn't let the bad blood between me and Papadokas prevent me from going to his father's Palace Theatre as often as I had money, and I remember that the Fox Movietone newsreel that preceded each show made it clear that the country was in trouble. I didn't quite understand what it meant when the stock market crashed in 1929, or precisely why that event led more than a few fellows in New York City to jump out of high windows, but I did know why it mattered when manufacturing plants in New Britain closed and people suddenly were out of work.

All over town, men who formerly spent their days bent over their shop floor duties now stood idly on street corners, smoking and talking and trying to figure out how they and their families could survive. In our family, my mother cooked and cleaned and looked after my nephew Bobby. And the rest of us, thank God, continued to bring in some cash money. My sister Nanajan worked in a laundry, then took a job in a shirt factory that remained in business; Maria found good work operating a stamping machine at Corbon Locks, and I continued to make afterschool deliveries for the butcher and do odd jobs for Mr. Page and anyone else who needed me on the weekends. We always had food and were able to pay our rent, new clothes or shoes were as rare as diamonds. But it wasn't long before our luck took a bad turn.

Although she knew better, one day Maria neglected to turn off her stamping machine before she began to clean it. A blade caught the rag she held in her hand and violently whipped it into the cutting blades. Two of her fingers were chopped off below the first knuckle, and although she was fine after a doctor stitched up the stumps, her boss threatened to fire her for her mistake and when she returned to the plant she was afraid of her work in ways she never had been before.

It wasn't long before we were forced to move again; money remained very tight and the one thing we could repeatedly do to ensure we had enough for food and other essentials was to spend less on rent. We went to a house on Grove Street, then, just as soon as I felt I knew where I lived again, we moved again, this time to a battered old house with peeling paint on East Main Street—a place that burned to the ground just a month after we arrived.

We had gone to Bristol on a Sunday afternoon to visit my sister Sophie and her family, and Sophie's husband Al had driven us the short distance back home to New Britain. We saw a huge cloud of smoke as we drove into town, and were surprised by all the commotion on Main Street when we turned the final corner toward home, then my mother began to shriek when she realized that the house in flames was our own. The fire department was battling a blaze that had begun on the third floor, and by the time we arrived, had made good progress. We stood in the street and watched helplessly, realizing that the second floor, where we rented, would be drenched with water by now, and even if nothing we owned was burned, it likely was very wet.

We spent that night in Bristol with Sophie and Al, then returned the following day, and when we were allowed to go inside at last, the whole of our house was soaked and it stunk so much of smoke and fetid water that we could barely stand to be inside. We salvaged our clothes and my father's instruments, which still hung on the walls; my violin was safe as could be inside its case, but our beds and a sofa and much of the furniture was destroyed.

Yet our bigger problem was that it would be months before any of the three homes in the building would be habitable again, and we had no place to live. That night, back at Sophie's house in Bristol, all of us squeezed into their home — who knew for how long? — and it soon became obvious to my mother that we had only one option.

My brother Polous had finally reached the United States from Russia. In the tumult of the Russian Civil War, he had been imprisoned for six months simply for attempting to leave the country, but in 1924 he and his family had successfully journeyed to Germany, yet it wasn't until August 1925 that they reached New York City, where he had accepted a position as a physician at Manhattan State Hospital on Ward's Island. My mother spoke with Polous by telephone and he assured her that he would find an apartment for us close to his home in The Bronx. "We will live near Polous," my mother announced with authority as she hung up the phone, and that was that.

I didn't much like this brother who was almost old enough to be my father, nor did I want to leave my jobs or my pals or my school or the haunts that had made New Britain feel like my true home by now. But I knew better than to argue. My mother had made her decision, and we were moving to New York City in the midst of this time that everyone said was so depressing, and that was a circumstance I simply couldn't escape.

*

I was seventeen or eighteen when I entered Morris High School. I still wasn't very tall, but I was muscular and strong as hell, and the truth was that I felt far more American than Assyrian any more. My English was as accent-free as anybody's and a place like New York City—which had overwhelmed me when we arrived by immigrant ship a decade before—now seemed like the best place in the world for a young fellow like me, even in a time when so many people struggled to make ends meet.

When I couldn't find a butcher or a dairyman to work for, I opted to start shining shoes. A guy could set up his little shop on any street corner in the city; all you needed were the tools of your trade and a box for the gentleman to rest his shoe on while he read the paper and you polished his shoes to a bright sheen. I often took my violin out on the streets with me; it was a way to get a bit of attention in the hustle and bustle of the city streets, and a way, too, to pass the time, practicing scales and playing parts of pieces I had memorized. I could practice my violin in between shines and could work anytime—after school, in the evenings, all day long most Saturdays—and because I still imagined myself becoming a famous violinist one day, I liked to hop on an IRT train and travel to heart of Manhattan, where I often shined shoes outside Carnegie Hall.

One evening in the spring of 1931—the weather dreary with intermittent rain and few passersby interested in shoe shines—three men in fine suits came out a side door of the hall and walked near the spot where I was working. One of them noticed my violin case, and no doubt it was amusing to them to think that a shoe shine boy might be a musician, and, out of curiosity, they stopped to chat with me. "What do you have in there?" the fellow with a thick moustache asked, speaking in an accent I guessed was German and pointing at the case.

"Violin," I answered. "I'll play it for you for a nickel."

"By all means," he said, and I opened the case, but before I could tuck the soundboard under my chin, he asked if he could hold it. I gave it to him, and he looked it over, then adjusted the bridge a bit, plucked the strings, and turned the tuning pegs, and I could tell he knew what he was doing. I gave him the bow, and he played the first few bars of a light little piece I'd never heard before.

"I'd say you're a true violinist," I announced, and the men who were with him laughed, and one of them explained to me that he was one of the best violinists in the world, in fact.

"Have you ever heard of Fritz Kreisler?" his friend asked.

I shook my head no, and the man said, "Well, it's Fritz Kreisler who's playing your violin."

Mr. Kreisler put out his hand, and said he was pleased to meet me. I told him my name and shook his hand, and he told me he was impressed with me. "It can't be easy to shine shoes and still have time to practice," he said, and I told him I didn't think I'd ever have enough time to be the player I truly wanted to be.

"You know how you get to Carnegie Hall, don't you?" the third man asked, and the others laughed as if it were an inside joke, but then Mr. Kreisler had a question for me about shining shoes.

"You're going to have a hard time making any money in weather like this tonight, aren't you?"

I agreed, and he said he had an idea, suggesting I walk with them to the restaurant to which they were headed. It wasn't far to a place on 52nd Street called Leon & Eddie's, and the man at the front was a fellow they knew named Toots Shor. I guessed he must have gotten *his* name mangled at Ellis Island, and as I shook his hand he gruffly called me "kid" and said he was happy to meet me.

Mr. Kreisler asked Toots if there was a place near the entrance where I could shine shoes for a while, and Toots thought it over and decided there was. The four men went in to dinner and Toots took me to a spot near the door and provided a chair and I went to work for the several men that night who wanted to look their best before they went in to dinner.

Before long, Toots brought me a plate of pot roast and potatoes and string beans, and I must have looked worried about how I would pay for it, because he waved his hand and said, "Don't worry, kid. It's on your Carnegie Hall buddies."

I enjoyed my dinner, and shined some more shoes before I saw Fritz Kreisler and his friends again on their way out of the restaurant. They wanted to know how business had been, and I told them it was as good I as could have hoped. Mr. Kreisler wanted to know what I planned to do with my violin playing, and I didn't quite know what he meant. "Do you want to play professionally one day?" he asked the second time, and I told him that was my dream.

"Well, I'd be delighted to support your dream," he said, taking his wallet from his coat pocket and handing me a shiny silver dollar. I'd seldom seen one and I was flabbergasted. But before I could thank him, his charity seemed to nudge his two companions into similar generosity and each of them gave me a dollar coin as well. I couldn't believe it. Three dollars was a fortune, and as I rode the IRT back to 68th Street that night, I couldn't wait to tell my mother that playing the violin wasn't simply a pastime—it had begun to earn us real money.

*

Although he didn't tip me again, Fritz Kreisler did stop to say hello on the following days when he saw me shining shoes outside Carnegie Hall. He lived in Berlin, he explained, and was only in town for a series of concerts. But there was something about New York that he loved, and he said he couldn't think of a better city in the world for a musician at the moment. Ill winds were blowing in Berlin, he said, and I wasn't sure what he meant, then he added that his hometown of Vienna once had been the world's greatest musical city, but it no longer was.

When I asked him what a kid like me might do to really make something of the violin, he thought for a moment, then had a thought: a better place for me to shine shoes might be outside the Metropolitan Opera at 39th and Broadway. At first I thought he misunderstood, thinking that I only was interested in more money, but then he continued. "Outside the Met, you'll meet some of the greatest singers and musicians in the world. It's early in the opera season, and they are there every day, practicing, performing—many more of them than here at Carnegie. Get to know them like you did me. They live here. They will know of teachers, or of conservatories that might accept you. That's if you're quite good, of course."

I told him I was getting better, at least, then asked if I could play something for him. He was in a hurry, I could tell, but he nodded his head and I quickly began to play a passage from a Mozart sonata I'd begun to learn back in New Britain. He listened— really listened in the way a musician can—then held up his hand to stop me, and the gesture made me think he hadn't liked what he'd heard.

"I must be off, my young friend," he said, "but yes, by all means, go to the Met and meet everyone you can."

The moment Fritz Kreisler turned the corner and was gone, I packed my violin and my shoe shine kit and headed off for Broadway and 39th Street. I'd never heard of the Metropolitan Opera, but I trusted his advice, and sure enough, lots of people came and went from the imposing, yellow-brick building, and plenty of them needed shines. I kept my violin case in a spot where passersby could readily see it, and I played a bit when I wasn't attending to a needy pair of shoes, yet no one asked me about my violin or my playing on that first day—or on any other. But in the end, I was indebted to Mr. Kreisler because I did take up a new line of work at the Met.

A week or so after I'd moved my shining operation south, a fellow stopped one day and asked if I'd run a quick errand for him. When he added that there would be a dime in it for me, I said sure, and I went to the delicatessen he told me to and bought the pastrami sandwich he wanted, and when I mentioned his name back at the entrance to the Met, the guard let me in and showed me to his dressing room. The sign on the door read "Edward Johnson" and he turned out to be a tenor, and a famous one at that. He was from Canada, but he'd lived in England, too, he told me when I asked about his accent, and we agreed that New York was one hell of a fine city. As I turned to go, he wanted to know if I'd like to fetch his sandwich for him every day. That chore was easy to say yes to, and before long, I made delicatessen runs for ten or a dozen singers and musicians in the hours before their evening performances.

I became a constant enough presence in the bowels of the building where the dressing rooms were located that people knew my name and the guards would always wave me right through. I was shy, at first, about walking in on a group of women in various stages of dress, and I got more than an eyeful a time or two, along

118

with my share of ribbing. "Come on in, George," someone would say. "Nothing in here that you haven't seen before, I'll bet. A looker like you has got to have a girlfriend."

Their teasing made me blush every time, but I enjoyed it as well—it beat the hell out of Katherine Page telling me to stay away. And I began to think that maybe before for too long, one of the girls I knew in The Bronx might let me touch instead of just look at those delights I'd glimpsed at the Met.

*

George Edgar, 1931

George, Nanajan, center, and Maria, early 1930s

George, Nana Khatoon and Polous, August 17, 1930

*George standing in rear, with his nephew and namesake, George Edgar
(Polous's son), left, and nephew (Nanajan's son) Robert "Bobby" Marshall,
October 10, 1931*

As far as my subsequent amorous discoveries were concerned, the move from Connecticut to New York City proved that God had decided to reward me not only for those years of my bad complexion, but for every trouble of every kind I'd endured up until then. In New York City, soon after opera singers began to let me see them sans their dresses and petticoats, the girls I'd gotten to know in my neighborhood somehow decided I was worth their romantic time. It may have been the height of the Great Depression, but 1931 was a year in which I had a spring in my step quite a bit of the time.

First there was Edda Biddle, who lived a floor below us, and who suggested out of the blue one day that she could show me the basement of the three-story building where we lived. Stacked high with trunks and boxes, the place was dank and musty and smelled like sour milk, but it turned out that Edda had other things to show me besides the basement itself. I was awkward and nervous and my brief performance didn't impress poor Edda, but at least from that day forward, I could call myself a man without having to lie to do so.

Sometime after my father died—and back when we were still in New Britain—my mother had taken it upon herself to talk to me about sex, at least to tell me I must never come home and announce that I had gotten a girl pregnant. I didn't really know what she was talking about at the time, although I assured her I'd never do the thing that had her so concerned. She must have understood that her awkward little talk with me didn't really connect, because not long thereafter, a neighbor we were friendly with stopped me on the street one summer day, gave me a watermelon to pass along to my mother, then said, "You know, your mother thinks I ought to give you a little talk about the birds and the bees." When I didn't know what he meant, he became flustered. It was clear he had hoped I could assure him there was no need to discuss things further because I already knew all there was to know.

"Well," he continued when he realized he had to instruct me, "the gist of it is, when your thing gets stiff, don't stick it in a girl. You got that?"

I got it, but like virtually every other young man on the planet, in the coming years I increasingly wanted to do what our neighbor had told me *not* to do more than anything I could possibly imagine. At the very least, my two-minute liaison with Edda Biddle proved to me that this was an aspect of living I was keen to further explore, and soon thereafter I was miraculously offered another opportunity, this time by a girl who lived on the floor *above* us. Her name was Bernice Stringer and, oh, what a beauty she was—with long brown hair and beautiful creamy skin and pointy breasts that seemed to lead her wherever she walked. She dressed in the latest fashions and always looked very sharp, and one day after we'd walked home from school together, we walked upstairs to her house and discovered that no one was home.

Bernice wanted to show me her bedroom, and I was game, and once inside she pushed me against a wall and pressed herself against me. I could sense every inch of her it seemed, even through her clothes and mine, and I was transfixed. I'd never really kissed a girl before but Bernice demonstrated the procedure in the most captivating way, then pulled me down on the bed. In a flash, up came her skirt and down came my trousers and we proceeded to do precisely what my mother did not want me to do, and life seemed wonderful in every way. Bernice was a goddess, and she wanted me, and I was far more poised, shall we say, this time, and I must have been at least an adequate lover because although no real romance ever developed, Bernice and I continued those rendezvous every so often throughout my years at Morris High.

My buddy Andrew Losey was a generous guy who had a girlfriend he liked to share. She was the kind of girl who seemed to feel all the more special following a session with three or four guys in a row than she would have with only one. There were occasional times, too, when I would meet a new girl on a Sunday afternoon and find a way to have sex with her before supper. But I didn't really fall in love until I met Lydia Turner. My brother Polous knew a Mr. Simmons who directed the Hebrew Orphan's Asylum in The Bronx, which operated a summer camp in the Catskills. Mr. Simmons needed camp counselors and Polous recommended me, and I spent an idyllic summer prior to my senior year in high school at the camp—sleeping in the dorm with the younger kids who would come to the mountains for two-week visits, and spending my days as a lifeguard, baseball coach, and hike leader.

Every Saturday night, the counselors were free to travel to nearby towns for dances and movies and dinner, and every night of the week determined and clever couples could find ways to meet after lights out for the kinds of intimate interactions that couldn't take place during the day. Lydia was the camp's dietician, and was older than I was and decidedly mature, it seemed to me—and we met so regularly in the still of the night that we didn't leave much time for sleep. She was sophisticated and intelligent and stunningly good-looking, and I adored making love with her out in the forest, in a storage room off the big industrial kitchen, and even once in a motel room on the outskirts of a Catskills town. But more than that, I loved simply being with beautiful, alluring, dynamic Lydia. We could talk about anything under the sun, and we left no topic undiscussed; she was captivated by the fact that I played the violin and believed I could become a great violinist even more than I did. And at the close of the camping season that September, Lydia and I were certain we wanted to marry.

Although I told people I was eighteen, I was probably at least three years older, in fact, and Lydia was twenty-four. Her parents lived in The Bronx as well, and when we returned from the Catskills we were eager to introduce each other to our families and share our very good news. When I met her mother and father on a Sunday afternoon, they were quite polite, even rather friendly, and as we discussed our plans, her mother asked if we'd spoken yet with Rabbi Lepsis about starting conversion classes. I was confused by what she meant, but Lydia immediately understood and explained to her parents that we hadn't discussed our faiths, and didn't understand why I would need to convert, in any case. Lydia's father stayed silent, and her mother went white before she explained that they would never sanction a marriage between us unless I converted. I seemed like a fine young man, she assured me, but an interfaith marriage was simply out of the question.

My mother's reaction to our announcement was equally negative and rather more unrestrained. "No Jews in family," she announced in very clear English, then turned to me and continued to speak in Assyrian. "Sargis, I'm shocked that you would bring a snake into our family."

"That's a terrible word to use," I whispered to her in Assyrian. "You don't like discrimination against us, but then you do it yourself. What's the problem, anyway? Jesus was Jewish, wasn't he?"

"Do not blaspheme, Sargis," she sternly replied, and when we left my mother's house—and the place where I still lived, of course— Lydia wanted me to tell her everything my mother had said. Because I'd never kept anything from her before, I told her in detail.

"A snake? She thinks I'm a snake? That outrageous," she shouted. I told her I agreed with her, but explained that it seemed unlikely that my mother would change that opinion soon. I didn't know what we should do, but Lydia was quickly clear about our only option. "You'll convert," she said matter-of-factly. "The classes are simple, I think."

I did my best to help Lydia understand that I couldn't possibly convert while my mother remained alive, explaining how precious our Assyrian identity was to my mother, telling her, too, about the genocide perpetrated by the Turks, about the fact that an Assyrian homeland no longer existed, and how people like my mother believed it was our duty to marry within our own race and keep it strong and alive no matter where on earth the winds had blown us. I shouldn't have been surprised when it seemed to Lydia that I was telling her I cared more about Assyrian ethnic purity than I did about her, and she was angry and we found ourselves in the midst of our first real fight.

At the door of her parents' house, she said, "Would you like to come in and learn more about converting, or have you suddenly become afraid of snakes?" I told her once more that, for me, converting was as impossible as becoming Chinese.

"Impossible for you, or for your mother?"

"What's impossible," I said, "is to shame my mother by converting while she's still alive."

"Then you *are* afraid of snakes," she haughtily announced, and slammed the door, leaving me on the step, confused and anguished and longing to be back in the Catskills again, where life and love had been idyllic for the whole of a summer.

Unlike my relationships with my father and my older brother—men to whom I was forever connected but who I found difficult to love—my emotional connection to my mother was deep, one I instinctively nurtured and protected. Together we had secreted a dead soldier through the darkened streets of Tiflis; we had endured an entire train ride wondering whether we'd ever see each other again; we'd slept crammed together in the stinking hold of ship as we crossed the Atlantic, and I'd done my best after my father died to make sure she felt secure in the strange new world of New Britain.

I was an American now; there was no other word that better defined me as my high school years flew by. But my mother— Khatoon—was a fiercely proud *Assyrian,* and Urmia in northwestern Persia remained her truest home. Although I found it difficult to explain to Lydia why it was so critically important to my mother that all her children marry other Assyrians and raise Assyrian children, it was a perspective and a deep emotion that I readily understood.

When I saw Lydia again in a few days, we both were quiet and awkward and a bit stunned by how dramatically everything seemed to have changed. The idea of marrying anytime soon no longer seemed imperative, and by Christmastime that year, we saw each other only occasionally. I remember the weather was warm again when I learned that Lydia was ill and in the hospital. I tried to visit her, but her parents wouldn't allow it. Yet a couple of weeks later, the family's rabbi found me at home and told me that Lydia's condition had become grave; she might not survive and she desperately wanted to see me, and he had persuaded her parents to allow me to visit her briefly. I couldn't believe how small and frail she looked in her hospital bed, but she was able to smile and she held my hand throughout the short time we spent together.

I told her I was sure she would be better soon, but Lydia knew the truth—she was about to die and this would be the last time we would see each other. It was clear that she continued to love me, and I knew in that moment that I still deeply loved her as well, yet I was about to lose her forever. Just a year before, we had spent a magical summer together and we imagined a future in which we never would be apart. But I already knew well that dreams didn't always come true and that, in my life at least, I often lost those I loved the most.

Los Angeles, 1975

MY MOTHER HAD become a realtor and a move to Los Angeles seemed to make sense, and my sister and I were game. We settled in Hollywood, and I liked the big city just fine, and my mom soon met a great guy. Somehow, she'd had enough of the kinds of men who needed to vent their rage on us, and Jim Kelly, a musician, was always great fun. My mother joked that with Jim around it was like having three kids instead of two, and it often felt like that was true, and I know it must have been a joy for her to see our domestic life turn simple and optimistic for a change. It was nice to finally be around a man who liked me, and I liked him as well.

But as promising as life seemed in Los Angeles, the one thing it clearly lacked was Poppy. I missed him terribly and it wasn't long before I'd figured out a way to get back to Santa Barbara virtually every weekend. A dozen Greyhound buses a day made the 90-mile journey between the two cities, and I carefully memorized the timetable. My mother would drop me off at the downtown Greyhound station early on Friday evening, and Pop would always be waiting at the station in Santa Barbara when I arrived. We'd go home, he would fix dinner for my grandmother and me, and then the two of us would watch television in his den while she listened to talk radio in the front room—the kind of right-wing stuff that he just couldn't abide. When I finally wanted to sleep, my grandfather would stay in the den and practice the violin and I'd fall asleep in his bedroom to the distant sound of the music he made.

On Saturdays, I would simply shadow him—going everywhere he went and pulling all the stories from him I could as he worked in the yard, ran errands, or went to the Y to swim and work out. Tears would come to his eyes when he reminisced about the pets that had been dear to him in his childhood, and his special rapport with animals continued in California. He always had cats and dogs and songbirds, and I particularly remember the cockatiel he trained to sing along to its own cacophonous tune as he played *the violin. In his garden shed, he would tap the floor with a shovel and I would watch in astonishment as mice emerged from their holes to be fed on cue, and it seemed there were always hundreds of pigeons sitting on the overhead power line in the yard, waiting for the moment when Poppy would throw them seed.*

Mimi would always insist that we go to church on Sunday, and although Pop never seemed particularly eager, he would acquiesce. I knew I didn't want to go, but if Poppy was going, I certainly was as well, and instead of making me leave him to join the kids in the Sunday school, I got to sit beside him during the entire service, even at the price of sitting through a sermon that might as well have been in a foreign language. I had no idea what all the religion was about, but at least I was with him, and it wouldn't be many more hours before it was time for me to get back on a bus bound for Los Angeles. Late in the afternoon, we would climb into his '69 El Camino and head for the bus station. He often would let me steer from the passenger seat for a few blocks, and he always gave me two quick kisses on the forehead as he said goodbye.

Chapter 6

Money to Burn

THE 1930S WERE tough times for almost all Americans, but, for immigrants like us, they sometimes were too reminiscent of the lives we thought we had left behind when we arrived in the United States. My brother Polous, who had lived in Russia until 1925, and who always paid close attention to the ongoing plight of Assyrians in Russia, Persia (now Iran), and Iraq, had become secretary of the Assyrian National Associations of America in the early 1930s. When the Iraqi government began a systematic massacre of Assyrians living inside that country in 1933, he worked tirelessly—speaking, writing letters, and lobbying every government official who would meet with him—to try to help end the bloodshed. Although Polous and I often were at odds, I was proud of his commitment to our people, and proud, too, of how he represented those of us who were Assyrian immigrants in the United States.

It was obvious to everyone in our family that our move to The Bronx had been the right one when we learned in letters from other Assyrians still in New Britain that dozens of plants and factories in Connecticut had closed since we had left. Jobs of any kind were almost nonexistent. Yet although it was never easy in New York, we found myriad ways to bring in a few dollars each week, and, for a stretch of time, we even operated a business at home.

Specifically because my sisters were seamstresses—a craft they had learned from our mother, who was very much an expert with cloth and thread and needle—they were approached in the winter of 1932 by a fellow from a sporting goods company who needed to have forty-dozen baseballs sewn very quickly. He brought a supply of bare balls to our house, as well as leather covers that were already cut to shape and punched for stitching. My sisters' job—one we all quickly joined—was simply to sew the covers over the balls. They had to be very tight, the seams perfect, and the tail of the thread tucked out of sight to mask any evidence of where the stitching began or ended. We all got the hang of it very quickly, the sporting goods man liked the quality of our work, and we spent nights after dinner for several months stitching baseballs, my mother becoming intrigued enough by what kind of game employed such a strange little orb that we vowed that one day—just as soon as we'd saved up some money—we'd go to Yankee Stadium and watch our homemade balls get thrown and batted around.

My shoe shining days came to an end when, rather miraculously, it seemed, a tobacconist hired me to work behind the counter in his small Bronx shop—selling cigars, cigarettes, loose tobacco, and rolling papers, with the odd pipe or two going out the door on rare occasions—and I earned a steady salary, something prized above all else. My mother found it hard to believe that a shop whose focus was smoking products did not sell hookahs like the one my father had given her—that water pipe something she cherished more than any other possession, I believe.

Although it wasn't the kind of work that got me out into the city—something that always filled me with energy and the pleasure of being part of that sea of people—I liked the shop and the stream of customers, and my boss was a gruff guy named Irv Rosenfeld, who always treated me squarely. One day, out of the blue, Irv said, "Listen, George, the boss is coming in today. He don't like to be spoken to or bothered, so just mind your own business."

The fellow owned many of the businesses and all the buildings in the immediate neighborhood, Irv explained, and he would be making an inspection of several of his enterprises that day.

When I asked how I'd know it was him, Irv simply barked, "You'll know."

A while later, two men in heavier coats than the weather required came in without a word and positioned themselves on either side of the door. They were followed in only seconds by two more who walked through the shop to the entrance to the backroom, where they similarly stood guard. Finally, a fifth man entered, wearing a coat with a mink collar over a fine suit and polished spats. He marched straight to the cash register, opened it, and began counting the cash inside.

Nobody but Irv and I was ever allowed to open that cash drawer, and I blurted out, "Hey, you're not supposed to be in there."

When the man looked up at me, I was worried. I'd never seen a more sinister expression on a man's face in my life. "What's your name?" he demanded. Then he wanted to know where I lived. I told him I lived just around the corner on 68th Street, and he said, "Well, you're a tenant of mine, then. Those are my buildings. You're a brave little punk for talking up to me like that. Am I right?"

I told him I guessed I was, and he asked if I knew who he was.

"Dutch Schultz, I think," I said, looking him in the eye.

"How do you know that?" he asked.

"I keep my eyes open," I told him. "That's how I stayed alive in the old country."

"Well, you're right, son. What would you say to doing a bit of work for me from time to time?"

The look on my face must have communicated my excitement, and he was quick to add, "Nothing dangerous. Just a little errand running. Nice and safe and simple."

A week later, the door to the shop opened and the body guards marched in, just as they had before, followed by Dutch Schultz, and he outlined three "runs" he wanted me to make for him—a trip to the post office to mail a package, another to give a guy an envelope, and third to deliver flowers to a beautiful gal who I assumed was one of his girlfriends.

I accomplished these kinds of errands well enough over several weeks that I earned his trust, it seemed, and Dutch made me one of his regular "runners." The pay was good, and he never asked me to do anything remotely risky, and working for him made me feel like a kind of big shot, I have to admit. But then, one day, he had a different sort of errand for me and he wanted to be straight with me about it.

"I got to pay off an important guy, and I can't risk him thinking I'm doing anything more than just passing him his money." He opened a big leather valise he carried and showed me the leather briefcase inside. "You're gonna take the IRT down to Amsterdam Avenue, and meet a guy making a call in a phone booth." I must have I blanched because he quickly asked, "You have a problem with this George?" And I replied, "No sir, Mr. Shultz."

Next, Dutch Schultz carefully explained where I would get off the train, how I'd climb up out of the station and walk across the street to a newspaper stand, where a tall man would be waiting in a phone booth beside it. "You ask the man, 'What time is it?' If he says, 'Time to have a Lucky Strike,' just give him what you're carrying. Nothing to it."

But I was nervous as hell as I rode the rattling IRT car south to Manhattan, and more anxious still when I climbed up to the street and into the bright sunlight. People filled the sidewalks and stalled taxis honked their horns in the street. The comingled smells of car exhaust and roasting chestnuts filled the air, and despite my apprehension, something about Manhattan always filled me with an expectant kind of energy.

Just as I spotted the man I was to meet and started to cross the street toward him, I heard a hail of machine gun fire and saw him slump inside the phone booth. Then, somehow, the bullets sparked a fire in the stacks of newspapers. In a flash, all the papers were ablaze and next the whole of the stand caught fire. People were terrified and I was frightened, too, but because the bullets had stopped, I opened the valise, pulled the briefcase from it, and threw the empty valise into the fire before I ran back down to the station.

Dutch Schultz was waiting for me when I got back to the tobacco shop. He'd clearly already heard that the man I was meeting had been shot and he wanted to know whether I'd reached him before he was gunned down. I explained what had happened, then handed him the briefcase—still full of cash. He opened it, and his eyes got big and he said, "Is this all of it?" I nodded, yes. He wanted to know why I'd thrown the other bag into the fire, and I said, "Well, so it would look like the money got burned in the fire. Doesn't that help you?"

"Son of a bitch," Dutch Schultz said, looking at me with a touch of admiration. "Pretty smart for a guinea kid." Then he laughed. "You may just be the most honest guy in the fucking city. What's to keep you from pocketing my money and telling me it burned up with all the papers?"

I said I'd have a hell of a time trying to explain to my Assyrian mother where all that money had come from, and he laughed again, then took two crisp hundred dollar bills from the stack and insisted I take it—and I gladly and gratefully did.

I knew my mother would find a windfall of two hundred dollars equally hard to believe, so I kept the gift a secret. Every so often, I would spend a bit of it on something I needed—a new pair of shoes, or trousers, or a sweater I admired, and on special occasions I would bring home lamb shanks so my mother could make Assyrian dulma. She certainly noticed those purchases, and when she pressed me to explain where the money was coming from to pay for them, finally I told her the truth. By the time I did, Dutch Schultz himself had been murdered—at the Palace Chophouse across the river in Newark—and because he was gone now, I thought perhaps she wouldn't worry too much. I told her all the money I'd ever made was for the family, and the same went for Dutch Schultz's money, too.

*

It may have been the heartbreak of the end of my relationship with Lydia Turner, forced on us by her parents and my mother, or it may have simply been my awakening into adulthood and the poverty, corruption, and injustice I witnessed every day in New York, but for whatever reasons, I began to want to return to Russia, and I expressed the desire often enough that my mother commanded me almost daily for a few months that I *must not* follow through on such nonsense. I had lots of cousins in Russia still, but it was a *communist* country now, she reminded me angrily. In those days, however, communism still held great promise for young people around the world—and, increasingly, I was one of them.

In the midst of the Depression in New York, it was hard for me not to look around and wonder where was the tangible evidence of America's greatness and the freedom and opportunity it offered all its citizens. And everything I read seemed to further my sense that this nation wasn't all it pretended to be. In school, teachers tried to convince us that America was a place where brotherhood soared supreme, but where was the brotherhood in three hundred years of slavery in this country? Where was the justice in the lynching of Negroes in the South that continued into the present day? Where was the freedom and humanity in the labor of children in West Virginia's coal mines? If brotherhood existed in America, I told anybody who'd let me talk, I sure hadn't seen it yet.

My mother regularly tried to remind me that the Tiflis I remembered fondly was a city in which I had been shot—and I still carried the scars to prove it—a city that was caught in the midst of a brutally violent revolution, and now was under every bit as much repression after the war, she suspected, than it had been before. It was true that my memory of the big sense of freedom I'd experienced in Russia had much to do with the fact that, when I lived there, I had been a small boy whom people largely ignored and let do as he pleased. It was probably true as well that the very same life I'd lived there before would have very little appeal to me now, but somehow I was both nostalgic about that faraway place and filled with the kind of indignation that was common in kids my age.

Everyone in my family continued to work hard, and we weren't destitute, as many in New York were. We had a roof over our heads, at least, and the overt racism suffered by blacks in the city was something we experienced to a significantly lesser degree. Yet undeniably, I had a chip on my shoulder as I entered adulthood, one that had been firmly planted as long ago as the time I when I threw the rich kid Papadokas off the gymnasium bleachers for making fun of my clothes. I hated the presumption on anyone's part that I was inferior or beholden in any way, and even my brother Polous seemed to think he had a leg up on me just because he was eighteen years older and a physician who wore a fine suit.

The hard and dirty work I'd happily done as a kid now didn't set so easily with me, particularly when I could plainly see that, here in America, the money you earned often seemed to have less to do with how good you were at your work than who your friends were. If you fell in love with the wrong girl, somebody was sure to get in your way, and if you tried to be the best you could be at something, surely someone would trip you up along the way just to watch you fall.

Perhaps because my father had such a low opinion of me; perhaps because, as an immigrant, I was inescapably an outsider as I'd begun my formative years; perhaps because my acne and poor kid's clothes had instilled in me an insecurity I hadn't yet shaken off, I was determined as hell in my early twenties to make my mark and prove I *wasn't* inferior to anybody who ever dared to think otherwise. I was never a spectacular student, but I was a true athlete, I'd discovered—as had the coaches at Morris High who increasingly were impressed by how strong and agile and fiercely competitive I was. I could call myself a musician, too, and proudly did, and I practiced playing my violin in every free hour I could spare, complimented and encouraged by a violin teacher named David Hirsch, who lived nearby in The Bronx and whose lessons I worked hard at the tobacco shop to afford. And as my broken heart began to mend, I also was able to remind myself that I'd turned into the kind of guy who young women found it easy to look at—and sometimes flirt with—and it seemed increasingly unlikely that I would spend all of my life wounded and alone.

*

The 1935 Morris High School yearbook from my senior year attests many decades later that I was a popular guy. I was voted the Best Boy Athlete and received the Faculty Medal for academic achievement, and dozens of classmates, male and female, signed the book and wished me well—most of them mentioning how well I swam, or what a fine gymnast or ball player I was, or how I'd be a better violinist than Heifetz one day, or even what a ladies' man I'd become.

I'd been a hard-punching Golden Gloves boxer when we still lived in New Britain, but it was gymnastics that caught my attention in high school in The Bronx. A coach named William Strobel had told me I'd be good at gymnastics, but I knew next to nothing about the sport. When I agreed to visit gymnastics practice one day, I was amazed to see how well-muscled these guys on the rings, horizontal bars, and side horse were. They looked like Greek gods, as a matter of fact, and I knew I wouldn't mind looking like one myself, and when Coach Strobel suggested at the end of the practice that I try the rings and bars, I was stunned by how difficult they were, and by how little strength I actually had.

Over time, I became an excellent gymnast and I loved the precision, strength, concentration, and even the endless practice it required. The sport of gymnastics, in fact, shared much in common with the art of the violin, I discovered, and something in me was drawn to it immediately and throughout my high school and college years, and I always brought to gymnastics the same passion I did to music. As a side benefit, it was great, too, that I did get into by far the best shape of my life. I was buff enough that many of my friends called me "Tarzan," a nickname in which I took real pride, and one that helped prove I was a "somebody" in ways that perhaps my clothes or my immigrant status did not.

As a way to improve as quickly as I could at gymnastics, Coach Strobel suggested I spend time at the New York Turnverein at 85th Street and Lexington in Manhattan. The Turnverein, which is the German word for sports club—and purportedly its sole focus—was operated by German ex-patriots and gymnasts, but my nephew Bobby, ten years younger than me and now a budding gymnast himself, soon discovered that the gym had something of a split personality. It was, on the one hand, a terrific place to train and receive feedback and coaching from some of the best gymnasts in New York. People at the Turnverein were dedicated to a high-minded gymnastics ideal that greatly appealed to me. But, on the other hand, many of them were Nazis, at least in spirit and public trappings, and I found it hard to believe that people I respected believed Adolf Hitler, who'd recently come to power in Germany, was something of a savior. I knew full well that Jews in Germany were beginning to be stripped of their civil rights, and I knew, too, that I wanted no part of an ideology that believed in an ethnic ideal that didn't include Jews or Negroes or Assyrians, for that matter.

There were days when I would arrive at the Turnverein on a Saturday morning, ready to get to work, only to be met by a parade of brown-shirted young Nazis, who had marched out of the gym and down Lexington Avenue, their intention to draw the anger of anti-Hitler New Yorkers as obvious as their brightly polished knee boots. One of the young Germans, Wolf Hufer—perhaps the best side horse vaulter I ever saw—tried to convince me that Nazism would return Germany to greatness, and would change the world. I liked the guy and loved to watch him in the gym, but I finally told him to cut out the political harangues, I wasn't interested.

Those intensive workouts at the Turnverein helped me earn a spot on the varsity team within a year of taking up gymnastics, and then I made the Morris High swimming team as well. I was a natural swimmer, and entirely self-taught, and I'd discovered a C-stroke that made the most of my strong arms and helped rapidly move me through the water. My grades never matched my best scores on the rings or my times swimming the hundred-meter freestyle, but that was okay with me. I was "Tarzan," and my classmates, coaches, and teachers respected me, and nothing seemed more important than that.

*

I was a good enough athlete, in fact, that it seemed possible that I could receive an athletic scholarship to college. My brother Polous had begun to try to convince me that I ought to study engineering, and although I really wanted to focus on music, I couldn't muster much of an argument with him when he talked at length about the range of work engineers did and what high demand they were in. When I learned that New York University's campus in The Bronx had an aeronautical engineering program, my skepticism turned into a targeted goal. I'd fallen for airplanes and the idea of flying long before—although I'd never actually been in a plane—and if I could design, test, and build aircraft someday day, then sure, I'd become an engineer.

With the help of Coach Strobel—who continued to believe in my potential and, I'm sure, pulled a few strings on my behalf—I was accepted at NYU and offered an athletic scholarship that paid my tuition. I continued to live at home, and the University Heights campus was an easy commute, and Irv Rosenfeld at the tobacco shop was glad to adjust my work hours to my class schedule. It was the fall of 1935, and the Depression continued its stranglehold on America, and the German Third Reich continued to flex its ominous muscles in Europe, but my immediate problem was that my engineering studies were harder than *anything* I'd ever done before.

I thought I was a smart enough guy, but I nonetheless had to spend three or four hours studying for every hour I spent in class, time I could only borrow from hours when I would otherwise sleep. So, I didn't sleep much, and I studied late into most nights, finally falling asleep with my head slumped over my books until it was time to be up and off to the Heights campus, where I would begin another day overwhelmed by the complexities of the engineering trade and struggling mightily to get grades that included at least a few Cs. If playing the violin was difficult—and joining the NYU orchestra had quickly demonstrated to me how truly hard it was—engineering, in comparison, included all the difficulty and virtually none of the joy.

But the world wasn't a joyful place as the year 1936 commenced, and like virtually everyone in my generation, I recognized that I had to make tough decisions, stand by them, and sacrifice in whatever ways I was forced to in order to make a life for myself. I'd long since surrendered the fantasy of returning to Russia, and if I had a bright future as an American, it would also be as an engineer. I accepted that reality, made the most of it I could, and studied so hard and long I thought my eyes would fall out of my head.

*

I found time, somehow, to continue to swim and compete in gymnastics, and I was good enough at both that I began to consider trying out for the teams in each sport that would compete in the 1936 Summer Olympic Games in Berlin. In large part because I'd quickly become a constant presence in the pools, gyms, and locker rooms of the NYU athletic department, I'd gotten to know a number coaches and trainers—and they liked me and the kinds of things of which I was capable—and soon I was offered a job, one that allowed me to say so long to Irv Rosenfeld at the late Dutch Schultz's tobacco shop and remain on the campus all day.

My responsibilities in my new work included cleaning and maintaining sports equipment, opening facilities in the early mornings, and officiating intramural games of basketball, volleyball, and baseball between competing fraternities. I got to know quite a few of the fraternity fellows, and some of them pushed me hard to join them, but I didn't have the extra money a fraternity membership demanded, and, just as importantly, I wasn't drawn to their segregated lifestyle. I spent enough time studying in frat houses with friends who also were studying engineering that I understood that, in the frat life, you woke up with your "brothers," shaved beside them, ate with, played and drank and sang with them, and too often cleaned up their vomit—all to the exclusion of anyone who hadn't pledged to the two or three Greek letters you had. For an immigrant like me, who'd always had to struggle to prove that I was part of the

American crowd, it didn't seem to make sense now to live a life that tried to make you believe you were above it. I didn't see much difference, in fact, between the Germans at the Turnverein, who so righteously touted their Aryan "purity," and the fellows in the fraternity houses who believed that going Greek had made them superior to those of us who had not.

I made as much money as an athletic department lackey as I had at Irv Rosenfeld's; working for the university helped me keep my scholarship, and, to be honest, spending lots of time in the locker rooms and on the fields was something I thoroughly enjoyed. During the fall and early winter of each year—while both the NYU and Fordham football teams were playing at Yankee Stadium—legendary Yankee baseball players like Frank Crosetti, Bill Dickey, Tommy Henrich, Joe DiMaggio, and Lou Gehrig would come to the Heights campus to work out, throw the ball around, and have some batting practice. The players would show up in fancy sports cars and sometimes wouldn't bother to stub out their cigarettes or cigars while they worked out, and nobody, I quickly learned, could swear like those famous baseballers could.

One time, Howard Cann, NYU's head basketball coach, found me in the gymnasium office and asked me if I had a few minutes. I told him sure, and he handed me a catcher's mitt and told me Lefty Gomez needed someone to catch his pitches. I told him I'd never played anything but the outfield, but he said it didn't matter. When he introduced me to Lefty, the two showed me how to squat and hold the glove and wait for the ball to come to it, but I quaked in my boots for the first few pitches Lefty threw. I got the hang of it after a while, but my left palm was swollen up like a balloon for most of the following week.

Lou Gehrig was a very good-looking guy, and friendly as well, and one time on the NYU ball field, we struck up a conversation while he was waiting to bat. He asked if I played and I said I'd been a centerfielder, telling him, too, that I'd played football during my sophomore year, but then had devoted myself to gymnastics and swimming, and I was impressed that he didn't make fun of the latter two sports. He was a smart enough fellow to know that their challenges were every bit as significant as baseball's— maybe more—and I remember that he added, "You'll save your knees, too, and you'll be glad you did. Nothing matters like your health does." He was right, of course, and only a year later he had to quit the game because he'd contracted ALS, and in just two more years he was dead.

*

A Young and studious George at N.Y.U., 1936

*George as a lifeguard Poses with other camp counselors at Camp Bowdoin,
New Hamburg N.Y., 1939*

George as a lifeguard at Camp Bowdoin, New Hamburg N.Y., 1939

Coach William F. Strobel stands next to George and the Morris High Gymnastic Team, 1935 N.Y.

David A. Armstrong

Lifeguard George Edgar, Camp Bowdoin, New Hamburg NY, 1939

Like so many young men, I mightily wanted to be a sports star, and I'd made such strides on the rings and parallel bars and in the fifty- and hundred-meter freestyle that in my freshman year at NYU I was eager to try out for the 1936 Olympics. My hope at the time was to qualify for either the American gymnastics or swimming teams, but in the fall of that year, Avery Brundage, head of the U.S. Olympic committee, ruled that only citizens would be allowed onto the teams and that permanent residents—like me—would not.

It was a dream I reluctantly—and a little angrily—surrendered. I'd lived in America for fourteen years by then; I spoke English without an accent and had a hell of a lot more to show for myself than many native-born people did, and it rubbed me a little raw that just because no one in my family was a citizen yet, I couldn't compete for an American team.

I flirted with the idea of going to Canada, where, I'd been told, citizenship wasn't an Olympic prerequisite and where my chance of making either team might even be better. Maybe Canada, rather than a return to Russia was my fate, I told my mother and sisters, but they reacted to that idea with as much shock and dismay as they had to my proposal to return to Tiflis. What was *wrong* with me, they asked. Wasn't I grateful for my life in America?

For years, we hadn't had the money to hire an immigration lawyer to help us with the documentation we needed to file our citizenship papers. And then, when we did have some money, other things always seemed more important, and citizenship took a backseat. My mother, in fact, remained a little apprehensive about citizenship, still afraid that if we drew attention to ourselves we could be deported on account of her bad eyes, or my smart attitude, or something else. And she was genuinely fearful, too, about the possibility that I would simply disappear one day, leaving behind only a note that included a forwarding address in Toronto or Tiflis.

David A. Armstrong

In the end, I had to reassure her for weeks that winter that I wouldn't leave for Canada or anywhere else. I would have to surrender my scholarship if I did, and lose my job in the athletic department, and leave the family to which I'd been a steadfast support since I was a kid. No, I wouldn't go to Canada, I promised, but that decision meant that neither would I have the opportunity to go to Berlin, where, I liked to imagine, I might have stepped onto a podium the following summer and had a laurel wreath placed on my head and a medal draped around my neck.

*

Britain had gone to war against Germany and Japan was rattling its sabers in the East in the summer of 1940. I was about to graduate from NYU and my prospects looked bright, but it was impossible not to imagine that world events might well affect me very personally before long. Yet little did I know that on a sultry night in June of that year, my world *would* change, but for the most intimate kind of reason.

I was studying in my undershirt late in the evening when my sisters Nanajan and Maria returned home from a short trip to Grand Central Station in Manhattan, where they had gone to meet Ann John, a distant cousin whose family had known ours well back in Persia. Ann lived in Chicago and had come to visit for a couple of weeks, specifically so we could meet and perhaps fall in love, as both families hoped we might. I came out of my room to greet her, we shook hands with a sense of something rather electric passing between us as we did, and only nine evenings later, I asked her to marry me.

A year before, my mother had taken the train to Chicago to visit Ann's family, and she'd had her first introduction to Ann when her brother Joel had taken her to a department store to see the amazing new televisions that had recently reached the market. When a car commercial appeared on W9XZV, Channel 1, Joel made sure she paid close attention, because the beautiful young woman standing beside the car was his sister Ann. My mother was impressed, and she assured me when she returned home that although she hadn't actually met her, she'd seen a tall, stately, and remarkably good-looking Assyrian girl on *television* in Chicago, a young woman who deserved a fine young man like me.

I didn't make much of my mother's enthusiasm at the time, nor did I later when she announced that, following an exchange of letters with her parents, Ann was traveling to New York in the early summer to visit. She had many suitors, my mother had been told, but no one she'd met so far was the perfect man for her. Her brother Joel, in fact, wanted her to marry a friend of his who was a physician—although he *wasn't* Assyrian—and the prospect of that union remained up in the air when Ann agreed to travel to New York. A career spent modeling in television commercials was unthinkable to her family, but it was suitable work while she waited to find her husband, and no one objected when it was agreed that, because of my impending final exams, she would come to New York to meet me, a circumstance that was quite unusual.

Except for noting that strange exchange of electricity as we shook hands, my first impression of Ann was that she was absolutely gorgeous—something I'd already suspected when I'd been informed that she had been crowned Miss Assyria at the 1933 World's Fair in Chicago. She was as tall as I was, with sparkling eyes and beautiful dark curls and a way about her that was rather formal and relaxed at the same time. I learned as we all sat down to tea and chada, a sweet pastry that my mother had baked for the occasion, that Ann also was outspoken, funny, and very sure of herself—and she certainly wasn't intimidated by me. At the end of the evening, my brother-in-law Peter, the always disagreeable guy who had married my sister Maria, took me aside and sternly warned me not to get any ideas; his close friend, he said, would marry Ann John, and he planned to introduce them the following day. I told Pete to go to hell, and he said he'd kill me if I touched her, and then everyone went to bed while I went back to my books to study for the exams that would be the culmination of my college career.

I'm not sure whether Ann ever did meet Peter's good friend, but I do know that in the following days, my concentration on my studies was sorely tested. With either Nanajan or Maria or both as our chaperones, we toured the city from the Battery to all my haunts in The Bronx. We went shopping, and visited the university and, of course, I wanted to take her to a movie or two. There was new picture called *Broadway Melody of 1940*, starring Fred Astaire and Eleanor Powell, that my sisters and I were eager to see, and it seemed to be exactly the right thing when Ann said, almost unbelievably, that she'd never seen Fred Astaire in the movies. But then she explained that that was because she'd never seen a movie, and her parents had made her promise, in fact, that she wouldn't see a movie or a show while she was in New York. I'm sure my jaw dropped before I said I was sure this was another one of her jokes, but she assured me it wasn't. "Our church is strictly Christian," she added, "and they don't allow shows." I was quick to retort that our church was strictly Christian, too, but we also liked to have a good time now and again, but Ann stood her ground, yet she wanted us to know how much she liked New York and what a grand time she was having, and she hoped we would understand that she just couldn't betray her parents.

"Not even to watch Fred Astaire dance?" I asked and she laughed because no, she said, in her church dancing was forbidden, too.

*

In the following days, the rigid rule of Ann's religion didn't further interfere with our plans, but I couldn't help but ask her more about a kind of church that sounded rather tough-minded and backward to me. Wasn't life a little dull, I wanted to know, with so many delightful pursuits forbidden?

No, she assured my sisters and me, on Sundays there were two sessions of Sunday school, then children's Sunday school, which was always fun, followed by the preaching service, and a Bible study, and then later a fellowship service to end the day. When I said I'd never heard of Assyrians that didn't dance, she explained that this wasn't an Assyrian church but rather one to which her parents had converted before she was born, things began to be clearer to me. This was an *American* church, and I'd heard that there were lots of churches like these, particularly in the South and Midwest where everybody seemed to spend their time terrified that a bit pleasure would intrude into their otherwise sober lives.

I told Ann that it seemed to me that we were plenty religious in our family. My mother was actually something of Bible expert, I said, explaining that Assyrian priests commonly visited to talk with her about the scriptures. I didn't want her to think that the only people who could rightly claim religion were those who forbid everything, and she assured me that no, she thought people should make their own decisions about what to believe and what religious rules to obey.

This rather sharp distinction between each family's beliefs and practices seemed, I remember, rather more substantial than anything that ever had stood between me and Lydia Turner, in fact, and I knew I just didn't entirely understand how and why people so often used their backgrounds and religions to hammer wedges between themselves. The differences between us might have been more than enough to make me change my otherwise entirely positive impressions of Ann, but they did not. I'd become captivated by her in only a few days, and, at the time, I was sure her family's fundamentalism wasn't the first subject on which I should focus.

Four nights before she was scheduled to leave, somehow Ann and I were able to spend some time alone. To this day, I'm surprised my mother allowed it, but after supper on a very hot night, we walked up to our building's roof and enjoyed the breeze. She sat on the parapet, and the street was six floors below, and I put my arms around her and told her I'd keep her from falling. She moved into my touch, and welcomed it, and we kissed—a long, lingering, and dizzying kiss at whose conclusion we had to sit on the warm roof tiles to compose ourselves. Half a moon lit our faces, and her smile was radiant even in the soft light, and that was the moment when I asked if she would become my wife.

*

My mother and sisters must have conferred below and agreed that it was time for Ann and me to be allowed a bit of time alone, and so they allowed us to talk for a long time after I asked the question, one she didn't immediately answer.

I wanted her to know that, as an engineer, I wouldn't have money to burn but neither would I struggle to find a good job, and she agreed. She knew, too, that I wanted to fly and still dreamed of being an internationally recognized swimmer and gymnast. More importantly—as far we both were concerned—was the fact that I remained committed to the violin. I told her how Alexei had given me my first lessons on board the *King Alexander*, how Jan Kaminski had assured me back in New Britain when I was just a boy that I was a true violinist, how the extraordinary Fritz Kreisler himself had encouraged me, and how David Hirsch, the fine violinist and teacher who lived just around the corner, contended that I was one of his best students.

Ann asked me if I could play for her, and I said, of course, I would; it would be my honor. Then I added that I certainly didn't want to rush her in responding to my proposal.

If we were to become engaged, she said, I would have to come to Chicago to meet her family, and I assured her it would be my pleasure and that I could arrange to do so soon after my graduation.

If we were to become engaged, she said, I would have to commit to becoming a born-again Christian, and I said I could do that, too, although no doubt with a bit less fervor in my voice.

If we were to become engaged, she said, there would be dozens of plans and decisions to make, not least of them the city we would choose for our home, and I explained that, almost certainly I would be drafted into the army and who knew where the army might send us. I had joined the ROTC in my junior year, with the hope that I would enter as an officer, and I explained that if all went well, she would be an officer's wife from the outset.

I apologized for the suddenness and directness of my proposal, and for the fact that I hadn't yet bought a ring. I said I guessed it was an engineer's kind of proposal, and Ann laughed. She told me she would be honored to carefully consider my proposal, and that it wouldn't be long before I would have an answer, and we kissed again on that New York night and suddenly the whole of my world was changed. I didn't hear the sounds of violins playing in the sultry darkness, or somehow imagine Fred Astaire dancing across the rooftops, but I knew nonetheless that I had just experienced one of life's transforming moments, and I felt light, and joyful, and very much alive.

Santa Barbara, 1979

I MUST HAVE been about ten when Pop gave me a children's violin, and I felt very grown-up to have been trusted with such an important gift. He immediately taught me how to cradle it in my hand and tuck it between my shoulder and chin, how to wrap my fingers around the neck and press the strings against the fingerboard, and how to draw the bow across the strings. I remember being intrigued to learn what an ancient instrument the violin was, and how it was the only instrument in orchestral music that hadn't evolved from its original form—something that made it seem eternal and powerful somehow. I took violin lessons for several years, and Poppy and I would play my little pieces together sometimes, but I think he knew early on that I had neither the talent for the instrument nor the passion for it that he possessed, and he never pushed me to take it more seriously than I did. Nor do I remember feeling guilty for failing to become a musician—something I can imagine might have disappointed him.

It was about that same time when Pop began to let me experiment with his 1959 Contaflex 35mm camera. I understood from its weight and complexity that it was much more than a toy, and I began to take pictures as often as I could. Pop and I loved to watch old black-and-white movies together on television, and as we watched I took photos of the screen, carefully framing my shots so that I could capture only the image on the television I collected those photos as my own custom-made movie stills. It was a quirky sort of hobby, but I was an odd kid, and I felt so grown up on the day Poppy took me to Tony Rose Cameras and bought me a Canon Super 8 sound camera and a Super 8 sound projector.

Before long, I was constantly making short movies—still aiming my camera at the television on occasion, but also filming our afternoons at the beach, the trips we took in the car, and everything else that caught my eye, then projecting the apprentice pieces that my grandfather dutifully admired. My mother, sister, and I had returned to Santa Barbara to live and the city *itself became my muse. If I wasn't exactly an auteur, at least I was enthusiastic, and I know Poppy was pleased that his investment had engendered a kind of passion in me for the first time. Yet looking out at the world through a viewfinder also kept me isolated, and I remained solitary, disconnected from the kids around me, and always awkward unless Poppy was by my side.*

But then I discovered football, or perhaps football simply took hold of me, and for the first time in my life I really excelled at something. Athletics had always been enormously important to my grandfather, of course, and it was Poppy who encouraged me to train hard, work diligently in practice, and treat the games like the elemental contests they were. The years I spent in the Youth Football League were my introduction to comradeship and team spirit, and by the time I was in high school I had grown big enough that I played on the defensive line, and I loved knocking the stuffing out of every quarterback and running back I could get my arms around. I was quick and strong and aggressive as hell and Poppy couldn't have been prouder.

I created real friendships for the first time; I became an all-league player, a rather cocky member of the jock elite; I was popular with both boys and girls in ways I could never have imagined before, and Pop seemed to take a kind of personal pleasure in the fact that I even became something of a teenage ladies' man. My whole family got caught up in watching the Santa Barbara Dons do battle in the sea-moist air on Friday nights at Peabody Stadium—Poppy, my mother, faithfully attending all of my games, my mom screaming bloody murder from the stands, Pop praising my performance as we advanced all the way to the state championship undefeated.

I remember that at one game during my sophomore year, I saw my grandmother Betty in the stands. I didn't expect her to be there, and a man I didn't know was sitting beside her, yet my instincts told me it was Harry Armstrong, my father. We met briefly after the game—the kind of introduction that left both of us feeling nothing more than awkward.

A couple of years later, my mother shocked me one day by telling me that my father wanted me to come visit him. He lived in Lake Tahoe and had mailed her a round-trip airplane ticket. I was old enough that I certainly could travel on my own, but my mother wasn't sure the visit was a good idea, although she didn't want to prevent me from seeing my father. My grandmother Betty was dead set against me not going, but I was curious, of course.

I was met at the Reno airport by the man who managed the small apartment building where Harry lived, and on the drive up to Tahoe City, he and his friendly wife cautioned me that Harry wasn't in very good shape. He really wanted to see me, but he was nervous about it, and, well, he had been drinking, they explained. They opened the door to his apartment for me, and although it was the middle of the afternoon, all the drapes and blinds were tightly closed and it was quiet except for the clank of a noisy fan. I poked my head into the living room and kitchen, then found Harry passed out in his bedroom. The sheets surrounding him were covered with vomit and a bucket beside the bed was stained with vomit, too.

I remember the manager's wife putting her hand on my shoulder and saying, "I'm sorry you're seeing him like this. He just didn't know how to handle you coming to see him." I felt sadder for her than I did for myself. She seemed to care about him, yet to me, Harry was just a dead-drunk guy lying in his own filth. I knew what the Vietnam War had done to him, knew about his broken body, the seven major surgeries and the addictions to heroin, then methadone. But he was just a guy who life apparently had treated pretty unfairly, just as he once had abused my mother and me. He wasn't a man who was my father.

I walked around his neighborhood that evening, found a hamburger for dinner, and slept on the manager's couch that night. The next morning I found a payphone, called the airport, and booked an early flight home.

Chapter 7

Ann

LESS THAN TWENTY-FOUR hours after I proposed to Ann, she stopped suddenly in the middle of the sidewalk as we were walking down Fifth Avenue in Manhattan. She turned to me, took my face in her hands, and said, "George, I *will* marry you. I *will*. And we will have a wonderful life together."

Ann didn't tell me she loved me in that moment, nor did I speak those words to her—either that afternoon or the night before. Yet both of us, I know, simply decided in those first few days of our acquaintance that somehow we were right for each other and that together we could create a family.

The bombing of Pearl Harbor and the United States' entry into World War II was still six months away, but the threat that the country soon would be enmeshed in a momentous war was one that thousands of young people like us understood very personally, and Ann and I were far from the only couple in America that June who saw some urgency in setting our grown-up lives in motion as soon we could. I don't remember being consciously aware of that hurry, but as I reflect on those days many years later, I can't help but recognize that, in addition to pledging a desire to marry each other, we each were expressing the hope that no matter how upside down the world was about to become, we would survive and live full lives.

When we returned to The Bronx for dinner that evening, I announced that I had proposed marriage and Ann had accepted and a celebration immediately commenced. Ann was a good sport when the group of us—including my mother and sisters and nephew and brother-in-law—did a bit of impromptu dancing, and my mother even got out the bottle of vodka she kept in the freezer and poured small glasses with which everyone but Ann could toast the great news. Ann hugged each member of the clan who had been a stranger just a few days before and accepted their congratulations, and my mother had tears in her eyes when she hugged me, and I was pleased that without specifically intending to do so, that I had found a way to make her very happy.

I'm not sure why it didn't seem appropriate to have Ann join us, but the following day my two sisters and I went shopping for an engagement ring. With part of my meager savings, I purchased a platinum ring with a half-carat, round-cut diamond, and an Assyrian priest blessed the ring for us before Ann began to wear it. It was a heady time, one of those when you're sure nothing will ever go wrong—and thank God for them, because life includes many obstacles and we were about to experience our fair share.

*

Ann John, Miss Assyria, Chicago's World Fair, 1933

David A. Armstrong

Ann, front row right, dressed for Chicago's World Fair, 1933

Ann, left, in traditional Assyrian attire, World's Fair, 1933

Above, Ann, summer 1934; below, Ann holds her Brownie camera, 1935

Ann at the Yacht Harbor (Note the puppy in her hands), August 23 1936

Above, Ann and girlfriend stay cool, below, Ann and a girlfriend sunbathe

Above, Ann and girlfriend going out, 1941; below, a smiling Ann, 1943

George and Ann, engaged to be married, on the back porch of George's sister's home, 1942

If Ann had been an instant hit with my family when she first arrived from Chicago, I made something less than a stellar impression on highly protective Joel and the rest of her family when I arrived to visit a few weeks later. Everyone was cordial enough to me, and unlike the trouble I'd had with Lydia Turner's family a few years before, the fact that I was Assyrian and a Christian worked significantly in my favor. But the problem was that I wasn't the right *kind* of Christian, a mark against me about which I'd already been informed, of course. And neither was it to my advantage that I was, as Joel saw it, poor.

Ann's father was a successful building contractor and Joel was a dentist with a thriving practice. Ann's parents lived in a fine home on Karlov Avenue that Ann's father had built; Joel lived downstairs, and the family spent much of the summer in a cottage on Fox Lake. Ann's younger sister, Florence, had a remarkable soprano voice and she and I spent lots of time sharing our love of music. They were a close-knit family, all of whom genuinely seemed to enjoy being in each other's company—and that was a circumstance that seemed natural enough to me. But no amount of advance notice could have prepared me for the zealotry the John family brought to their religion, and—if I hadn't really fallen in love with their beloved Ann—the first Sunday I spent more than seven hours in church with them would have sent me running.

There was no question, as well, that my own piety was an issue with which the Johns wanted, even needed more information. Because they were Assyrians, at least I didn't have to explain the kind of religious environment in which I'd been raised—it was one in which Ann's parents had been brought up in themselves—but they made no secret of the fact that they wanted to hear some rather specific theological responses from me to their questions. When Joel asked me what kind of relationship I had with God, I was momentarily stumped, but then was able to shape an answer he seemed to find at least acceptable. And when Ann's father rather bluntly asked on the second day of my visit whether I had accepted Jesus Christ as my personal savior, it seemed for a moment that the whole question of whether he would sanction his daughter's marriage to me hung on my answer.

"You're asking if I'm born again?" I responded.

"I'm asking precisely what I asked," he said, a bit impatiently.

I didn't want to simply and honestly answer no, but neither could I go on at effusive length about a relationship with Jesus; I barely knew the man. After a few uncomfortable moments, I finally managed, "Well, as Ann's future husband, I look forward to doing so."

It was a response that appeared just barely acceptable, and Ann's father let it go at that, to my great relief, and we moved on to topics about which I was less tongue-tied, such as my plans for a career in engineering, the importance of music in my life, and how important it was that Adolf Hitler and his armies were stopped.

By the end of my stay, no one in Ann's family had announced that I would be an unsuitable mate for her, and Joel had gone so far as to say something about how he was looking forward to having a "brother," and as Ann tearfully bid me goodbye at Chicago's Union Station, she assured me that I had passed muster in every way. I hadn't considered prior to meeting her and initiating our whirlwind courtship what it would be like to have "in-laws," but now that the prospect was very much at hand, it seemed to me that, although I might have preferred a livelier and appreciably less virtuous bunch, I was glad to add them to my life, at least if Ann was the centerpiece of the deal.

*

Ann's mother, Salby Joseph John & her father, David Peter John

Ann's Sister-in-law, Clara, her brother Dr. Joel David John, their children, Esther and my namesake, David Alan John.

I had been a weak enough student that in order to graduate, I had to attend summer school and prove my mastery of computational fluid dynamics, equations of motion, terminal velocities, and the like, but I had been allowed, nonetheless, to graduate with my class that June.

I hoped Ann could return from the Midwest for the cap-and-gown ceremony on the broad green lawn of University Heights campus, but something or other got in her way. Yet even without her there to see me accept my soon-to-be degree, it was a fine day—all of us who were completing our studies tossing our mortar boards high into the air, everyone in my family crowding round me to tell me how proud they were of my accomplishments, even my brother Polous hugging me firmly and telling me he was sure I'd have a fine career.

I telephoned Ann in Chicago at the end of the afternoon, informing her that her betrothed had indeed become an aeronautical engineer—at least for the moment and just by the skin of my teeth. She told me she was very proud of me, but then, because the cost of a phone call was significant in those days, she wanted to talk about setting our wedding date. There were mountains of things to accomplish between now and then, she explained, and the sooner we set a date, the quicker she could reserve the church and purchase a dress and select her attendants and begin to plan the reception. And it was with that particular conversation that we initiated what became more than six months of disagreement, misunderstanding, and sometimes even anger about where and how we would marry.

As far as Ann was concerned, there was little to come to terms with. A solemn wedding in her own Chicago church, one in which she was attended by many bridesmaids, and which was followed by a formal reception, was the only wedding imaginable. For my part, if I was going to be married—to Ann or anyone else—the occasion seemed to warrant a party. I favored a simple ceremony in New York, perhaps even a civil one, followed by the kind of music, dancing, feasting, and revelry that would seem to my family and me to suit the magnitude of the occasion. Ann and I had starkly opposing ideas, we discovered, about how we would be wed, and we proceeded to argue the subject out in letter after letter from June through the following January—communications that always included professions of love and fidelity and eternal commitment as well, but which often set off some real explosions.

As the discord and tension mounted, Ann began to question whether I truly loved her, if I couldn't simply acquiesce to her request for a wedding of her choosing. Weddings traditionally were planned and hosted by the bride's family, she reminded me, and she felt it was an affront to them all that I wouldn't agree to every plan they made for us while I was faraway in New York. In turn, I wanted Ann to carefully consider whether she really wanted me or a wedding. If it was the latter, no doubt she could find many young men who would meekly accept the wedding they were informed would be theirs. Yet if it the latter, I repeatedly wrote, didn't *my* desires and *my* family's traditions amount for anything?

By the beginning of 1942, I'd come to the conclusion that it wasn't just being married in Chicago that mattered enormously to Ann. I was convinced as well that she couldn't be happy living anywhere other than the place where her family was. "Honey, remember this," I wrote on January 19th, "neither you or any other power on earth will ever drive me an inch closer to Chicago. If you are harboring an idea that first you'll marry me and then get me to Chicago to live, you'd better forget it." My bluntness was both a personal and family trait, but it was coupled with an ability to give in on those occasions when I ultimately recognized that it was in my best interest to do so. And less than a month after I wrote those defiant words, Ann and I were married—in Chicago, in her family's church, just as she had wanted to since we'd become engaged.

I gave in, in the end, simply because I couldn't bear the thought of losing her. And although I was the sole member of my family in attendance, my many distant relations who lived in the Chicago area came out in force. Many of them were strangers, but they rallied round me as if I were their son or brother, and despite the fact that they eagerly attended—expecting a *wedding*, after all— none objected in the slightest when the reception didn't include a moment of dancing, just as Jesus himself would have wanted it, Ann's clan wanted us to suppose.

Ann looked radiant in her modest, lace-trimmed gown, her beautiful black hair framing her face, her veil cascading behind her, and I felt a bit like Fred Astaire himself in my white tie and tails. People applauded as we walked arm-in-arm down the aisle at the close of the service—husband and wife. At the downtown hotel where the reception was held, there was a single *small* glass of champagne for anyone who cared for one, and the dinner was sumptuous, and late in the evening everyone still in attendance escorted us to the elevator and shouted their congratulations and best wishes before we went up to our room.

Each of us showered, then Ann dried and fixed her hair while I waited in bed. She wore a sheer and beautiful gown, but told me not to look at her as she prepared, and I laughed and reminded her that the whole idea was not only that I looked, but also that I liked what I saw, and I assured her I liked everything very much. We were both awkward and uncertain and Ann literally shook with apprehension until, somehow, other emotions overtook her. I did what I could not to hurt her, but we did make a mess of the towels we'd placed on the sheets, and after we cleaned up the bed and ourselves, we made love again, and this time we both were at ease and enthralled and sure we would be in love like this forever.

*

Wedding Day, February 8, 1943

Wedding Day, February 8, 1943

A few weeks later, my family hosted a second gathering at a reception hall in Yonkers, and on this occasion, the restraint of the Chicago celebration gave way to the jubilance of a more traditionally Assyrian affair, replete with mountains of delicious Urmian food, music from Persia, Turkey, and Russia, and even a showy ensemble of Russian dancers, who leapt, spun, squatted, and kicked their boots high into the air to the delight of all of us who watched. Ann, bless her heart, understood that she had no alternative but to dance the day away as well—to songs by Tommy Dorsey, Glen Miller, and Benny Goodman—and dozens of men took their turns hand in hand with the beautiful recent bride. My mother, into her seventies by now, danced with me perhaps half a dozen times, and she warmly accepted the congratulations of hundreds of kin and near-kin, and because I was her last child to be married, she approached the occasion with a sense of completion of her life's work that was wonderful to see in her eyes and on her life-worn face. And when it was time for the traditional ring dance, so many people pinned money to our clothes that we ended the day five hundred dollars wealthier than we had begun it—a fortune, and enough money that we would be able to rent our own house or apartment, if the army didn't have other ideas about where I would live in next few years and how I would spend my days.

Immediately following summer school, I had accepted a job at Republic Aviation in Farmingdale, on Long Island, where I was the junior member of a team designing the machine-gun mounts for the wings of the P-47 fighter. I shared a house with a group of young engineers, and several of us were in the same sort of limbo. It seemed to make sense to the company—and to us—for us to remain on the job indefinitely as part of the nation's defense. The United States formally entered World War II in December, of course—an event that had immediate consequences for millions of Americans, and I was one of them. Virtually the moment Ann and I were married in the winter of 1942, the draft board in The Bronx began to threaten to induct me immediately.

Over the coming months, the management at Republic made repeated requests in letters, telegrams, and telephone calls to the board, insisting that I was far more valuable helping design fighter planes as part of America's sprint to build its military might than I would be in the army. But as luck would have it, the head of the New York draft board to which I was assigned was an entirely disagreeable fellow named Henry Lutz, an engineer himself and one who had been fired by Republic for incompetence some years before.

When I appeared before Lutz and the board in The Bronx in May 1942—just three months after Ann and I had moved into a little apartment near the Republic plant—the balding man with eyeglasses as thick as Coke bottles looked me over briefly and announced that he knew a lot about Republic Aviation. The company was lousy with engineers, he said, and could readily do without me. At a break in the hearing, I telephoned the manager of the North Smithfield plant, who had been working hard to secure my deferment, but when he heard Lutz's comments, he quickly surrendered the effort. "The son of a bitch is having fun with this," the manager told me. "And I'm sorry, George, but I don't think there's another thing we can do to keep you stateside."

Ten minutes later, a self-satisfied Lutz presented me with my induction notice, one that gave me just fourteen days to report to the army's east-coast induction center at Fort Dix, New Jersey. I visited my family before I took a train back to Long Island, and my mother and sisters assured me that they would love to have Ann live with them until I'd completed basic training, and, I hoped, had received my officer's commission and been stationed somewhere where she could join me. I wasn't sure how Ann would receive that invitation, suspecting that perhaps she would quickly opt to return to Chicago, but she was married now, and I was her husband, and somehow that fact had altered her outlook. The prospect of surrendering her new groom for a house full of Assyrian women wasn't her first choice, that was certain, yet we were at war and Ann certainly understood that everyone was making sacrifices, and so could she.

She said much the same thing to me on a platform at Penn Station in Manhattan two weeks later, her cheeks wet with tears. "Well, this is life," she acknowledged, "and we're in the middle of it. You have to fight the Nazis and I have to stand by you and wait for you." I promised Ann I would be faithful to her, and would love her forever, and that just as soon as I received my commission, we would be together again. It was far more certain that I'd be sent overseas—I might be, but it wasn't impossible that the army would assign me to a munitions or aircraft company like Republic Aviation.

"You married an aeronautical engineer, after all," I told her, proud and sad and eager to see where this life would take me.

*

Despite the terror of my first association with the military back when I saved my mother from one of the tsar's soldiers in war-torn Tiflis, I thoroughly enjoyed my ROTC training at NYU. I *liked* something about military regimentation and organization, liked the fact that you generally knew precisely what was asked of you and that, if you did that task competently enough, you would be rewarded. I liked the crisp and manly uniforms, the short army haircuts, and, given the independent streak that had been with me throughout my life, it's surprising that I was also perfectly comfortable being one among a sea of soldiers. If all went well, of course, I would become an officer, and instead of accepting orders, I would give them, and the idea of leading men—in training, in planning and executing, and even in combat—was one I found appealing.

I was one of the few guys I knew who actually liked to drill, and was among the many who enjoyed the hours spent at the firing range. The semi-automatic M1 carbine had only been in general issue for a short time, and it was a remarkable weapon with which I quickly became proficient. At two hundred yards, I could empty its eight cartridges into the heart of a target time after time. Because of my engineering degree, it seemed virtually certain that I would end up helping build infrastructure as part of the war effort—whether at home or at the front—but if I had been signaled out for the infantry, I knew, I would have readily accepted the role, particularly if I could begin each day with an M1 on my shoulder. But before I did any fighting—or helped erect a building or make a road, for that matter— I had to survive basic training, and that proved to be a challenge, particularly when a drill sergeant with a dirty mouth chose to insult my wife.

Following a few days of induction processing at Fort Dix, a group of fellow officer candidates and I were sent by train for basic training to Miami Beach, of all places. Our barracks were beachfront hotels and the mess halls were converted restaurants, yet my weeks there were anything but a holiday. The summer heat and humidity were absolutely stifling. We were issued salt pills to help combat dehydration and it wasn't unusual for a 180-pound man to lose ten pounds of water weight between morning reveille and supper. The mosquitoes were as big as bumblebees, the burning sun relentless, and everyone agreed that the army appeared to have issued an order that no good-looking women were allowed within a hundred miles of the beaches where we grunted and sweated and trained.

My army pay was $48 dollars a month, a sum so paltry I could send virtually none of it north to Ann, but I did make some additional money by taking in ironing. My sisters had earned their livings sewing, altering and ironing clothes for nearly two decades by now, and I'd learned plenty during those years to allow me to charge officers at the base ten cents for ironing pants or a shirt, and twenty-five cents for a full dress uniform—and even more if the job including mounting bars or sewing on stripes. Not once did anyone make fun of my little enterprise; it was essential work that only I and a one other guy knew how to do, and I remember enjoying writing to my sisters to thank them for all their help in preparing me for the army.

I didn't make any money at the job my years in the NYU athletic department readied me for, but it did save me some pounds of sweat and help my chances of earning a commission when a company commander put me in charge of daily calisthenics for three separate platoons. Every morning, I would stand on a shaded platform in the center of a grassy field with a microphone and loudspeaker in hand and put 120 men through their paces. I worked them hard, but my fellow GIs preferred taking orders from me to the sadistic barks of a drill sergeant, and the commander was impressed enough that he agreed that I could experiment with rifle drills as well. By the time every soldier in those three platoons was tossing his carbine high into the air on precisely the same beat, and catching it in unison a second later, my stock as a drill instructor and officer candidate had risen sharply. But those achievements were jeopardized, I have to confess, by my lifelong inclination to react with force whenever I believed I was wronged.

As I stood at attention on a particularly sweltering Miami day, a drill sergeant approached me and began to shout at me to stand up straight and pull my shoulders back, the kind of order I'd endured dozens of times before. Then he noticed my wedding ring, and asked me if I missed my wife.

"Yes, Sergeant," I shouted back, as I'd learned to do.

"Well, you can forget about her, soldier," he retorted. "She's fucking somebody else by now."

I wasn't going to let *anybody* talk about Ann that way, and against every rule in the army's book, I spoke up, telling the son of a bitch that he was abusing his rank and had no right to talk like that to an enlisted man.

"I've got a right to fuck her myself, if I want to," he shouted, and a millisecond second later I hit him so hard on the left jaw that I relieved him of a couple of teeth. The drill sergeant fell to the ground, holding his bleeding mouth in pain, and I was about to kick him in the balls when an officer grabbed me.

"That's enough, soldier," he shouted, and quickly a couple of MPs grabbed me and marched me to a guardhouse. I knew I was in serious trouble, and was waiting in the blistering heat to be taken to a court-martial arraignment when the MPs returned and announced that they were escorting me to meet with the company commander instead. In the thirty minutes since I'd struck the blow, the drill sergeant had begged the commander for a chance to lay his fists into me, and the commander had heard from the witnesses he spoke with what had provoked my punch, and he decided to let us fight it out.

Still under guard, I was marched to a gymnasium the army had converted from a hotel ballroom and stripped to my waist. The drill sergeant took off his shirt and a circle of men surrounded us and somebody barked, "Okay, settle this." The drill sergeant came at me, and we circled for a few seconds. But before he threw his first punch, I motioned to him and asked if he thought it was safe to fight with that shoulder. I couldn't believe my luck, and in the millisecond it took him to glance at his right shoulder, I landed another right hook to his left jaw, just where I had the first time, and he went down again. But this time, nobody pulled me away, and I had the pure pleasure of giving him a licking like he'd never had before. The bastard was tough, however, and he didn't surrender, and he still wanted to fight when three of his buddies finally pulled him away, thoroughly beaten and shamed.

I was battered a bit, but not badly, and delighted by the chance to give him what he deserved, yet I was sure I was still in for what the army politely calls "discipline." But the commander—who had been in the mood to watch some fisticuffs, it appeared—simply walked up to me and asked me if that finished the matter, as far as I was concerned. I told him it did, and he ordered me not to get into a similar circumstance again, then walked away.

Both the drill sergeant and I spent two days in the guardhouse—in separate cells—and on the third day, when an MP came to tell me I was free to return to my unit, I passed the cell where the sergeant still sat, and he growled out at me, "I'll get you. I'll find you somewhere." I didn't understand what "somewhere" meant until my buddies ultimately gave me the news that he had been transferred to another camp because he continued to vow to anyone who talked to him that he would kill me. I would have guessed that an inductee like me would have been the one sent elsewhere, but that was what the army, in its wisdom, chose to do instead.

I received no other punishment, nor was my army career in any way thrown off track. My reputation among my fellow officer candidates grew rather dramatically on the heels of the "altercation," and, as a particular bonus, I knew that a certain drill sergeant wasn't likely to defame another soldier's wife for a very long time to come.

*

One day during my tenure in the equatorial heat of Miami Beach, another drill sergeant—one with whom I'd never tangled—found me finishing supper in the mess hall and presented me with a telegram from my sister Nanajan. "ANN GONE TO CHICAGO," it read, "TELEPHONE SOONEST." And when I reached my family by phone a few minutes later, my mother was able to confirm for me what those six words already seemed to explain: Ann hadn't been easy to live with, she said, although, God himself knew, she and my sisters had tried their best to make the situation work. Ann took offense at even the smallest issues, and made constant demands, and now—today—she had packed her bags and departed, leaving a note saying only that she was returning to Chicago to live with her parents.

I didn't try to call Ann because, I presumed, she was on a westbound train at the moment, so I did nothing more for the time being than imagine whether the thing that had set them at odds was religion, someone's perceived untidiness, food preferences, or perhaps the amount of money Ann could contribute to the household. I was dismayed to think that the arrangement had collapsed so quickly and, it appeared, dramatically, and my thoughts immediately cycled back to the fear I'd had before we were married that Ann couldn't be happy anywhere other than Cook County, Illinois.

When I received a letter from Ann two days later, she outlined in great detail the transgressions she had had to endure. The rudeness, abrasiveness, and insensitivity she had encountered on 68th Street in The Bronx had been the worst insults she'd ever encountered, and although she loved me, she said, she couldn't wait in that crowded and inhospitable New York apartment for me to send for her.

I was far enough away that I was spared the job of refereeing this fight—and the time for any sort of reconciliation between them seemed to have passed already. When I finally spoke with Ann at her parents' home, her outrage was gone but she had no interest whatsoever in reconsidering her move. She loved my family, she assured me, but she simply couldn't live under the same roof with them. She had tried her best, but my mother, in particular, she said, had made her life miserable with her constant disapproval of virtually everything Ann did or said. She hoped I understood, but even if I could not, her decision was final.

The last thing I wanted to do was join the battle on either side, and it was easy enough to imagine why it had been such an oil-and-water arrangement from the outset. I knew all of the parties involved well enough to imagine some of the fireworks that had erupted between them, it went without saying, and from distant Miami, I promised Ann that we would settle somewhere together just as soon as the army determined where it wanted me.

A few weeks later came official word that, because of my ROTC training and my performance in basic training, I had been accepted into officer candidate school at Fort Belvoir in Virginia. The months I would be stationed there were a short enough time that I couldn't realistically move Ann to the southern end of the state to join me, but at least we could see each other as often as I could secure a leave and catch a train north to Chicago.

But Ann and I did find a way to be together not long after my graduation from officer candidates school in the spring of 1943, when I was sent to central Oregon's Camp Adair to join the newly activated 70th Trailblazer Infantry Division, where I was assigned to the 270th Engineer Combat Battalion as a reconnaissance officer. I had a few days furlough before I had to report, and spent them with Ann and her family at their cottage before she and I eagerly boarded a train, traveling someplace new together for the first time in our married lives. It took forever, it seemed, to cross the prairies and Rocky Mountains and finally arrive in Portland, and we were exhausted when we arrived at last in Salem, where good fortune was waiting for us.

I was a second lieutenant now, and instead of living in barracks at the camp, I had requested housing, arranged by the army, in one of the nearby towns or cities. And when Ann and I first saw the house we would rent very inexpensively, we couldn't believe our eyes. It was two stories tall with four great columns supporting its front porch. It had spacious rooms, hardwood floors, a modern kitchen, and was heated by sawdust, a fuel in plentiful supply in central Oregon, we quickly discovered, driven by a thermostatically controlled auger into a basement furnace. The house was a palace, and no doubt Ann had charmed someone on our arrival at Camp Adair, something she regularly did with no intention at all. Yet we remained a little afraid that there had been a mistake in offering it to us until a supply clerk stopped by to check on us and assured us that, yes, this was our new home.

I joked with Ann that she had indeed found a worthy husband if she'd been able to move up from the very cramped quarters on 68th Street to a mansion like this in only a little more than a year, and although she still didn't find anything funny in retrospect as she looked back on living with my family, she did agree that this house in Salem, Oregon would be a wonderful place to really begin to *live* together. We had no certainty about how long I would be stationed there and anyone in the armed services understood that hundreds of thousands of additional American personnel likely would have to join the fight overseas if Hitler was to be routed in Europe and the Japanese conquered in the Pacific.

Like almost every young American couple in the spring of 1943, we understood that the time we had together was precious and that we could depend on it and no other. My training commitments at Camp Adair were challenging and intensive, but they still allowed me relaxed and joyful time at home. Ann dove into nurse's training—and found she both liked and was wonderfully suited to it—and still she found a way to make our home special to us in every way. On cool and rainy nights by a crackling fire, we huddled together and planned our post war lives, and we conceived a child in that house—something we worked at with the delight of young people for whom the novelty and meaning of sex was endlessly fascinating—and we both were thrilled to imagine our twosome soon becoming a real family.

Ann and Second Lt. George Edgar at their new home, Salem Oregon, 1943

Above, George laughs with family; below, poses before shipping off to war.

From left, Nanjan, Maria, George, Nana Khatoon & Sophie

*Nana Khatoon says goodbye to her son George before he goes off to war,
1109 Clay Avenue, Bristol Connecticut, 1943*

I had discovered since my induction into the army that engineering, which had been an enormous challenge to me academically, came rather easily to me when it came to its practical application. As an army engineer, I seldom encountered any subject, assignment, or obstacle that stumped me. Since the day I'd flirted with a court-martial when I landed a blow on a drill sergeant's jaw, I hadn't been involved in any scrapes, and my superiors liked me and the kind of soldier I was becoming in ways that already marked me as a leader on the rise.

It was an irony that wasn't lost on many of us engineers that we spent as much time learning how to blow things up as we did building them. We became highly proficient in planting land mines; we could dependably level any structure that wasn't made of solid concrete, and when there was a need for precision, not only could we dependably drop the largest Oregon firs, we could also land their trunks on a target.

My platoon and I prided ourselves in impressing the Trailblazer's captains and colonels with the efficient and effective way we rigged explosives for everything from Jeeps to tanks and bridges to landing strips and airfields. In the midst of a war game that lasted a stretch of days in the dry early October of 1943, we successfully wired both abutments of a single lane country bridge that spanned a small a tributary of the Willamette River. Colonel James Niles, head of camp's engineer corps, had inspected our work himself and found it acceptable, and he and I were standing on a nearby bluff together at the moment when our red team was set to "blow" the bridge to prevent the enemy blue team from crossing it.

As our war games protocol required, everyone had cleared away from the bridge soon after a couple soldiers on either side of the river strung red-flagged ropes across the ends of the bridge to mark it "destroyed." But what my men had failed to do—and what I, inexcusably, had not personally checked—was that the actual explosives had been disarmed just as soon as they had been inspected.

"Prepare to blow the bridge," I barked into my field phone, and I had a quick reply from one of my men that the detonations were ready. Then, no more than an instant after I reported back, "Roger, proceed to take it out," I saw two gigantic clouds of dust rise at each end of the bridge, followed almost immediately by the sounds of an explosion that assaulted my ears.

"Jesus Christ, what the hell's going on?" Colonel Niles asked in disbelief, and my stomach suddenly turned with the horrified understanding of what indeed had just occurred. It took a full minute or more for the dust to settle enough for the two of us to see from the bluff that the bridge no longer spanned the waterway. Its wooden trusses, in fact, were floating down the river. Small debris, some of it still red hot, began to fall around us, and without saying a word, I raced toward the site of the explosion to see whether anyone had been injured.

Within a few minutes, I'd determined that, by some miracle, no one had been close enough to the explosion to be injured, and I discovered as well that most of my men thought the bridge's destruction was funny as hell. I might have found it humorous, too, if I hadn't just come very close to killing a fellow soldier or more, and if Colonel Niles hadn't quickly informed me that he would defer any disciplinary action to the camp's commander, Major General John Dahlquist.

When I met with the general the following day, he wanted me to know before he said anything else that he had been fielding virtually constant phone calls from county commissioners, state legislators, and individual farmers and ranchers who found nothing about the bridge's destruction laughable in any way. "You've played hell with their livelihoods, Edgar, not to mention that you put my ass in a sling with the locals," he wanted me to know, then he asked how long it would take to get a makeshift bridge across the river.

I was an engineer, and by now I knew how to build bridges out of whatever materials lay at hand, and I assured the general that my men and I could have a temporary structure spanning the river in place in twenty-four hours.

"I'll give you twelve," he coldly announced. I said nothing more, staring at him in hopes he'd reconsider, but to no avail. "Now get out of here," he barked. "You're wasting your time and mine."

If we had been in the Saharan desert, my army career likely would have ended six hours later, but because there were so many enormous old trees at our nearby disposal, we were able to fell the stout ones we needed, and make a bridge out of them in just under fourteen hours. Neither General Dahlquist nor Colonel Niles dressed me down for missing my deadline, nor was I officially reprimanded. But on November 8, I was demoted to the role of "administration officer" for the 270th's Company B, and then was transferred exactly four weeks later. I can't help but partially credit my survival in the long year and half that lay ahead to the respect I gave to explosives from that day forward, and I knew full well as I departed the 270th that the bridge that we blew to smithereens on my watch was precisely the reason that I was off to Europe.

*

Although it was officially a subject about which we were ordered not to talk, increasingly everyone in the army knew that an invasion of Europe was imminent. Privately, my fellow engineers and I openly shared our certainty that we would be part of that invasion. But on December 8th, 1943 it suddenly appeared that perhaps I was the only soldier among the Trailblazers whose help would be needed in Europe. My orders were simple: I would report immediately to

Camp Reynolds, Pennsylvania, where I would prepare for "trans-shipment to a cold climate" early in the new year.

It was news that both excited and troubled me, of course, but it was hard to put an optimistic face on it with Ann, except to assure her that I was a clever and talented Assyrian kid who had survived a lot by now, and that I could guarantee her that I would do what I could to help knock out the Nazis, then I'd be back as soon as I could to kiss her and our new baby.

Ann and I traveled together across the country, and we had two weeks together in New York at Christmastime before I shipped out. We returned to a few of the places we'd first visited on those days two and a half years before when we fell in love, and I can't remember why, but she took a taxi with me to the pier on the day we had to say goodbye.

The cab driver wouldn't take my money when he learned where I was headed, and he offered to wait for Ann and return her to The Bronx. She and I held each other closely in the swarm of people whose lives mirrored ours at that moment. We both were tearful, and we smiled as bravely as we could, assuring each other we would write as often as possible, and asking each other to be safe. I patted Ann's belly and reminded her I had a hell of a reason—*two* reasons—to get back home, and I closed the door of the cab, blew her a kiss, and turned and went off to war.

Santa Barbara, 1984

WHEN SHE MOVED to Santa Barbara in 1956, my grandmother hoped the change would be a tonic for her poor health, but it not. She'd had a kidney removed back in Chicago, and she remained chronically ill long thereafter. She was on dialysis for decades and spent as much as half of every year in the hospital, my grandfather always assuming the lion's share of the household duties, shopping for groceries, cooking, and cleaning. Because of her infirmities, they were able to spend far too little time together enjoying what Santa Barbara had to offer. Occasionally, they would attend concerts together, and friends regularly came to dinner at their house, but otherwise Pop filled his life with all the pursuits he could fit into each day, while Mimi remained at home, her life as an invalid a far cry from the enchantment the beautiful former Miss Assyria once imagined her life would be.

In the late summer of 1984, my grandmother met with Pastor Nelson from Trinity Baptist church in Santa Barbara. She wanted to know whether she would be committing suicide if she chose to discontinue dialysis—something that would rather quickly lead to her death. Her faith remained as strong as it had when my grandfather first met her four decades before, and something the pastor said led her to announce to us all soon thereafter that she no longer wanted to continue her fight. With the whole family's reluctant support, she discontinued dialysis in early August, and we collectively said goodbye to her during the week before she died.

A child of the Depression, my grandmother insisted that as little money as possible would be spent on her funeral or burial. She was cremated, and I remember that as we were leaving my grandparents' house to board a boat and take her ashes out into the Santa Barbara harbor as she had requested, Pop suddenly thought of something and asked us to be patient for a few minutes before we left. We waited outside, but we watched through the open living room window as he placed my grandmother's ashes *on the fireplace mantel, got out his violin, and played Mozart's "Violin Concerto No. 4," one of her favorite pieces, for her a final time.*

Chapter 8

Returning to War

THE CUNARD LINE'S *RMS Aquitania* was much grander than the ship on which I first crossed the Atlantic back when I was a boy. Dubbed "the ship beautiful" when it made its maiden voyage in 1914 because of a showy opulence that surpassed even the ill-fated *Titanic*, the *Aquitania* had ferried soldiers during the first world war, then had been pressed into wartime service again in 1940. By the time it steamed out of New York Harbor on January 12, 1944 with me aboard, it had been stripped of all its luxuries and had carried hundreds of thousands of U.S. and Canadian soldiers across the Atlantic, and I was simply among the next ten thousand who were off to Europe to try to save the world, if it could be saved.

As we sailed past the Statue of Liberty, I couldn't help but remember the first time I'd seen the huge copper lady—back at a time when, as a young boy, I thought coming to America meant that I would never see the chaos, brutality, and horror of war again. Yet I agreed with millions of others that a madman in Germany now was bent on controlling the world, and that young American men like me had a duty to stop him if we could, and I was proud as the Statue of Liberty receded from sight that I had become both an American and a soldier.

It wasn't long after the *Aquitania* had moved into open water that I became starkly aware that my second crossing of the Atlantic would be only marginally more comfortable than the first. Although my fellow commissioned officers and I were forced to sleep in narrow bunks that were three tiers high, at least my status as a second lieutenant earned me quarters on the ship's B deck—fully five

195

decks above the unluckiest bastards, who were forced to contend with the crossing so far below the ship's waterline that they might as well have been fish. And as we imagined what might lie ahead, few of us on any deck believed we had much to complain about—except perhaps that we still had no official word about where precisely we were headed.

*

After several days on the ship, I discovered, like so many others that playing poker virtually around the clock was the only thing that really helped the time pass. I certainly preferred the late-night poker tables to my bunk, where the snores and farts and body stink of the men around me could make the nights long and very miserable. And I was running the table one afternoon when the news raced through the ship that we were in sight of land.

As a so-called "pool officer," on what the army dubbed a Fast Fleet Replenishment Ship—men like us would "replenish" units already in Britain that were in need of particular expertise or simply more manpower—I was soon called into a meeting where I learned that the land we had sighted was indeed Scotland. In a little less than two hours, the *Aquitania* would steam into the Firth of Clyde, west of Glasgow, and would dock at Greenock at dusk. The following morning, a complex disembarkation would begin and we would work fast to ensure that both personnel and supplies were off-loaded from the enormous ship before the day was out, the former cruise liner sailing back across the Atlantic for another load of soldiers as quickly as it could.

*

Second Lieutenant George Edgar

David A. Armstrong

R.M.S. Aquitania

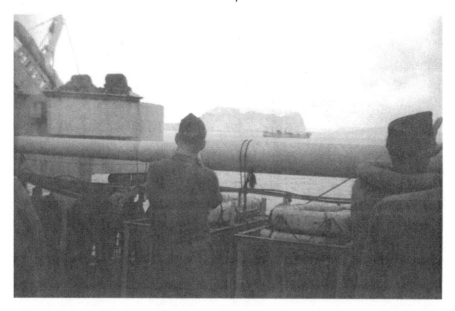

George's first photograph of the European continent, January 1944

I spent the next four months attached to several different replacement depots in Scotland and England. I was delighted in mid-April when I learned that at last I'd been given a permanent assignment, and that in four days' time I'd be shipping out to a place called Kingwood Common in Oxfordshire west of London to join a bridge building outfit called the 989th Engineer Treadway Bridge Company.

My formal orders guaranteed me $5.25 for food and lodging during the three days I was allowed to spend in transit to England. I packed my duffel on April 17, then took a train to London—a city that was very unlike New York, yet which shared with it something that seemed to hang in the air, something you breathed in and that let you know you were in one of the world's great places. Yet New York had been spared the horrors of the war—at least so far—and areas of London that had been blown to pieces in the blitz reminded me much more of Tiflis than they did anything else. And like the Russians, the Londoners with whom I came in contact seemed resigned to leading difficult lives for a long time to come.

In the short time I was in the city, I managed to see a Brahms and Mozart concert at the Prince of Wales Theatre, and a chamber concert that featured Schubert's "The Trout"—a piece I'd always loved—and although I knew it was a little crazy, I also bought a violin. I saw it in a pawnshop window just off Piccadilly Circus; it was a Gibson—the American company that was far better known for its guitars—and when I couldn't help but go inside and have a closer look, the fellow behind the counter quickly nudged me to buy it. It had belonged to a U.S. Army band member on furlough who had pawned it in advance of what he hoped would be a wild London night, the pawnbroker explained, but he had never returned for it. I agreed with him that the soldier probably simply forgot where the pawnshop was located on the morning after; then I tuned it and played it for a moment, and I liked its sound. When the pawnbroker offered to sell it for just two pounds and throw in the leather case stamped "U.S." in gold letters—telling me, "A good price for you, 'cause we ain't going to make it without you Yanks"—I told him I'd buy it.

It wasn't until I'd taken a train to Reading, then hitched a ride on an American supply truck to Kingwood Common, that I began to consider how in the hell I thought I could pack a violin across France. And neither could I imagine what the men of my new company might think of a second lieutenant who would arrive for his new duty with his foot locker in one hand and a violin in another.

*

Many of the men of the 989th were farm boys from Kansas, I discovered a few hours later. They were gangly, square-jawed fellows who sure knew how to work, and who spoke few words, and I quickly knew that these guys and I could build a bridge or two together. The company's commander was a first lieutenant named Arnold Maeker, a west Texan with whom I initially struggled to build a rapport. Maybe it was because, as an immigrant New Yorker, I seemed to him to be a little exotic, or perhaps it was because his dry and laconic high plains ways were strange to me. But I'd been in the army long enough by now to know that it was made up of many types and kinds of men, and I felt sure that Lt. Maeker and I would end up hitting a common stride.

I was quickly certain as well that a number of the men I would command were exemplary soldiers, fine engineers, and good fellows to be with. I would be in charge of the company's second platoon, and my counterpart in the first platoon was Jim Conyers, a fisherman's son from St. Simon Island, Georgia, who was a bona fide engineer as well and no more inclined to make a career of the army than I was. Lt. Conyers and I had similar command styles; it was important to each of us, for example, to really get to know our men, but we understood, too, that the butterbar we wore on our chests was the army's way of reminding them—and us—that they were *not* our equals. I liked Jim immediately—we could talk plainly with each other and didn't have to dance around difficult issues—and I felt lucky to have him beside me.

Ray Herman, a baby-faced Minnesotan and my second platoon sergeant, proved right off the bat to be the kind of soldier who would do what I needed him to do without complaint or confusion. He and I would become something of a team, I was sure, and that suited me just fine. Jim Conyers's sergeant, a German-born guy named Ludwig Balzerski, immediately impressed me with the thoroughness of his bridge building skills and his toughness—yet it was going to be more than a little strange to have a veteran of the German army as one of my sergeants. I didn't know yet, but I suspected that he was Jewish and that his family had escaped the Nazis, and that he had volunteered for the U.S. army seeking some measure of justice. Whatever his story was, it seemed that the fact that he was a native German speaker certainly would come in handy down the line.

The three dozen men whom I commanded in the 989th's second platoon and an equal number in the first platoon had been in training for nearly two and half years by now—in Kentucky, California, Tennessee, and New York, prior to coming to England. They knew how to have a good time together—that I quickly discovered—but they were all business when it came to getting a bridge built. By the time I arrived, in fact, the men of the 989th's two platoons had constructed and disassembled more than thirty bridges spanning the River Thames and its tributaries, each one built at breakneck speed with inflatable rubber pontons, steel saddles and interconnected treadways hauled to the water's edge in eight-ton, rubber-tired transports called Brockways, massive trucks with power steering and pneumatic brakes—features that still were virtually unheard of on civilian vehicles. The procedures these fellows followed in laying ponton bridges was virtually identical to the methods we'd used back Fort Belvoir, so my job, as I saw it, wasn't to institute change so much as it was to simply ensure that we could lay a bridge faster and more precisely on one day than we had the day before, and that on the following day, we were faster still.

Collectively, we'd all been so well-trained that we could construct 650 feet of M2 treadway bridge in about four hours of daylight—and in only six hours under blackout conditions at night—and because we were just engineers with pencils tucked behind our ears, after all, it was brain-engaging and physical work we often truly enjoyed. But Treadway bridges were essentially assault bridges—we would often be under heavy fire until we got one completed and our infantry could cross it and rout the Germans who were firing at us. Building bridges was going to be dangerous work. But that said, not a man among us wished he'd become an infantryman instead of a bridge builder, and we all took real pride in the fact that our wartime contribution was going to be *building things* that were absolutely vital to the Allies advancement toward our collective goal.

*

It had become a secret only in name that the Allies soon would invade the European mainland. It was an invasion that had been in its planning stages for more than two years by now; nearly a million soldiers had been amassed in southern England, and it seemed certain that the Allied commanders would choose to begin the assault on the French or Belgian shore early enough in the year to ensure that we would have plenty of time to defeat the Germans before the harsh northern European winter settled in.

Just a few days after I'd joined the 989th, however, Lt. Maeker announced that we would be laying another bridge across the wide Thames the following day. By now his men had bridged it so often they could almost do it in their sleep—little of which they'd gotten of late—and before dawn the next morning, we began the day by moving the whole company and a mountain of equipment to the grassy banks of the river in the fleet of big Brockway trucks that the mechanics in the outfit babied like they were their own hot rods back home.

As each huge truck reached the river, a detail of men quickly off-loaded the massive un-inflated rubberized canvas pontons—or floats, as we called them. When the tubes of each ponton were fully inflated and resembled enormous Polish sausages, a team of enlisted men led by Sergeant Herman began the saddle assembly procedure, using a crane to place wide, steel-bearing plates directly atop the float and readying it to receive the two sections of 12-foot steel treadway it would support.

With the help of an inboard powerboat—which acted much like a tugboat moving a barge up a river—each raft was pushed toward its destination with a kind of precision I'd never seen before by a driver named Alva Hard. A Tech 5 from downstate Illinois, Hard was already something of a legend among the men of the company, and I could see why. Throttling his motor, cranking the rudder to starboard and port, and maneuvering each several ton raft as if it were nothing more than a paper boat on a pond, his deft touch was something to behold. And according to Conyers, I hadn't seen anything yet.

Our work was being surveyed that day by Colonel Daniel Spengler, the commanding officer of the 1110th Engineer Combat Group and a West Point grad and South Pacific veteran whose old school toughness was legendary among the engineers. Col. Spengler had said nothing as he watched our progress, and I was a little worried as he walked up to shake my hand that something about the job had displeased him. I offered him a quick salute and braced myself for a dressing down, but all he offered was, "Not bad, lieutenant, not bad. But next time, shave about thirty minutes off the operation."

I assured the colonel before he drove away that we would do so. After a quick lunch and a minute or two of nap for most of the men, it was time to *disassemble* the impressive floating bridge we'd spent the morning laying across the Thames.

*

The River Thames, about an hour outside of London, just before the 989th began their bridge-building exercise, May 1944

In the first days of June, we were issued K-rations, French currency, and heavy-oiled outerwear designed to repel chemical weapons. We packed and repacked our rucksacks, repeatedly oiled our boots, and stockpiled as many packets of cigarettes as we could scavenge, and it fell to me to check with each of my men to make sure they had filed their wills. Like many soldiers both higher and lower than me in rank, I found it increasingly hard to get a good night's sleep; I tossed and turned like a rat in a paper bag most nights, thinking of Ann and our baby, who, I knew, would be born any day now, thinking of my family and of my carefree boyhood years in New Britain and even of Constantinople, where I first had escaped the tumult of war and had grown excited by all the possibilities the world seemed to offer. But after evening chow on June 4, Lt. Maeker called me into his quarters to give me arresting news.

The lieutenant was about five years younger than me, maybe more, and no doubt that was part of the awkwardness between us. He was my commander, but he was also just a kid, and I instantly could tell that he was about to give me an order that he wasn't entirely comfortable with.

"Edgar," he began, as he motioned for me to take a seat in a folding chair, "you're being temporarily assigned to the 1110th. You're going to be part of an advance party of engineers—most of them officers—who'll arrive on the mainland just a day or two after the invasion gets underway. There's an obvious need to know as much as we can before we put the rest of these engineers in harm's way. And it looks like it's sure as hell going to be nasty."

"Yes, sir," I responded.

The lieutenant sat down at his desk and looked me in the eye. "I'll be honest. They want just one officer from the 989th and I picked you. You'll be commanded by Colonel Spengler, who you met at the bridge site the other day, and he's as good as they get."

My head spun with the news, but no, I told him when he asked, I didn't have any questions. I wanted to say I wasn't entirely thrilled to be leaving the 989th no sooner than I'd been attached, but before I could say something that might have set him off, Maeker explained that I'd be rejoining his bridge builders just as soon as they arrived in France, and that he wanted me to have a site ready for our first bivouac, as well as a secure spot for a command post, and he made it clear that I'd also better know the roads and bridges in the area every bit as well as if they were in my hometown.

It was obvious that Maeker had selected me for the job simply because I was the newest officer in the outfit, and if I was killed in the days to come, my death would have scant effect on the cohesion and safety of the men of the 989th. I couldn't blame him for the decision—it was the smart thing for him to do as commander and, frankly, I would have made the same choice if the responsibility had been mine.

What neither Maeker nor I knew that day was that the largest amphibious assault in history was less than forty-eight hours away from its commencement—an invasion in which more than 150,000 British, U.S., and Canadian troops would surprise their German adversaries by storming the shores of Normandy. In order to defeat the Germans, a massive invasion of the European mainland had to be mounted and had to succeed, but gaining the first few yards, then miles of the French coastline was going to come, all of us knew, only at great cost.

*

Before I jumped in a jeep on the morning of the 5th for the short drive to Sonning, a village on the Thames a few miles east of Reading, where Col. Spengler and the 1110th were based, I had just a moment to say a few goodbyes. I double-checked that I had stuffed everything I would need for the weeks and months ahead in my pack; I left my violin in my foot locker and asked Sergeant Herman to look after it, and he assured me he understood how important it was—at least to me if nobody else. When I reported to the 1110th's commander at his desk in a ramshackle country estate that stood beside the river, the first news Colonel Spengler had for me was that I would be joining an engineer reconnaissance detail led by him, but that there was no way to know how long it would be before we took our turn wading onto a beach that had been liberated by the first wave of invading soldiers. We might go within a few days if the invasion began in a day or two—and *if* it went well. But if the initial thrust onto the continent was hellish and slow, it might be a week or two, or even longer, before our advance party was deployed.

"Looks like we're about to get this fucker started," the colonel said with a curious mix of nonchalance and excitement, and I was surprised when he didn't seem to be in a hurry to get me out of his office. He offered me a cigarette, in fact, and asked me where I hailed from and where I'd gone to school. And when he discovered that I'd been an athlete at NYU and had been mentored by Howard Cann, the university's legendary basketball star and longtime coach, he reacted as if we'd been buddies and teammates who hadn't seen each other since some long ago championship season.

Spengler—at least six feet three inches tall, and with a neck and shoulders like Sampson—had been a letterman in his freshman year at little Juniata College in Pennsylvania, then had accepted an appointment to West Point in 1928, where—he proudly told me—he ultimately became an All-American football player. I explained in turn that I'd been a gymnast at NYU, and had been good enough that I might have made the 1936 Olympic team if I hadn't been prevented from trying out because I wasn't a naturalized citizen yet. At that, Spengler snorted and growled, "Who the hell made that idiot decision?"

I told him it had been an Olympic bureaucrat named Brundage, and that information really shot the steam out of his ears. "Fucking wormy bureaucrats," he cursed, "I'd take a single soldier like you over ten dozen of those fuckers every time," and I took his implied compliment as proof that he was a pretty decent guy.

Spengler's voice was deep and commanding and it seemed certain that anyone who met him would come away from the encounter certain that he was not someone to cross. He remained a jock at heart, I could quickly tell—and so did I, if I was honest with myself. Both of us were the kind of men who held great athletes and coaches in at least as high regard as we did men like Bradley or Patton or even Eisenhower, I suspected. Before Spengler finally sent me on my way—telling me he'd see me tomorrow down on the channel coast—he made me promise to write Coach Cann and give him his best regards. The NYU basketball team was the odds-on favorite to win the NCAA title that year, Spengler knew, and he wanted the coach to know that from far across the Atlantic he was pulling for him to win.

*

The world was a different place on the afternoon of June 6th, when Spengler and his contingent joined the rest of us in the advance party at the marshaling area at Hiltingbury, outside of Southampton, because the invasion—so long anticipated by millions everywhere—had begun at dawn.

It was a profoundly important day, and Spengler, a "full bird" colonel and the highest ranking officer among us, appeared calm and resolute as he spoke to our recon group in a makeshift officer's mess in a Quonset hut—yet he was also clearly troubled by the bits of information he'd received so far. Reports still were scattered and little was confirmed, but the assault on the two beaches to which American forces had been assigned on the Normandy's

Cotentin peninsula was proving to be brutal, particularly at the cliff-backed beach the Allied commanders had dubbed Omaha. Big waves still pounded the whole of the Cotentin coast in the aftermath of a heavy storm; the soldiers struggling ashore with heavy packs on their backs had been met with massive German resistance, and already hundreds of bodies of American fighting men floated on the surf and lay on the sloping sand.

Over the next two days—during which time I did little more than pack, then repack the K-rations, life belt, cigarettes, chocolate, canned heat, water purification tablets and vomit bags that were issued to the many thousands of us who soon would cross the channel—several times I also took my wallet from my pocket and looked at the photo of Ann I kept inside it. I tried to imagine how much bigger her belly had grown in my absence, yet by now it was certain, wasn't it?, that Ann had become a mother—or she was very much overdue. There was another possibility as well, of course, but it wasn't one that crossed my mind. In the aftermath of the kinds of injury and death Allied soldiers had begun to suffer on the shores of France, it was hard to imagine that the simple birth of a child could ever go awry.

And if Ann was a mother by now, it meant that I was a *father*, for heaven's sake, and that was a prospect that made me grin broadly as I looked at Ann's beautiful smile in the photograph. I felt far away from her, and the experiences I was about to have were ones that she could not have comprehended, yet nonetheless, we remained very connected—of that much I was certain—and I knew we would be fine parents. Ann would become the kind of mother my own mother was—loving and protective and always constant—and I knew I could find a way to be substantially different from the sort of parent my father was. I had made enough of my early life that I'd become a second lieutenant in the United States Army—and that was something of which I was unapologetically proud—and surely I also could do a decent job of raising a child, if only I could do what was asked of me in the months ahead and return home in a single piece.

Ann and I had decided before we said goodbye in New York in January that, if the baby was a boy, his name would be Gary, a name we had selected for reasons I honestly can't recall. A girl we would call Georgeanne, her name a blending of our two names with an extra "e" at the end because Ann thought the name looked incomplete without a bit of a flourish, just as she would be a blending of us in blood and bone. I kissed Ann's photograph before I tucked it away and I wished to hell that this waiting soon would end.

Then, late in the afternoon on the 9th, Spengler's sergeant found me in the smoke-heavy officer's mess, bearing the news that we would board a troop transport at 0030 that night. We would cross the channel with the soldiers of the 298th Engineer Combat Battalion and our principal mission—in addition to providing reconnaissance for the hundreds of engineer troops that would follow us—was to ensure that all the roads and bridges were made passable in the small port city of Carentan.

*

Those of us who comprised the advance party boarded a channel steamer in the Southampton harbor shortly after midnight on June 9, and we were met with strong wind and choppy seas as we journeyed out into the open channel. The small ship—packed to its gunwales with soldiers—was filled with a kind of tension that hung in the air like a fog. Everyone onboard, you could feel, was both frightened and excited at the same time, and conversation grew quiet and many men preferred simply to sit alone with their thoughts. Dozens became seasick during the night, and the strong stench of vomit did nothing to make the hours pass quickly; no provision had been made for feeding us anything other than the K-rations in our pockets and packs, and the only sleep most men got was a catnap or two using a buddy's shoulder for a pillow. The moods of the men around me didn't improve at mid-morning when word quickly spread that, because of the crush of troops and equipment waiting to come ashore at Omaha and Utah beaches, we might be forced to wait off the Normandy coast for the rest of the day. Naval ships and boats of every size and shape pitched in the rough sea, and seeing them reach far away from us in every direction made it easy to understand the traffic jam.

Despite the fact that it was June, the day was overcast and raw, and squalls of light rain periodically enveloped the ship. It was far from pleasant to be out in the bad weather, but it was worse in the holds below deck, and as darkness began to fall—and it became all but certain that we would spend *another* night on the steamer before we would leave it—I stood near Col. Spengler at a railing near the bow of the ship, watching thick columns of black smoke rise from the distant shore. It was impossible to know what exactly was burning, but it was troubling sight, and it seemed very unlikely that the fires were making life easier for the men who had already landed. No doubt the Germans were throwing everything they had at the defense of the peninsula, and that truth became even clearer when a squad of German Messerschmitts appeared in the darkening sky and began to dive at and strafe a cluster of Allied ships in the middle distance. At about ten o'clock, the whole of the English Channel seemed to light up in explosive fire, and we could hear the screams of battle-station whistles and alarms on all the ships that surrounded us. Within minutes came the unmistakable sound of German Stuka bombers, their sirens howling as they dove. But the assault quickly was met by anti-aircraft fire from American and British battleships that were part of the huge armada, and although we remained well away from the action, I wondered whether Spengler would suggest we go below.

But the colonel wanted to observe everything that he could, and we must have shared a whole pack of cigarettes while we watched. When Spengler asked me about my family, I opted to tell him much more than I often did in answer to that question, and he seemed genuinely interested to hear that I'd seen war before. He pressed me for my childhood memories of the Russian Civil War and the revolution and he slapped me on the back when I described how I'd saved my mother from the tsarist soldier, adding "You were a tough little shit, weren't you?" before he noticed my repeated yawns and told me to follow him. I stayed close to his heels as we made our way down two decks to his cabin, where he opened the door and motioned toward a narrow bunk. "Here," he said, "Test this thing for me. I got some good sleep last night but I'm way too keyed up tonight."

I must have looked at him uncertainly because he quickly added, "*Sleep.* You'll be no goddamn good to me tomorrow if you're dead on your feet."

The colonel turned to go; I closed the tiny cabin's door, then promptly followed his orders. With the ship rocking in settling seas, I slept soundly through the rest of the night, despite the tension and my uncertainty about what lay ahead. And I remember being a bit amazed as I drifted off that someone of Spengler's stature would go out of his way for somebody like me. I took it as the good omen it was, and vowed to pass the favor along to somebody else when I had the opportunity. Over the years, my quick-to-flare temper had sometimes led people to think I was an immigrant asshole bent on some sort of retribution for all the trouble he's had, but the truth was that the person I wanted to be—and hoped I was sometimes—was one very much like the football player and fine soldier who had just surrendered his bunk for me.

*

213

The clear, early morning skies had given way to a heavy and ominous overcast by the time we began boarding landing craft at noon on Saturday, June 10, which would ferry us into Utah Beach. The twenty-three of us in Spengler's advance party—comprised of a representative from each of the companies and battalions attached to the engineer group—stood in a restless and uncomfortable queue that was hundreds of soldiers long, waiting our turn to transfer to a LCI, a boat whose flat hull could deliver two hundred men directly to the beach. When the LCI was filled with soldiers, it pulled away from the ship and we remained five or six miles offshore, and all of us struggled to stay balanced on the stamped metal decking—each of us loaded with packs on our backs and chests that together surely weighed a hundred pounds. I couldn't imagine how we would manage if the LCI dropped us more than a few feet away from the sloping sand.

From my position near the starboard ramp, I had a clear view of the broad and chaotic beach that lay ahead of us—the twisted wreck of heavy timbers, concrete pillars, railroad ties, I-beams, and the huge steel cross-arms dubbed "hedgehogs" that still blocked the shore except in those spots where our fellow combat engineers had blasted wide lanes through them during the previous four days.

As we drew nearer the shore, the LCI's captain suddenly reversed the propeller to slow us, apparently wary of something he saw ahead, and dozens of dozens of us fell to the deck with our heavy packs. We managed to get to our feet again as the LCI came to a halt, and I heard the whine of the motors that would begin to lower the ramps. In only a few seconds, both long ramps slapped the surface of the water, then disappeared beneath it and it was suddenly clear that we weren't going to wade into shore. We were going to swim.

I followed the first men into icy water and it instantly rose to my neck, but before I was forced to start paddling, the toes of my boots found the sand. But almost immediately I was treading water again and I struggled to keep my head above the salt water that stung my eyes and filled my mouth. My carbine was wrapped in a plastic bag but I held it high and lunged forward as best I could, and now I heard the frightened shouts of dozens of men who were faring worse than I was. When my feet found firm sand beneath me at last, I spun around and saw wild confusion as soldiers frantically jettisoned their rifles, packs, helmets, the gas masks and oiled coveralls designed to keep them safe from the possibility of a German chemical weapons attack—anything that was weighing them down—in the struggle to the reach the shore. Col. Spengler, mad as hell at the LCI's captain and as thoroughly soaked as the rest of us, barked orders to salvage the gear that hadn't yet sunk beneath the surf, and several men rushed back into the water to retrieve it as best they could.

It was a shock to see the bodies of so many dead American soldiers still floating in the surf and lying on the beach seventy-two hours after the invasion had begun—hadn't someone been assigned to retrieve and bury them?—and the bodies made it clear, if we needed the reminder, that our months and years of *practicing* war now had ended. We encountered no German fire on the chaotically busy beach, where hundreds of us continued to storm ashore and struggle across the sand and the grassy dunes that stood behind the beach. And the small unmanned blimps that rose high in the sky along the length of the beach, and which were tethered by steel cables, made it impossible for German fighter planes to strafe us there. But inland, the rising smoke, the heavy booms of mortar rounds, and the chilling noise of German fighters dropping low to strafe Allied positions were all the proof we needed that we were headed directly into the heart of the fight.

We traveled on foot the few miles to the place near the village of Hébert where a temporary command post had been established, and where Colonel Spengler was warmly greeted by his old friend Lt. Col. Ray Liedike, who had arrived the day before and who briefed us on the disappointing progress of the invasion's initial mission. We had collectively succeeded in getting ashore, the colonel proudly said, but only at great cost, and now it appeared that pushing into the interior was going to be even tougher.

*

As we began to make our way toward Carentan—Col. Spengler always ten or twenty yards out in front as we slogged through flooded fields—we heard the troubling news that our casualties had been heavy everywhere during the invasion's first six days. But by the time we reached the outskirts of Carentan a few days later, the mood was very different. Those of us in Spengler's advance party had helped open the roads that led into it, and we were greeted as heroes as we rode down the town's main thoroughfare. The people of Normandy who lined the street were thrilled to see us in their midst, despite the massive damage their small city had suffered during the three previous days of fighting. Women rushed out to offer us bread and eggs; old men formally saluted, and I was charmed by the small children who weren't quite sure whether they should offer us the V for victory sign or the Hitler salute.

It wasn't until the morning of the 15th that at last those of us in Spengler's advance party were able to begin the bridge and road reconnaissance we had been sent to do. The colonel had bitterly chafed at having to wait while the airborne infantry troops cleared enough of the area of German holdouts to make the reconnaissance relatively safe. He was an engineer but a proud soldier as well; if he had his way, we would be doing what we could to rout the Jerries as well. Spengler, I discovered, was far gruffer, hard-headed, and sometimes downright meaner than I had known before. The genial athlete and bright engineer could also be a son of a bitch, but so far at least, he'd seen no reason to direct any of his ire at me. For virtually every hour of the next three days, Spengler made sure we were relentlessly at work. Despite the ongoing danger—incoming German artillery and sniper fire remained a constant threat at virtually every place on the peninsula the Allies now controlled—we scoured every corner of the area surrounding Carentan, the twenty-three of us working in teams of four and five as we scouted bridge locations, surveyed German damage to towns and villages, marked roads for repair, updated maps, and established supply dumps for the heavy equipment and bridge building supplies that had begun to arrive in convoys from Utah Beach. Spengler often ordered me to join him as his driver raced their jeep from site to site, and that was fine with me because I enjoyed being with him. Sure, he barked at me often throughout each day, but he wasn't a bit tougher than my father had been. And although he was just a few years older than me, sometimes his fierceness actually reminded me of my father—except, of course, that my father had never once asked me to join him on an important task, nor was it ever his habit to tell me I'd done a good job, something Spengler was quick to do.

*

The staff sergeant who served as the colonel's aide found me on the afternoon of 17th bearing the news that Lt. Maeker and a dozen men of the 989th had reached the coast and would move inland the following day. Their arrival meant that my temporary assignment was over, and I couldn't help but suspect that I would have had a wild ride if I continued to serve immediately under Spengler. But because he commanded the 1110th Engineer Combat Group—to which all of us were attached—I'd still encounter him often, particularly on those occasions when a number of engineer companies and battalions would work in concert to get a big job done.

When I found the advance group of the 989th on the outskirts of Carentan on the afternoon of June 18, they had been joined by seventeen new enlisted men and a new lieutenant named Bill Baker, all of whom had been assigned to the unit as replacements despite the fact that we currently had our full complement of personnel—the army expected the bridge builders at the front lines to suffer heavy casualties, it seemed. I liked Baker, a sharp kid from Columbus, Georgia, right off the bat. He'd been trained to be a leader of an infantry platoon, and it worried him that he didn't know the first thing about engineering, but something about him made me think he would be a quick study and that we were now lucky to have him. Lt. Maeker agreed as he walked up to Baker and me, giving the new guy an encouraging pat on the shoulder and warmly shaking my hand as he told me in his west Texas drawl that it was good to see me standing upright.

In advance of the rest of the company's arrival from England in a few days, he explained that our first collective chore was to establish a bivouac in a field near Carentan that had been the site of a fierce battle soon after paratroopers landed in the predawn hours of D-Day. The bodies of the American soldiers who had been killed in the firefight had been removed, but it remained littered with the corpses of German defenders that had been rotting in the summer sun for almost two weeks. It was grim, nauseating work that we had no choice but to accomplish, we began by digging a long, narrow pit about three feet deep in the dark and fertile soil, then we drug the bodies toward it as carefully as we could, quickly discovering that arms tore free from torsos and that feet were likely to come away if we pulled too firmly on a boot. The stench of decay was horrible, and there wasn't a man among us who didn't wretch at least once during the disgusting hours we spent burying our enemies, and it was no easier to feel respect or sadness for a dead Kraut than it was for a live one at this point.

The bivouac grounds continued to reek for days afterward, despite the green wood fires we lit in hopes that the thick smoke would carry the smell away. And when the rest of the company joined us on the following two days—now giving us our full complement of six officers and 135 enlisted men—I remember that a number of guys who were newly arrived commented that they never imagined that war would smell so bad.

*

On June 20th, ten days after I'd entered France, the men in my second platoon and I finally bent our backs to some bridge building when we lent the 300th Combat Engineers a hand building a Bailey bridge on the outskirts of Carentan in the midst of a heavy, three-day rainstorm.

Maeker—traveling with Lt. Baker to help him get a feel for the kind of work we did—went to the site as well where Major John Tucker, the commander of the 300th, and his engineers were working hard to complete a timber-trestle bridge across a canal. I had been supervising our crane and compressor equipment in support of the 300th, and I had returned to our jeep for smokes when an artillery shell screamed out of the sky and buried itself in the near bank of the canal before it exploded. The concussive blast blew Maeker and Baker to the ground a millisecond before the shell's shrapnel shot through the air only inches above their bodies, and they escaped unharmed, as I did, because I was protected by a low rise. But in the minutes that followed, the artillery fire grew intense, and terrifyingly accurate, and men repeatedly ran from the bridge's nearly completed deck to try to protect themselves from getting hit—something that incensed Major Tucker, I could see, even though he was well aware that Maeker and Baker had just barely escaped with their lives, and fifteen more men already had been wounded, by my count.

Tucker had served with Col. Spengler in the South Pacific two years before and had become his protégé of sorts—both of them old-school army engineers who would gladly strip you down to buck private if they disapproved in the slightest with the way you carried out an order. To make his point that the bridge would be finished and finished *now*—regardless of how heavy the shelling was— Tucker strode out onto the bridge and shouted at the top of his lungs that the next man to leave the bridge before his work was done would be court-martialed. Yet the angry warning was barely out of his mouth before an incoming shell slammed directly onto the bridge deck and blew Tucker to bits.

Col. Spengler was at the Carentan bridge site that day, and he, too, had watched helplessly as Tucker was killed. Despite the shock and the personal loss, he had stayed to see the completion of the bridge, and before the tragic day was over, Spengler had ordered the men of the 300th to erect signs at either end of the permanent bridge that read, "Major John E. Tucker Bridge, Constructed by the 300th Engineer Combat Battalion." I certainly understood the gesture, yet as far as I was concerned, naming the bridge after Tucker simply honored his life and his service; I couldn't help but think that his desire to demonstrate his bravery to both his men and to Spengler had needlessly cost him his life.

There was nothing more elemental than life and death, I was reminded that day, nothing more complex, and sometimes nothing simpler. My platoon sergeant, Ray Herman, had been with Maeker as part of the 989th's first wave, and I'd been happy to see him two days before. But somehow, he'd forgotten to give me a telegram I'd received at Kingwood Common the day after I'd been temporarily reassigned. It may have been the prospect of ending up dead that at last had reminded him as we had crouched together in a hole near the Bailey bridge's abutment, but whatever the reason, I had been surprised as hell when he pulled a telegram from his pocket. "Sorry, lieutenant," he told me, "I completely forgot this. It came for you just after you headed over." Then he waited while I opened the wrinkled envelope and read: CONGRATULATIONS DAUGHTER BORN BOTH FINE LOVE CLARA JOHN. The message from Ann's sister-in-law didn't mention the baby's date of birth or what Ann had named the baby, but the news was wonderful in any case, and Herman was genuinely glad for me. No doubt his own family seemed very far away as well, and while we remained together in a damp hole in the ground in France—waiting for the all clear whistle that would allow us to get back to work—he promised he'd find cigars for all the officers and NCOs in the outfit just as soon as we were back on our feet.

The telegram had proved it, but it still took a bit of time for the news to sink in that I now had a *daughter*. Ann, I was sure, would have named her Georgeanne—a combination of our two names with an "e" added for a bit of feminine flare—just as we had planned, and the precious little thing was beautiful—that much I was certain of without even seeing her.

*

David A. Armstrong

Major John Tucker Bridge, June 27, 1944, seven days after he was killed
(Photos courtesy of Jan Ross and Brad Peters 300th C. Eng curators)

From left, Lieutenants Conyers, Baker and Edgar, France 1944

*George's Platoon Sgt., Ray Herman, left, and his driver,
Private Maloy Thompson*

Above and middle, the 989th on the move in France; bottom, George's 989th convoy waits for orders to advance; George's jeep is in the foreground

I was more than a little surprised a few evenings later when Spengler found me and ordered me to join him on a night mission, shouting nonchalantly, "Hey, Edgar, we're going on recon. Get your shit and let's go." Impromptu reconnaissance was something he was already renowned for; instead of sending his subordinates out to scout for bridge locations or check on German damage to the local infrastructure, he was always eager to do the job himself, even when it called for traveling behind enemy lines. The army has enough invested in colonels that they're under orders to take every precaution to stay alive, and none of his superiors was happy about the personal risks Spengler took on these night missions, but neither had anybody forbidden him to go out, at least not so far.

When we reached a bridge that crossed the Douve outside the town of Picauville, Spengler ordered his driver to stop. Germans still held much of the ground on the opposite side of the river, he knew. He wanted to get across but was afraid the bridge might be mined. I suggested that I could take a flashlight and wade underneath the bridge to check, and that was fine with the colonel.

While he and his driver waited, I quietly waded into the shallow and chilly water and made my way under the old stone and timber bridge, and, sure enough, the thing was mined from one end to the other. I had a pair of wire-cutters with me, and it was a simple enough to disarm each of the mines that were strapped to the wooden stringers, and soon I was sure the thing was now safe to cross.

When I returned to the jeep and explained to Spengler what I'd found and what I'd done, he wanted to have a look for himself, and didn't mind getting wet to do it. "Jesus, Edgar," he whispered as we neared the shallow river's opposite shore, "If we'd driven across with these still wired, they'd have never found a piece of any of us." But although the colonel now was as sure as I was that we could safely cross the bridge, he opted not to do so, apparently chastened by the mines and suspicious that the Germans would have more surprises for us if we ventured on—Spengler demonstrating real caution for the first time I'd ever seen.

Over the next few nights, Spengler repeatedly asked me to join him for chow in the officer's mess, and although he remained a much higher-ranking officer than I was, it felt like we were building a real friendship. I was late getting in on the evening of July 7, and when I arrived at the mess tent Spengler was ready to head out on another last minute mission. "Let's go have a look around La Haye-du-Puits, Edgar," he barked, and I quickly replied, "Yes, sir." But the colonel's sergeant spoke up, pointing out that I hadn't eaten yet. "Sure. Get some grub, Edgar," Spengler responded, motioning for me to sit as the two of them headed off.

At about four o'clock the following morning, Sergeant Herman woke me with the news that Col. Spengler was missing. The details weren't yet clear but Spengler's sergeant had returned to the 1110th's command post with some very worrisome information. As they drove to the outskirts of La Haye-du-Puits the night before, Spengler had decided that, without support, it was simply too dangerous to go into the town where a number of German holdouts were believed to be in hiding. But it remained vital to assess what kind of engineer work would be needed to clean up the town and its roads and bridges, and so Spengler had set up an observation post outside the town.

Spengler and six infantrymen had finally determined it was safe to enter the town from the west, and they hadn't radioed with news of any encounters with Germans before Spengler appeared alone on a railroad bridge on the north side of town, where he was able to visually send an all clear signal to the men waiting at the observation post. Their orders had been to wait for the colonel to return, but when he hadn't after ninety more minutes had passed, his sergeant grew worried and radioed the command post for assistance.

I dressed quickly, grabbed my M1 carbine rifle, and Herman and I drove toward the command post outside La Haye-du-Puits just as the sun began to climb the sky. The early morning was still and hushed except for the noise of the jeep, and heavy dew bent the grasses in the fields low to the ground. When we joined the infantrymen outside of town, they explained that they had become separated from Spengler and had been unable locate him again. Then, they had heard a short machine gun blast echo through the otherwise deserted streets. I selected three of the men who'd been with Spengler to join us, and the eight of us who now went searching for Spengler again were armed solely with our pistols and M1s. But, as it turned out, we didn't need them.

We didn't encounter anyone who was hostile before we found Spengler's body slumped in a narrow street, the front of his chest etched by a line of machine gun bullet wounds. I knelt beside him, and it seemed impossible that this man who had been so vital and so constantly animated now lay utterly lifeless. His face was drained of its color and his eyes stared blankly into the morning light. I closed them, and I wanted to cry, but somehow I couldn't. Then, when I noticed that the Krauts who'd killed him had taken his West Point ring, I was hit by a wave of guilt that made my stomach turn. Surely I could have protected him if I had been there. And I was angry now, too. How in the hell had those infantrymen from the 79th Division lost track of this man? I was angry at them, at myself, and with Spengler himself. The big, gruff son of a bitch hadn't needed to die that day, I knew, and my tears finally did come when we wrapped his body in a rain poncho and solemnly carried it out of the town.

In the couple of weeks that followed, I heard rumors that the army had ordered an investigation into why a full colonel had been so poorly protected, but I wasn't surprised to learn from Maeker in late July that Spengler had received a posthumous Silver Star.

Combat awards were handed out pretty readily to dead men, I knew, and I spent plenty of time trying to decide whether, in fact, the colonel had been foolhardy or brave. The one thing I was sure of was that I remained deeply sorrowful that he was gone. I wrote to Coach Cann at NYU, giving him Spengler's regards, then sharing with him the news of his death. Both men had seen something in me they liked, that they thought was worth mentoring and encouraging, and for a guy whose own father had deemed him a bum, in both cases it meant a great deal to me. Spengler had taught me many things in the seven weeks since I'd known him; he had given up his bunk for me, helped me understand how to command my engineers, and had offered me true friendship. But now the "Old Man" was gone, and all of us who served with him were the poorer for it.

Valencia, 1988

AT THE TIME *my grandmother died, I had begun to try to find a way to turn my passion for movies and cameras into a career, yet I was off to a halting start. It was my uncle Paul who first had suggested the obvious to me—why didn't I become a cinematographer? His idea seemed to make sense, and in 1985 I was accepted into the California Institute of the Arts and moved to Valencia, a year after Mimi's death.*

Cal Arts was a terrific school for me, and I really got excited about making my way in the film world, yet with Pop on his own now, some of my attention necessarily remained focused on how he was faring alone. He had retired from Raytheon in order to be constantly nearby during my grandmother's difficult final year, and because he had always spent so much time caring for her, he now had lots of time on his hands. By now he was far less active than her ever had been, and the Santa Barbara Symphony had forced his retirement after thirty years in the violin section. His life was far too quiet, I'm sure, and at the end of each of my regular visits, I remember that he always asked if I really had to leave so soon.

Then, literally out of the blue, Pop's sister Maria arrived—and stayed. Maria's husband Peter had died many years before, as had their mother, who everyone knew as Nana Khatoon, in 1964. Their sister Sophie now was very elderly and their sister Nanajan had very recently passed away. Nanajan's son and Maria's nephew, Bob Marshall, wasn't in a position to take her in, and Pop was her brother, after all, so Bobby put her on a plane for California, and very soon after his decades of caring for my grandmother came to a close, he found himself taking care of his older sister, meeting all her expenses, and providing her a home.

Although Maria had lived in the United States every bit as long as Pop had, she'd never learned to speak English and I know that drove him crazy. He and his sister bickered in Assyrian as part of their daily routine and that habit might have continued for years. But one day, Pop came home to discover that Maria had rifled through his belongings and found a few old photographs of his early loved Lydia Turner—the young woman whom his family would not accept because she was a Jew—torn into small pieces on top of the bedroom dresser in which he had kept them tucked away.

Poppy was so outraged that Maria had gone through his things and crushed that she had destroyed irreplaceable photographs that clearly still meant a great deal to him. Lydia Turner had been dead for decades, of course, and my grandmother was gone as well, but somehow Maria was morally affronted that Pop retained her pictures and she destroyed them with the kind of self-righteous indignation and sanctimony that Assyrian widows too often wear like clerical robes. I wasn't present for what I know must have been an epic shouting match between them, but I do know that the next day Pop moved Maria to a nursing home where, at his expense, she lived until she died.

*

Throughout his life, my grandfather had always leapt forward to meet the dragons that stood in his path, and it was simply his nature to shape challenges into opportunities. In a an attempt to battle both boredom and too much time alone—and echoing his father's passion for building musical instruments—Pop opened a violin shop at his home to keep himself engaged with the world. He became an expert at repairing damaged instruments and it was common for him to sell a violin to a student for half its true value or to give a violin to a needy youngster in whom he spotted real promise. He began to teach violin lessons, and he became a familiar and beloved visitor to the campus of the Music Academy of the West, where he often attended concerts and looked after the musical needs of many of the students there.

I had followed my years at Cal Arts with a series of jobs as an assistant cameraman and then camera operator on Hollywood films, the kind of work that I'd have to do for some time if I really wanted to be a cinematographer one day. It was far from glamorous work, yet I was learning a lot and happy to be in L.A., but then one day I got the news that

Pop had suffered a heart attack. My mother, back in the U.S. at the time, had been with him in a Santa Barbara pharmacy when he suddenly dropped to the floor. She and a pharmacist were able to slip a nitroglycerin tablet under his tongue, an ambulance arrived quickly, and he survived. But he needed constant care for a while, so I put movie making on hold and moved back to Santa Barbara to be with him. I was on call twenty-four hours a day, and Pop was not the simplest patient to look after, but I was glad to be with him—except that I could do little to help ease his worry that his heart would fail him again.

Responding to his concern, his doctors ordered a home health nurse, and after two months I felt I could make plans to return to Los Angeles, but this time, Poppy begged me to stay. He agreed that he was making good progress, and understood that I had to get on with my life, but he was also confronting his mortality for the first time, and we both knew that we wouldn't be at each other's side forever.

I promised to return to see him constantly—and it was a promise I kept—and not long after I'd begun to make those weekly trips, I decided to bring a camcorder with me and videotape a series of interviews with him. The subject of our conversations would be his early life, I explained—his first years in Persia, Russia, and Turkey, his immigrant boyhood in Connecticut and New York, and the years he and his fellow engineers built bridges from Normandy to the outskirts of Berlin. I'd heard him tell the exotic stories throughout my life, but now I wanted to hear them again and in the greatest detail he could offer. And the reminiscing and taping proved to be a wonderful way for us to spend our visits together—Poppy at ease in his comfortable chair, often with a baseball cap pulled low on his aging forehead and his glasses perched low on his nose, remembering in vivid detail a cave he found stuffed with food long ago in Tiflis, the huge lizard he led on a leash through the streets of Constantinople, the money-running he did for Dutch Schultz, and the old school Army colonel named Spengler, who briefly became a kind of father to him before the colonel was killed.

Chapter 9

The River Lines

THE ALLIED SUPREME Command hoped to race across France just as soon as the peninsula was liberated, and if that were to happen, those of us building and repairing the infrastructure that would make that onslaught possible would need enormous amounts of supplies. The town of Saint-Lô had been all but destroyed; hundreds of French citizens had been buried in the rubble, and I remember the gut-clenching stench that hung over the city like a pall—a combination of chemical residue from the explosives, the dust from fallen buildings, and the rotting bodies that lay beneath them—a smell that vividly brought my early days in Tiflis and the chaos of the Russian revolution back into my mind.

I did my best to quickly learn the first name of every guy in the second platoon—and most of the men in the first—and I always tried to use them instead of their surnames. Early on, the four of us who were officers had received a liquor ration—a bottle of gin and a bottle of scotch for each of us—and from then on we never were out of booze, and I always made a point of sharing mine with the guys in the second platoon. And I never asked one of my men to clean my pistol or do my laundry or even fetch me a cup of coffee. It didn't seem to me that that was what the army had trained them for, and I knew those kinds of orders chafed the hell out of the guys who received them.

The only person in the company with whom I truly tried to be a good friend was Jim Conyers, my fellow platoon commander. We both had been made first lieutenants soon after Maeker's promotion to captain, and the fact that each of us led a platoon of these occasionally unpredictable engineers meant that we shared virtually identical responsibilities, and we tended to handle the same day-to-day headaches in similar ways. Like me, Conyers would much rather have a guy make his own best decision about something and risk his lieutenant's disapproval than be afraid to wipe his own ass without first receiving an order. Like Conyers, I thought it made sense to take exactly that approach with Captain Maeker, and Maeker, in turn, seemed to appreciate our willingness to act decisively. That was why the army was paying us the big bucks, Conyers liked to say. I respected him, depended on him daily, and it was remarkable how well a rural Georgian and an immigrant New Yorker got along.

But the man I spent the most time with during those months was almost certainly my driver, Maloy Thompson, a young private who had joined us as a replacement just a few days after the company reached Normandy back in June. Thompson was a born comedian and always had a story to tell or a funny take on the sorry state of things.

If Thompson was all jokes, Ludwig Balzerski was all business. He was the platoon's staff sergeant, one of our best bridge builders—as was my own platoon sergeant, Ray Herman—and Balzerski was every bit as German as any of the Jerries who were trying to kill us.

Ray Herman was as quiet as Balzerski was bombastic, and I couldn't have remotely designed or even imagined a sergeant who was as stalwart and steady and cool under fire as he was. And it had been Herman who had made sure back in June to bring my footlocker across the channel from England—a trunk that contained nothing of any real importance to me except my violin. It was hard to imagine when I might find the time to play it, but it was reassuring somehow to have it nearby. And if it were lost or damaged on the way, well, it wasn't a Stradivarius, after all.

*

In only twelve days, we advanced more than two hundred miles from Saint-Lô in Normandy to the banks of the Seine in the Île-de-France, the long truck-and-jeep convoy of the 989th alone sometimes stretching out for over a mile. Along the way, we built three short river bridges and a fourth bridge that spanned a blown overpass before finally getting the chance to build a masterpiece of sorts across the river the Gauls had long ago named the *Sicauna* or Sacred River.

The hopes of many of my men to be part of the liberation of Paris had been dashed when Eisenhower and his colleagues chose to bypass the city and the forces of the Free French Resistance marched on the capital instead. But American troops *would* take Berlin, we were told, and the news we received made it seem we might do so very soon.

*

By the end of the first week of September, it became clear that the Nazis were determined to defend the city of Metz in northeastern France's Lorraine region at all costs. Ours had become a war of the river lines, and it was essential to get a bridge built—followed by several more—if Metz were to be taken, and we were assigned to get the job done at the site south of Dornot near Arnaville. By now, we were veterans of both combat and building assault bridges, and after what we'd encountered at the Seine a month earlier, we thought we had seen everything the Jerries could throw at us. But, as we would soon learn at the Moselle, they remained capable of far more fury than any of us could imagine.

Bridging the 240-foot Moselle didn't appear difficult in itself, but the task was significantly complicated by the fact that we would need to deliver and offload a mountain of supplies and begin the bridge assembly in an area that was traversed by a canal banked by high levees that paralleled the river near its west bank. Added to that logistical challenge, Conyers and I explained to our men, was the fact that the Arnaville location was within eyesight of the German officer candidate school located high on a nearby hill. The young German soldiers and their commanders could look right down on the bridge site and take direct shots at us with the 88mm guns and 105mm artillery that were positioned at the school, and we certainly couldn't expect a warmer welcome from the young Krauts than they had given the assault troops at Dornot.

As both sides escalated the fighting, we joined the effort to ferry soldiers, ammunition, and jeeps for evacuating the wounded to the enemy side of the river on rafts that were simply two pontons with two sections of treadway strapped between them and lashed to a powerboat operated by Alva Hard. But once the jeeps reached the eastern shore, they bogged down on the muddy slopes of the hills that rose directly up from the river. Casualties at the bridgehead had to be carried back from the forward lines by litter men using field cots and Hard repeatedly crossed back to our side of the river, bringing with him seriously wounded soldiers in immediate need of more medical attention that the medics at the front lines could give them.

When Bill Baker took charge of moving our fleet of trucks that carried the bridge building supplies forward from a temporary depot on the west side of Arnaville, the Germans began to bombard the entire area—their shells aimed with frightening precision on Arnaville itself, the roads leading toward the river, and our staging area at its bank. Maeker and all of us were well-accustomed by now to working under hazardous conditions, but we'd never experienced fire as intense and deadly as this before, nor had any of the units of the Fifth Division. The Jerries pounded us from three sides, as well as from the officer candidate school, and attached time fuses to the shells so they would explode before hitting the ground—raining destruction across a wide zone, and bringing so much heat to both sides of the river that no place felt at all safe.

On our side of the river, Balzerski and his crews had only begun to offload pontons and inflate them when suddenly the eerie scream of incoming 88mm artillery shells made it clear that hell was about to rain down on us. As if on cue, every one of us dropped what we were doing and sprinted for some kind of cover—the back side of the canal levee, beneath a truck, a shallow depression in open ground—any place that might offer even a small bit of protection. When the shells hit, it felt like the end of the fucking world to me, and from underneath one of the Brockways, all I could do was hold my helmet tight and pray. The shells hit the ground with such earth-shattering force that, in the seconds following each explosion, it seemed impossible for more than a few of us to survive. Yet when the twenty-minute barrage was finally over, Conyers and I took a quick count, and only half a dozen men from the units supporting us, the 204th and 160th Engineers had been wounded.

Eight inflated pontons had been damaged badly enough that they would have to be replaced, but when Captain Maeker, Conyers, and I agreed to try to get to work again, the terrible shelling suddenly resumed, this time killing a fine kid named Clayton Forsythe when a shell made a direct hit on the air compressor he was operating. In only a few more minutes, five other engineer troops were killed, and eight more men were wounded, and a quarter-ton truck and a big Brockway were completely destroyed when they took hits that triggered massive explosions. For the next hour, shells rained down on us at five-minute intervals, during which time brave litter crews continued to evacuate the wounded as best they could.

*

First Lt. George Edgar ready for combat just before river crossing

989th's treadway bridge, left, Moselle River, September, 1944

After the battle, France, September 1944; below a French policeman looks on

Blown French railway bridge, September 1944

*Moments after the town was liberated; the man in the foreground is a
French resistance fighter, with two German grenades in his belt*

*Grave of T5 Clayton E. Forsythe, killed Sept 11, 1944
(Photo Courtesy of T5 Lyle L. Pascal, Second Platoon, 989th)*

It was hard to imagine how the situation could get worse. From safe positions on several high points at Fort Driant, the Germans could watch our every move and target their artillery and mortar fire with deadly precision. And it was Lt. Col. Walker himself who decided to hold off any further attempt to get either the Bailey bridge erected across the canal or the floating treadway bridge laid across the river until, somehow, our odds improved a bit. He called for the 84th Chemical Company to come up to the front and crank up its smoke generators to create a smoke screen that would give us at least some minimal cover, and by about 9:00 o'clock on that awful morning, the light wind carried a thick veil of smoke precisely over the top of us. But because the Germans already had us very well-targeted by that point, we also had to move the two bridge locations laterally by several hundred feet for the smoke cover to truly give us protection.

By late morning, we were back at work and Balzerski was singing the praises of the boys who made the smoke, and virtually everyone was less afraid than we had been since the operation had begun. But it seemed to Maeker, Conyers, Baker, and me that, while we had to get the bridge up and open as soon as we could, neither did we want to risk losing any more men, and Maeker ordered everyone in the company to consider his safety at every moment. By mid-afternoon, we had positioned less than half of the float and treadway assemblies of the twenty that would be required to span the river when the wind picked up, the smoke dissipated and we were exposed again.

I remember wondering as the bright sun began to bath us again whether God really cared who won this awful war. And sure enough, the Germans began to pummel us again soon thereafter, and I hollered at the men to get off the bridge and take cover till things quieted down, and as I reached a soldier from one of the units assisting us—a guy whose name I never knew—he shouted at me, "Right behind you, Lieutenant."

"Let's get the fuck out of here!" I told him.

"In a jiffy, Lieutenant," he responded. "I just need to get—" But before he could say another word, a piece of shrapnel ripped his face off. A millisecond later, I heard the sound of the explosion—the shell must have hit no more than twenty feet away—and I was blown off my feet but otherwise okay. I crawled to the sergeant and saw just a bloody mess where his head had been a moment before, and all I could do was drag his body off the bridge and find the cover that I wished to hell he and I had taken seconds before. There was far too much to attend to, even while we waited, for me to spend any time wondering why the shrapnel hit him instead of me, but I know it's a question I've asked at least a thousand times since that bloody day.

Alva Hard, the company's powerboat operator and a guy everybody thought the world of, had bravely ferried raft-loads of ammunition throughout the night to the contingent of infantrymen who remained on the opposite bank. Maeker, Conyers, and I were watching near the bridge's near-shore abutment when Hard took a truckload of ammunition onboard his raft, throttled his motor, and turned the raft into the current and toward the opposite shore. In the smoke and the darkness, we could hear his straining motor, then suddenly, the terrible whine of the 88s again. We could see the outline of Hard's boat in the darkness and Conyers and I began to scream for him to get to shore. Because of the roar of his motor, Hard almost certainly didn't hear our shouts of warning, and if he heard the incoming 88s, he only responded by turning his motor full throttle. We could hear his engine shift from a low groan to a loud wail, and even in the darkness, I could glimpse a bit of the white spray that now trailed in the boat's wake.

The 88mm shells began to hammer the far shore, then the water, and they were plainly advancing toward the spot on the near shore from which we helplessly watched. I couldn't tell whether Hard was in their path—I couldn't see him at all now—and then

Maeker, Conyers, and I had to dive for cover. As we did, suddenly there was a thunderous explosion and huge fireball as the ammunition he was pulling exploded—water spray from the blast reaching all the way back to the spot where we lay helplessly near the water's edge with the noise of rifle casings whizzing over our heads.

When the explosion of the ammunition finally stopped, we strained to hear the whine of Hard's motor, but heard nothing, nothing at all, and quickly knew that the kid must have taken a direct hit from a shell that ignited the ammunition he carried. When he didn't return to shore within a couple of minutes, Maeker, Conyers, and I briefly considered whether to send out another boat to see if we could find him, but as we talked, a ferocious new round fire came our way, and in thirty more minutes we agreed we had no choice but stop the construction and get everyone under cover once more, pulling all the way back to the west side of the town of Arnaville for the second time in only a few hours.

We didn't return to the bank of the Moselle until 8:00 the following morning, and in the morning light we found that our almost-completed bridge had been destroyed. And to no one's surprise, there was no sign of Hard—nothing except for a piece of human flesh that was imbedded in the remains of the powerboat we later pulled from the river. The guy who had somehow embodied the heart and soul of the 989th had been doing heroic work when he was hit—ferrying ammunition to the infantrymen who were doing their best to keep us all alive—and in the morning quiet, Maeker asked everyone in the company to offer him a moment of silent prayer.

But quickly the silence gave way to a flurry of activity. The Germans, we now suspected, had opted to throw every artillery shell they still had in their arsenal at us during the previous night, and the only response from them now was an occasional round of rifle fire. We couldn't be sure whether, or how soon, they would be resupplied, but this time it didn't matter because we had cleared the area of debris and completed a spanking new bridge by noon—the effort only accomplished at a price of thirteen combat deaths and a hundred soldiers wounded, just among the engineer outfits. Overall, the 11th Infantry who had been on the German side of the river fighting, and the units attached to it lost 107 soldiers, and 258 others were wounded—the highest casualties the Fifth Division would ever suffer in a single battle.

The Third Army's 5th and 95th Infantries didn't take Metz until early November, and by the time they reached the officer candidate school whose cadets had tried so hard to defeat us, the place was empty. They had graduated on October 9 and had been sent as replacement officers to defensive locations across the Western Front. The Germans, for whom we had new respect as well as utter contempt, were far from finished; we now knew all too fucking well.

*

During the September days, we remained bivouacked near the Moselle outside the village of Arnaville. We had time to lick our wounds and try to regain the kind of confidence that had gotten us so close to victory so quickly. But the truth was that we had been heavily battered by the German defense of the Moselle and its eastern shore. We'd been met for the first time by an enemy whose military prowess apparently exceeded our own; the Third Army had suffered its greatest casualties of the war to date in the fight to cross the river and those of us in the 989th had lost key members of our team.

The moods of the men in the company grew somber; war meant death, plain and simple, we now knew very personally, and I'm sure that virtually every one of us in the company had grown more reflective about our own mortality in the past few days than we had even during the first days of the invasion.

It may have been my own interior response to the killing we witnessed at the Moselle, but whatever the reason, for the first time since we'd arrived in France, I began to practice the Bach sonatas and partitas for solo violin that had been part of my memorized repertoire since I was a teenager. I played only in my tent and I always attached a mute to the strings—I didn't want my guys or any of the men in the company to wonder what in the hell I was up to— but the sound carried a bit nonetheless and a few of the fellows reported that although they didn't know beans about classical music, they enjoyed what they heard. One of the guys in my platoon confided once that my playing made him feel hopeful about the war and his future, but in ways he couldn't explain.

I know Maeker, Conyers, and Baker must have imagined I was becoming something of a loner—preferring to spend time alone in my tent with my violin to bull sessions and card games with them. Maybe I'd truly begun to be affected by the deaths of good men like Spengler and the guys we lost at the Moselle, but whatever the reason for my solitary sessions with my violin, none of my fellow officers razzed me about it. And I think that for me, the music—even as out of practice as I was—was a link to the best of humankind in the midst of a war in which we were often forced to act in blunt opposition to those ideals and during which we were often forced to spend nights in damp and dirty foxholes hoping we'd live to see the morning.

*

On September 26, Captain Maeker received word that the 989th was being detached from General Patton's Third Army and reassigned to Lt. Gen. Courtney Hodges's First Army, whose front line was the Dutch-German border area near the city of Aachen. Two days later, we prepared to move out in a long convoy of our own, ultimately traveling 175 miles north through Luxembourg and Belgium to the Dutch city of Maastricht.

As we were preparing our trucks for our departure from the outskirts of the town of Chambley-Bussières, a French woman and her daughter came up to me tentatively and asked if we could spare any gasoline. Although fuel was still in short supply, I found it hard to say no and asked her in English if she had a container in which we could put a gallon or so. The woman nodded, then turned to tell her daughter to run get a pot from inside their house, and I was astonished when I heard her speak in Assyrian.

"You're Assyrian?" I asked her in disbelief, and then the woman was as dumbfounded as I was—how could an American soldier speak to her in Assyrian? "*Khdeh lee b'Khzaytukh.* I'm so happy to see you," I told her. "I'm Sargis, but I'm American now. My family is in New York, Chicago. But I was born in Persia. How's it possible that you are here? *Min Ainee Atra tiyet*? What country are you from?"

"Well," she told me, "this is where we live now, where our family came when the Kurds forced us out of Urmia."

I told her my family was from Urmia, too, and that we'd been in the United States since the 20s, and when I opened my arms she didn't hesitate to give me a warm hug.

Mo eeleh Shimukh? I asked her. "What is your name?" She was Katherine, she explained, and her daughter was Lydia, and her husband—she shouted for him to join us—was Alexander. None of the three of us could quite believe that we had encountered each other in a hamlet in France in the middle of the war, but there we were. When I asked them if there was anything else they needed, explaining that we would be moving out in just a few minutes, the beautiful young Lydia, who looked to me to be about twenty or a little older, glanced momentarily at her mother as if for permission, then asked if we by chance had anything for cleaning teeth.

Sure, I told her, then I went to my first aid kit and found a big tube of toothpaste and a new brush. When I returned, Alexander had joined his wife and daughter and he was accompanied by a boy who couldn't have been more than three—Lydia's son Aram—whom they were raising in their home, Katherine explained. Alexander and I embraced in the way that Assyrian men always did, but which was more than a little unusual for an American soldier.

When Maloy Thompson, my driver, wandered over to see what the excitement was, he immediately seemed a little too interested in Lydia for my taste, and I whispered to him to leave her the hell alone—I didn't even want him talking to her if he was going to droll all over her, for God's sake. Her father appreciated my vigilance, I could tell, and he took me by the shoulders and asked what he and his family might do for me—or for us—in return. I quickly told him there was no need to reciprocate, but then I had another thought. Would they write to my mother and sisters in New York—in Assyrian—explaining our chance encounter, telling them I was well and giving them my love.

"I can write," Katherine volunteered. "Yes, it would be an honor to write to your family and tell them of your kindnesses to us." I wrote home often, of course—although the tenor of the letters that reached me from Ann made it appear that she didn't always receive them—and I knew she and my family would love to hear from this farmer and his wife in faraway France. I tore a page from the little notebook I kept in my breast pocket and wrote down their names and addresses then pressed the paper into Katherine's hands. I explained that my father had been a woodworker and made beautiful tars that people said were a joy to play, and that with my mother and sisters we had fled to Tiflis before we eventually immigrated to the United States.

There were dozens of things we might have talked about, things we could have remembered together from a time long ago. I was sick that I had only met these people with whom I obviously shared so much just minutes before I and the 989th had to set out for Holland. I grabbed my camera, took snapshot of the four of them—the two women in dresses and Alexander in a beret and his grandson wearing my officers hat—then I quickly hugged each of them again. *Khush B'shlama*, we wished each other, "Go in peace," and then Thompson honked the jeep's horn to announce that we had to be underway.

*

George's French/Assyrian Family, September, 1944
(Note, the boy is wearing George's hat)

After three major battles, George takes some needed rest, France 1944

Between battles, there was time for relaxation. Above, George and his men commandeer a roadster; below, George examines a lute

If France had been chaos and constant movement and more killing than a group of army engineers ever wanted to encounter, the Netherlands was something entirely different, and the ways in which we lived our daily lives changed dramatically. Instead of sleeping in tents—or foxholes or under Brockways when we were worried about artillery fire—and using slit trenches for latrines, those of us who were officers and a number of the enlisted men lived in private houses or in tents outside them as guests of their kind and generous Dutch owners. Beginning in early October and through the Christmas holidays, I lived with a family whose surname I strangely can't recall—a railroad man, his wife, and two teenage daughters—and was as warm and comfortable and amply fed as if I were in my own home. It was odd to rise early, share the coffee, bread, and cold cuts that I'd been able to scourge from our field kitchen as my contribution to our little "family," then go off to war as if it were simply my day job. And it was equally strange in that lull to "come home" from the war in the evening and acquiesce to their cheerful demands I play my violin for them as our evening's entertainment.

One of my men, Sergeant Havelock, an Ohio kid, was a pianist as well as a tall, fine-looking soldier and a hell of an engineer back while we were still in England. He was one of those guys who had an unusually wide array of talents and interests, and he was without a doubt the only man in the 989th who would have been even remotely impressed that I had met and been encouraged by Fritz Kreisler when I was a kid, or who knew what Mozart's music meant to the world, or who cared about *any* musicians, for that matter, beside the Dorsey brothers or Dorothy Dunn.

And what a pleasure it was to discover during our hiatus in Holland that the family with whom Havelock was staying had an old but still very serviceable upright piano in their home. They loved having him perform for them in the evenings after dinner, and I spent dozens of evenings there myself as the winter unfolded, the two of us soldier-musicians dressed in our semi-formal uniforms with our ties tucked into our shirts and sipping corn wine, all of us marveling at how well Havelock could play difficult Beethoven and Schumann and Mendelssohn pieces. Occasionally, we even did our best with a duet—my Gibson violin tucked under my chin but my playing embarrassingly poor because I so seldom was able to seriously practice.

*

One day in early November, Captain Maeker called a special meeting of the entire company for that evening at a small church in the town. He didn't explain the reason, even to his officers, and rumors flew for a few hours that the war must have taken a dramatic turn, although none of us could quite imagine what that might be.

With all 155 men in the company seated awkwardly, nervously, in the little church's high, straight-backed pews, Maeker opened the meeting simply by announcing that he had received a general order from headquarters of the army's XX Corps, which he wanted to read to the men of the company. "To T/5 Alva M. Hard, 989th Engineer Treadway Bridge Company," the communication began, "for distinguishing himself by meritorious achievement in military operations against the enemy at Arnaville, France, 12 September, 1944, is awarded the Bronze Star Medal." Maeker paused, and when he did, the little church was hushed. Instead of applause or shouts of approval, the men responded only with a deeply respectful silence.

For a long moment, the only sound in the little church was the clearing of throats of dozens of Hard's fellow soldiers, men who seldom cried—some of whom couldn't cry—but all of us profoundly moved as we remembered that terrible night once more, recognizing that Hard must have known he faced near-certain death, but that something more important than his own well-being had kept him on his mission.

*

At chow one winter day during the time we continued to ready ourselves for the big push into Germany, my sergeant, Ray Herman, found me with word that Balzerski, Conyers and I had been approved by headquarters of the XX Corps for Bronze Stars for our roles in bridging the Seine and Moselle rivers, awards that had been recommended by Maeker. I told him I doubted it, but Herman was insistent, and he was disconcerted. "Lieutenant, I gotta tell ya, I may not be an officer," he said, "but it sure as hell doesn't take one to know that you deserve more than a Bronze for what you did at those rivers." But I quickly dismissed the notion, telling him that everybody who was there on those days deserved a god damn medal.

Each of those men had performed outstandingly under those deadly conditions. But something nagged at me nonetheless. If I understood anything about the criteria that qualified soldiers for medals, it seemed to me that Hard deserved the Silver Star, if he deserved anything at all. The Silver Star was awarded for "gallantry in action," the Bronze for "heroic or meritorious achievement," and although the distinctions were subtle, I didn't understand how Hard's sacrifice of his life on our behalf didn't deserve to be honored with something more than the Bronze. If I was honest with myself, it simply sat the wrong way with me that Maeker apparently hadn't thought more of what Hard and the rest of us had accomplished when he made his recommendations.

The subject was no doubt still on my mind later that afternoon when Jim Conyers found me with an idea that he said just couldn't wait. A light snow had begun to fall, and earlier snow still blanketed the ground, and Conyers was eager to send a photograph of himself in the midst of the wintery scene to his family back in south Georgia, none of whom had ever seen snow, he told me, except in the movies, when it probably wasn't really snow at all. "Grab your camera, George, and come with me," he instructed. "I want a picture of me in my uniform out in all the white." He was already dressed in his semi-formals, and I changed into mine, then we walked to a field at the edge of the village of Schaesburg where the camera's lens would find plenty of snow in every direction, with the buildings of the town framing the background.

Despite his boyish pleasure in the moment, I couldn't get Conyers to offer me more than a thin smile—he was all military, after all—then he turned the camera on me. We were half a year into our part of the war, and we'd seen a hell of a lot by then, but somehow it was a special moment—both of us still very young, in fact, and proud of what we'd done and of the men we now could claim to be—and the snow powdered our shoulders and helmets and the war, for the moment at least, seemed blessedly far away.

Edgar and Conyers

Ellis Island, 2002

AS POP AND I *dove deeply into the interviewing process, I discovered— really for the first time—that in his early life he had been as fatherless as I had been, and that a longing to win people's respect was a desire that coursed through his veins as well as mine. I began to research the places and moments in time that Pop described to me, and I was continually amazed by how good his memory remained.*

Poppy had saved every snapshot, concert ticket, letter, and Army order he'd ever possessed, it turned out, and as I sifted through them—and then thousands of documents from dozens of other sources—the stories he told me came ever more to life. And all of them were true. Kurdish tribesmen did, in fact, sack the towns of Alwach and Anhar in October 1914; the American embassy in what was then called Constantinople was indeed housed in the grand and imposing Palazzo Corpi in the early 1920s; violinist Fritz Kreisler did live in Manhattan in 1931 and was sometimes known to dine at Toots Shor's restaurant, and by now I've also seen the brittle and yellowed "Morning Report" for the 989th Combat Engineers dated June 5, 1944, which notes that Lieutenant George Edgar had been ordered onto a temporary assignment with the 1110th Engineer Combat Group, one that would include a "SSV," short sea voyage—the crossing of the English Channel four days after D-Day.

Years later, when my then-girlfriend Nikki Carbonetta and I traveled to Ellis Island to research my grandfather's arrival in the United States, we both were immediately moved by what we encountered there, as so many people are. For Nikki and for me, this was the place where our family's history in America began to unfold, and standing inside the Main Building's Great Hall felt oddly like we were visiting a cathedral that had been the scene of the many thousands of christenings in its time. At the American Family Immigration History Center, it was a profound experience to view the page from the King Alexander's *manifest that affirmed that on*

July 2nd, 1921, "Sarkis Georghiz," listed as eight-years-old, had arrived from Constantinople with his mother, sister, and "brother," who was, in fact, Poppy's cousin Babajan Pera. By July 4th my grandfather was still waiting to disembark the King Alexander *and to be processed through Ellis Island.*

While we were at the center, we also researched records for evidence of Nikki's grandfather, who we knew had arrived from Naples in the early 1920s as well. At the close of a very long day of research, Nikki found me in the Great Hall, which was empty by now. Other tourist had started heading to the boat back to NYC Harbor. Late sun streamed through the huge windows and we savored the brief moment in that room by ourselves. Nikki had successfully found the ship's manifest that listed her grandfather's arrival and she carried a bag filled with photocopies. When I asked the date of his arrival she told me she'd been too pressed for time to look, but now she pulled out the documents, read one, then paused before she said, "July 4th, 1921."

Tears came to our eyes when we discovered that Giuseppe Carbonetta arrived at Ellis Island aboard the Duca d'Aosta *on July 4, 1921, the same day Pop had. And it was a thrilling thing for Nikki and I to think that my grandfather and hers where both in New York Harbor on the same day, watching the Fourth of July celebration and waiting patiently to become Americans.*

*

Following my acceptance into a master's in cinematography program at the American Film Institute in 1996, I won a trio of awards, including a Student Academy Award Gold Medal for my work in my thesis film, John. *Once I was out of school again, I continued to find good work, and for someone whose early life had been laced with perplexity and a particular kind of alienation, nowadays I was increasingly at ease with the person I had become.*

My mother now shared her time between homes and businesses in Puerto Vallarta and the island of Bali in Indonesia, and when Nikki and I finally found time to make a long-planned trip to visit her in Bali, something about the island's rich history and tropical mystery, its huge banyan trees, and the hibiscus, bougainvillea, jasmine, and water lilies that flooded our eyes with color, allowed me to shed some of the complexity of my relationship with my mother, and the two of us had time—far from the difficult memories that were always engendered in Santa Barbara—to simply acknowledge our profound connection to each other, not ignoring the wounds each of us still possessed, but recognizing that healing was a slow but important process.

It was during that visit that my mother shared with me her conversation with Pop in which he had spoken again about the terrible time in Tiflis when his friend Alexander was shot on the street and his mother was attacked by the Russian Dragoon soldier. Pop was tearful, she said, when he described Alexander as his first true friend, then recounted once more his horrible death in the middle of a city street. He was certain, he told her, that killing the soldier in defense of his mother came easily to him, in part, because it was a kind of retribution for Alexander's loss. "After he told me this," she explained, he cried and said, "your father is a murderer." I hugged him and said, no Pop, you were struggling to survive and you were only protecting your family. We're all proud of you and we would not be sitting here today if you had not done what you did."

My mother told me she hoped her words had comforted him, but she couldn't be sure, and we both agreed that childhood is a realm populated by both wonderment and dragons.

Chapter 10

Into the Fatherland

ON THE NIGHT of January 21, with the heavy winter showing no sign of abating and still more snow falling to remind us of that fact, we began the "infiltration" process of moving the company a small piece at a time across the border into Germany. We were relocating only about five miles east of Schaesburg, where we'd been bivouacked throughout the Ardennes offensive, and the town of Herzogenrath, where we now would be based—no more than a few hundred yards east of the Germany-Netherlands border—but the distance might as well have been hundreds of miles. For the first time since we'd landed at Normandy, the local citizens weren't delighted to have us in their midst. In France, Belgium, and Holland, we had been received as liberators; we had given people their lives and their freedom back and they had gone out of their way to offer us every kindness they could.

We were still bivouacked near Herzogenrath on February 19, and the winter ground remained brown except for the first tenacious grasses; the trees still were bare and the weather was cold, yet I remember the day we were awarded our combat medals as one of warm and meaningful celebration. Lt. Colonel William L. Rogers, the commander of the 1141st Engineer Combat Group, and Colonel Blynn of the XIII Corps had joined us to make the medals presentations, and—in their honor as well as ours—Captain Maeker had ordered a close order drill. Each of us wore his dress browns and helmet—we were in a combat zone, after all, and we wore our helmets even on occasions like these when they otherwise would have been quite out of place.

Col. Blynn first presented the Bronze Star and the Croix de Guerre, awarded by the Free French Forces, to Captain Maeker. Then, on Lt. Col. Rogers's order, the four of us who served under Maeker and had been awarded medals stepped up in a single row — Conyers, Newquist, Balzerski, and me. Each of us would receive the Bronze Star, and Balzerski would also receive the Croix de Guerre. Blynn took his time with us, offering each man a few private words and his personal thanks for our service, and I remember feeling truly honored as I saluted him, then stood at crisp attention while he pinned the Bronze Star on my chest.

An army staff photographer who had traveled with Rogers shot dozens of photographs of me and the others and we all eventually got copies, and they are photographs I've always treasured because for someone whose father had declared him a bum from the moment he was born, the moment was sublime.

Afterward, Maeker found me and wanted me to know that he'd actually recommended me, Conyers, Balzerski, and Alva Hard, the powerboat operator we'd lost at the Moselle, for Silver Stars. "But XX Corps thought better of it in their divine fucking wisdom," he quietly drawled, "the bastards."

There was little emotion in what Maeker said, but it meant a lot to me nonetheless. Neither a Silver Star nor a Bronze was proof in any way that I was better than one other fellow in the 989th, or somehow more heroic. I knew better than that. Yet the award did seem to certify that I had proven my father wrong, and that mentors like Col. Spengler had been right when they saw attributes in me worth encouraging. I was a decorated soldier now, and I liked the sound of that, and it seemed that for the moment at least, I could be justly proud.

*

The entire 989th in parade for awards ceremony near Herzogenrath, Germany, February 19, 1945

From left to right in front row, Conyers, Newquist, Balzerski and Edgar as they wait to be presented with the Bronze Star

Sergeant Ludwig Balzerski being presented the Bronze Star

First Lieutenant George Edgar being presented the Bronze Star

*George (second from right, back row) proudly poses
with the men of the 989th after ceremony*

A newly decorated George with his award ribbon on his chest

263

The Battle of the Bulge finally had come to a close at the end of January 1945, as the Germans began to withdraw east toward the Rhine River. Hitler, we read in the copies of *Stars & Stripes* that intermittently reached us, had pulled his entire Sixth Panzer Army out of the Ardennes and had redeployed it on the fragile eastern front against the Russians, leaving huge gaps in the German defensive lines in the west.

As warmer weather began to presage the coming of spring, we received encouraging reports that the Russians were pressing close to Germany's borders, and from halfway around the world came the equally promising news that McArthur's relentless island-hopping campaign was bringing the war ever closer to the Japanese islands. There was a sense of victory in the air, and all of us could taste it. For the first time since I'd read the telegram that announced her birth, I began to allow myself to imagine being at home with little Georgeanne and her beautiful mother—at home in a country free from war and personally free from the background apprehension that each day might be my last. Necessarily, I and the men I served and commanded were wise to focus only on the challenges and tasks immediately at hand. But as winter waned and spring was in the offing, I couldn't help but begin to imagine a time when the war was *over*. I wrote my first letter to Georgeanne, in fact, certain that her mother would read it to her despite the fact that language was still a year or more away for her. It was a letter that quickly spilled from my pen, and I marveled at how much I loved a little girl I'd never met when I read it again many years later.

> My Darling Daughter,
>
> I think that this is my first letter to you, and just for you. When Mommy reads it to you you'll probably wonder what it's all about. But someday you'll be able to read it without any help. You know, I have many pictures of you, Mommy

sent them to me. I can see you growing day by day. I look at you all day long and my arms are just itching to hold you. I want to hold you close to me and kiss that funny little nose of yours, and watch you smile. A smile at the right time is a treasure. Life was not meant to be sad.

I'm still in a country called Germany. It's a long, long way from you and Mommy. I'm still fighting that war I wrote you about in Mommy's letter once. Only the end of this war is much nearer. I'm well and I try to make myself as happy as possible. I always say, "I have a beautiful wife and daughter to go back to." And that's something worth fighting for, all by itself. I have seen many difficult times, but my love for you and Mommy has always helped me come through.

Before I started to write this letter, I was playing the violin. I played for Mommy and you, as always. I'm not very good but I love to play. I'll soon be playing you to sleep with soft lullabies. I hope you'll like them.

Love and regards to those at home. Here are my kisses for Mommy and you. My life is yours and Mommy's and my heart is always with you because I love you both forever.

Your Daddy and hubby, George

*

We bridged the Roer River at the end of February—but not without a hell of fight—and we were advancing almost as quickly and optimistically as we had in the breakout from Normandy, although the distances we traveled each week were far shorter now. But this time, we were in Germany—taking the fight to the Fatherland and winning at every turn, despite the fact that Hitler showed no signs of surrendering and that the increasingly down-spirited Wermacht troops remained fine soldiers and a formidable match.

During the month of March, we established a bivouac, then broke it down and moved on to the next roughly once a week, and the Germans continued to try to stop us with intermittent artillery fire that made us all wary and nervous—and reminding us all that even with the Germans in retreat, The Fatherland remained a dangerous place to be. I wrote home to Ann soon, as I often did, but for some reason, I told her I wanted her to know that I loved her "if I shouldn't make it home." They were the kind of words it wasn't fair to make her read, but somehow I needed to write them.

Near Rheinberg, we set about figuring out how to prepare a treadway bridge for construction in a brand new way. The broad width of the Rhine was going to demand more supplies of every kind than we had ever mustered before, including *ninety* floats and saddles and enough M-2 treadway to span 1,080 feet, more than three and a half football fields in length.

*

989th's staging area just before crossing the Rhine River, March 23, 1945

Rhine River Crossing, March 24th

One of the massive Brockway trucks on the way to the Rhine River

First Lieutenant George Edgar proudly stands in front his, and the 989th's, treadway bridge at the Rhine River, March 24, 1945

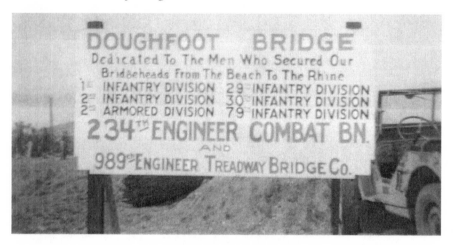

Stars and Stripes, *March 28, 1945, the pictures are of the 989th's treadway bridge across the Rhine*

"Used with permission from Stars and Stripes.
© 1945, 2010 Stars and Stripes."

With fully half of our pontons already inflated and saddled in the first hours of March 24, the Ninth Army's artillery divisions unleashed one of the heaviest single artillery barrages of the entire war. The Germans were waiting, of course, and they shot back with no small amount of firepower themselves, but they were dramatically outmanned and outgunned by now, and although we didn't know it at the time, many high-ranking Wermacht officers had even begun to quietly talk of surrender.

The first Ninth Army assault troops started across the Rhine in storm boats. Enemy fire was only sporadic, likely because the German forces were stretched thinly by now along a defensive front of nearly a hundred miles. It was a thought that charmed the hell out of me as we worked—the notion that virtually every German wearing a uniform along the western front was seeing the Allies coming straight at him—sprinting across the fearsome river that Hitler believed his forces would always hold, leaping over it as if it were only a piddling stream.

Because of the relatively light resistance from the enemy throughout the morning, Captain Maeker decided to get our bridge underway a good bit sooner than had been planned. And his plan worked like a dream—those heavy dump trucks rolling down a road we'd built ourselves, hauling floats and treadway assemblies ready to be dropped into the water, bolted into pairs, then ferried into position on a river that was wide enough to give us plenty of room to maneuver.

By morning, every one of us was dog tired but the job was all but done. The Germans apparently had lost interest in our particular bridge building exercise, but the thunder of distant guns made it clear that they were focusing their animosity on other Allied bridges instead. If they left us alone, we would complete our bridge and get traffic rolling across it by lunchtime.

Sign-builders for the 234th Engineer Combat Battalion—with whom we built the Rhine treadway bridge—had painted a piece of plywood white and lettered it to read: "DOUGHFOOT BRIDGE, DEDICATED TO THE MEN WHO SECURED OUR BRIDGEHEADS FROM THE BEACH TO THE RHINE." It seemed to me it was a fitting dedication— we wouldn't have built a foot of bridge under assault conditions if it hadn't been for the heroic soldiers who'd quickly reached the far shore of dozens of rivers by now and fought off the enemy while we did our work.

It didn't take long for news to travel that the assaults across the Rhine had gone exceedingly well along more than 200 miles of the river's length. And because we had served under General George Patton when we were attached to his Third Army back in the summer, it wasn't a bit difficult for my guys and I to believe the stories we quickly heard about Patton pissing into the Rhine the day before from the deck of a treadway bridge located 175 miles upstream from ours. "I've waited a long time to do that," he reportedly announced as the stream of his urine arced out into the water. "I didn't even piss this morning when I got up so I would have a really full load." But if pissing in the Rhine was Patton's way of celebrating the accomplishment of a long sought after goal, simply hammering that sign into the mud beside the west abutment of our bridge at Mehrum was somehow more appropriate to us and the kinds of men and engineer units we were. Those of us in the 989th were bridge builders, plain and simple, and that exquisitely long bridge bent into a subtle arc by the river's current—all 1,080 feet of it—that we surveyed with pride on that spring evening was a hell of a piece of work.

*

The March 28th *Stars & Stripes* ran a big front page photograph of our bridge spanning the Rhine, and the accompanying article made us sound like we were engineer wizards of sorts, but we didn't have long to bask in the limelight. At the beginning of April, we were moving again.

Everywhere, we saw long columns of defeated Wermacht soldiers walking toward prison camps and a future they couldn't be sure of, and on their faces was the kind of resignation that proved they'd known for a long time that they would lose the war. Everywhere, too, so-called "displaced persons" clogged the roads and highways, reminding me of the ragtag group of refugees I had been part of when I was a small boy and we struggled to find our way into Russia. These ghost-like figures who had been forced to work in Nazi slave labor camps now were free, desperate men, women, and children from many countries who had nothing but the clothes on their backs and no idea of how or whether they might one day return to their homes.

German citizens increasingly hung white flags from their windows and carried white handkerchiefs in the streets, and many were quick to announce to us in English, "Me no Nazi, me *anti-Nazi*." And everywhere now, German soldiers could see for themselves that the Wermacht was being routed by Allied forces. Soldiers deserted their ranks constantly and they were also increasingly quick to surrender.

As we passed through a small town whose name I don't remember early in April, traveling from Gohfeld to Herford, we had to negotiate our long convoy through streets so narrow our trucks almost scraped the buildings on either side. White flags hung from most of the windows, but the place seemed virtually deserted when, at a place where the street made a turn and each truck was forced to a crawl, an old German soldier with sergeant stripes and a grizzled growth of beard and a German private who couldn't have been older than fourteen came out of a doorway, each one carrying a stick with a white handkerchief tied to it.

I grabbed my carbine; Herman quickly leveled his Thompson at them, and our eyes darted in every direction, unsure whether this might be some kind of ambush. I shouted back down the line of trucks for Balzerski and warned the others behind us to beware of snipers, and when Balzerski made his way to us, he didn't have to ask for instructions from me. *Gibt es mehr von Ihnen?*, he demanded of the old soldier. "Are there more of you?"

The German sergeant explained to Balzerski that there were more, but assured him they all wanted to surrender. *Erzählt, dass jeder mit dort Händen auf herauskommt*, Balzerski quickly commanded. "Tell them to come out with their hands up." The bearded man turned and shouted Balzerski's order up to a second-story window, and soon doors opened everywhere—not just in that building but in every building nearby, and suddenly we were surrounded by a hundred or more ragged German troops, most of them old men or young boys, all of them beleaguered and apparently eager to do what they were told and be done with the war. I caught Balzerski's eye and was glad to see that he apparently was convinced that these Germans meant us no trouble, and I thought I saw a hint of grin on his face as well. And I knew how he felt. If these soldiers had been in another kind of mood, every one of us could have been killed.

Soon, the narrow street was filled with German soldiers and still men continued to file out of surrounding buildings. The few who carried rifles dropped them to the pavement the moment they came into view, and I watched as one man bent to put his rifle down, then looked at me and studied my face for a moment, before he came closer still. There was nothing menacing about him, but I'm sure I began to tense up, at least until he spoke my name. "George," he asked. "Is that you?

I couldn't believe it. It was Wolf Hufer, the side horse vaulter with whom I'd trained at the Turnverein in New York ten years before. Hufer had been one of the best gymnasts I'd ever encountered, and a decent guy, but I remembered, too, how enamored he'd been of the Nazis back in those days.

"What in the hell are you doing in that German uniform?" I asked, and he explained that he had joined the Wermacht soon after he'd returned home to Germany to visit his parents, but that now he regretted ever leaving the U.S.

"Not such a good time to be a Nazi, is it?" I asked.

"No," he said. "I rejected it soon after joining, but by then I could do nothing except try to stay alive."

I told him I was happy to see him, but I wished to hell he had rejected the Nazi bullshit back in New York a long time ago, and I explained that I couldn't let him go. He was now a prisoner of war, just like all the men with whom he had been hiding, and he said that yes, he understood that, of course.

I assured him that he and his fellow soldiers would be safe, but I wanted his word that no one would try anything funny in the time it would take for us to load them into our trucks and transport them to a POW camp. Hufer said I could count on him. He saluted me, and we shook hands, but then I had work to do. By the time each man had been thoroughly searched, we had counted 154 German soldiers for whom I would remain technically responsible until they were safely behind the stockades at the camp near Bielefeld where we delivered them.

But when we reach the camp, we were astounded to see an open field packed with more prisoners than we imagined had surrendered in all of Germany. The only thing keeping them there were the MPs who circled them and casually trained their machine guns on them. None of the Americans guarding the Germans appeared tense and all of the prisoners I saw at close range appeared happy simply to sit in the sun and smoke. For them, the war was over.

I found Hufer and took him to meet the camp's commander. I explained that I had known Hufer long ago in New York and that he spoke excellent English. "If you need a translator, he'd be a good choice," I said, and Hufer was quick to nod his agreement and he thanked me for the recommendation. I saw Hufer only briefly once more about an hour later as he and his fellow soldiers stood at a motley kind of attention in the camp's dusty yard. I gave him a little wave, and he lifted his chin in response, and then we were on our way.

*

As we advanced on the town of Gardelegen on our way to Kloster Neuendorf, we spotted a large column of black smoke rising in the distance, and then soon could see that the source of the fire was a long and imposing building surrounded by pastures. Its cinder block walls were still standing but its wooden roof by now had collapsed. Those of us riding in the lead jeeps stopped—presuming there was little we could do and that the fire by now only smoldered—and it was then that we were hit by a hideous stench, one that no one needed to identify or explain and one I'll never forget.

When I walked to the far side of the building, which I thought might have been a barn, I saw a large open trench at its flank, and at the bottom of the trench lay a huge heap of bodies—dozens of them, hundreds perhaps—that had been tossed into it like scrap. But the scene on the opposite side of the barn was even more ghastly still. There, lit by the bright morning sun, we could see charred heads and hands sticking out from under three sets of heavy doors, the bodies of prisoners who had tried desperately—but futilely—to escape the conflagration.

Maeker already had encountered the commander of the 405th Regiment of the 102nd Infantry Division, and had begun to hear a more horrific story than we had yet imagined. Ten days before, thousands of religious, political, and military prisoners had been pulled out of slave labor camps where they'd built munitions, then forced onto trains headed toward a destination their captors would not name.

Then two days ago, the train had been forced to stop at the town of Letzlingen because Allied bombers had destroyed the railway lines that lay ahead. The prisoners had been unloaded from the train and forced to walk the eight miles to Gardelegen, and those who were sick or lame had been shot where they fell along the way. When the SS troops guarding the prisoners heard from the frightened local residents of Gardelegen that the American Army was quickly advancing on the town from the west, they had marched the prisoners to a large masonry horse barn on an estate outside of town and had locked them inside, where they encountered knee-high straw already heavily soaked with gasoline. It had taken only the bolting of the doors and a single phosphorus grenade to transform the barn into a living hell.

According to the colonel with whom Maeker and I spoke, only a few prisoners had escaped before the doors were sealed shut, or managed to tunnel in the dirt beneath them. Those who managed to escape were shot as they ran away by SS officers and the great majority of the people trapped inside the barn—perhaps two thousand of them—had been burned alive.

The discovery of atrocities like the one we witnessed at the barn outside Gardelegen would become all too common in the weeks ahead. And a thread that seemed to connect them all was the degree to which the German people themselves claimed to have never had an inkling of the crimes done in their name. They were as horrified as we were, and they couldn't possibly have known, they assured us time after time. It was impossible to discern whether that was true, but it was hard to believe it could be. At Gardelegen, at least, the townspeople would never be allowed to forget what had taken place on a warm spring day just a stone's throw from their homes—just as my mother, my sisters and I would never forget what we had witnessed long ago in Urmia, when the Kurds and Turks destroyed our villages, kidnapped hundreds of children, and shot every able-bodied Assyrian Christian man they could find. People could become monsters, I'd known all of my life, and now I was reminded of that terrible truth once more.

We wanted to believe that the German people now were as eager for the war to be over as we were; we hoped they were resigned to the fact that Hitler's Third Reich was done, and at least some of them, no doubt, were. People in cities and towns seemed to be less wary of us, and everywhere soldiers now were surrendering in droves. It was a time of chaos; soldiers and citizens were in motion everywhere, and even among the defeated, you could sense something akin to an exhausted hope. Things would be different in the days and months to come, they seemed to know, and it was hard to imagine how they could be worse.

*

Not every German was ready to give up the fight, we discovered one day not long thereafter when Balzerski, Thompson, and I escorted a corporal from our motor pool to a local hospital, one that was bomb damaged but still in partial operation. The soldier had badly lacerated his arm when a jack collapsed as he was changing a tire on one of our Brockway trucks. I was sure he needed a doctor, if we could quickly find one, and I'd noticed a German hospital a couple of miles back. Our aid station was at least an hour away, so I'd grabbed Balzerski in hopes that we wouldn't encounter communication problems and off we'd gone.

The old hospital was so badly damaged that I was amazed its personnel could still care for the sick and injured; many of its walls and a substantial part of the roof had been blown to bits. We were met in a hallway by the facility's administrator—a stern, middle-aged woman who was clearly disgusted by the fact that we had entered her domain. When Balzerski explained that she had no choice but to cooperate and help us get aid for the injured man, she hissed at us in German, and she and Balzerski traded insults until I grew tired of waiting and told him to explain that I had a soldier who needed assistance *now*.

Balzerski told me the woman was outraged by the Allied bombing she had witnessed and the thousands of deaths it had caused, and she believed we were directly responsible. I told him to describe for her the horror we had just witnessed in the barn at Gardelegen; she listened briefly, then screamed the word "Lies!" at me in English, and suddenly I'd had enough.

I ordered Balzerski and Thompson to go find a doctor for the injured corporal, then grabbed the woman by her arm and led her into her office. When she attempted to pull away, I pulled out my pistol and shouted, "Halt!" But she wasn't deterred by the weapon. She spun, moved close to me and spit in my face, screaming "*Schwein!*" Pig!

Enraged, I slapped her face hard with the back of my hand and knocked her against her heavy desk, but was startled when blood began to trickle from her mouth. My anger instantly ebbed when I saw that I had injured her, but still she wasn't finished insulting me. "Murderer!" she shouted in English, "Americans burned those people!" And this time I charged her, pinning her throat against a wall with my left arm and pressing the pistol against her temple with my right. When she continued to try to escape, I spoke with whispered fury, "You fucking stop right now or I will kill you."

But the woman wasn't cowed. My .45 still didn't concern her, and she began to kick me and scratch at my face. I threw her to the floor, unintentionally ripping open her blouse as I did, and I was stunned as I caught site of the pale white skin between her breasts. She looked up at me with both terror and rage etched on her face — precisely the same expression I'd seen on my mother's face back when the Russian soldier was trying to rape her — and I shuddered to think that I might have been capable of the same crime.

In all the months of the war, I'd tried to treat everyone I encountered with a basic kind of respect — even the Germans — and I believed I largely had until now. But in exactly the same way that the Greek kid Papadokas's taunts that I was a "pimple face" had led me to throw him off the bleachers back in New Britain, this woman's utter contempt and lack of respect for me — coupled with her odious charge that *we* were responsible for the barn massacre — were things I couldn't let stand. Since back when I was a small boy, I'd had to suffer my father's scorn and disrespect, and surely in part for that reason, I'd always been quick to flash hot with anger when I believed I'd been treated unjustly or with no acknowledgment of my basic rights. Yet still, I might have killed the woman and I thanked God that something had stopped me.

I holstered my .45, then simply turned and walked out of her office. I found my men and waited impatiently while a war weary old doctor completed splinting the wounded soldier's arm. "Let's get out of this shithole," I dismissively announced to my men when the doctor was done, and we departed.

I returned the following day with a cardboard box full of food to try to make some sort of amends to the woman, but the hospital had been abandoned. And for days thereafter I was haunted by what had happened there, by the suddenness and scale of my rage and by my discovery that I, too, was likely capable of committing a heinous crime.

*

On the Road to the heart of the Fatherland, May 1945

A German anti-aircraft gun is destroyed, Germany, May 1945

A Stuka Dive Bomber after emergency landing, Germany, May 1945

David A. Armstrong

The Destroyed city of Breman, Germany, V.E. Day "Victory in Europe"
May 8ᵗʰ, 1945

At war's end, a very tired George. V.E. Day, May 8, 1945

We reached the banks of the Elbe River in the first few days of May. Then, on May 8, came the telegram we'd been waiting for since we waded ashore in Normandy eleven months before. A representative of the German High Command had signed the unconditional surrender of all German land, sea, and air forces in Europe, it read. "Effective immediately all offensive operations by Allied Expeditionary Forces will cease and troops will remain in present positions." It was signed simply "Eisenhower," and I remember how virtually everyone in the outfit wanted to take his turn and read it with his own eyes.

The Germans were defeated, and the war—our part of the war, at least—was over. There was clearly nothing else to do but celebrate, and with Captain Maeker's permission, Herman and I hauled out the last of our stash of French liquor, which we had hoarded for precisely this occasion. There was cognac and champagne and wine for everyone and there were broad smiles on faces on which I'd virtually never seen them. We were tickled to death not to be building a bridge across the Elbe—that would be work for somebody else, if it had to be done—and at that moment, the 6,263 feet of tactical bridge we'd built in France, Holland, and Germany seemed to add up to plenty of fucking bridge.

It wasn't a raucous party—somehow the occasion was too momentous for anybody to pay it disrespect by getting falling down drunk. Instead, it was an afternoon and an evening during which each of us in his own way celebrated the fact that he now stood an awfully good chance of seeing his family again, and that he would have a chance to make a life for himself and his wife and children in the way that far too many of our comrades would not.

We had lost a lot of men as we had fought to bridge rivers large and small in three countries. Given the fact that those bridging operations were almost always undertaken under assault conditions, we certainly might have lost dozens more, yet each of us was mindful of what we owed those dead engineers, and how this celebration was terribly muted by their loss.

For my own part, I couldn't be sure how many months it would be before I would see her, but finally I felt certain that I would get to meet my precious little Georgeanne, and to tell her how sorry I was for having had to miss her first year of life. I thought of my beloved Ann, and my mother and sisters, and I remembered America, the only place I'd ever lived where the guns of war did not thunder. I took my violin, and walked out into the trees in the moonlit darkness and I played what I remembered of a Beethoven cavatina. I doubt anyone heard me and for once I wasn't critical of how I played. I simply made the music I could, and I was grateful for that, and I remembered my father and tried to believe that at last he must be proud of me.

Los Angeles, 2003

THE MORE I learned from Pop of that extraordinary time he spent with the 989th Combat Engineers, the more I marveled at what he had endured and accomplished in his life. I began to understand that for Pop, the war had not been a brief and terrible interruption of his life, but rather the time when all the challenges and complexities of his entire life up to that point were suddenly forced into his consciousness. He had always known brutality and violence, he'd always struggled for acceptance and respect; he had a deep need to prove what he was capable of, and he longed for words of approval from strong and successful men. I'm sure that Colonel Spengler's death so early in the invasion was particularly hard on Pop because Spengler had so openly embraced him as a good man and a fine soldier. And I'm sure as well that by the end of the fighting, Pop knew how much the men who served under him respected his intellect, his leadership, and his friendship. Yet he only spoke to me about how much he admired them.

Poppy remained the most important person in the world to me. No one else offered the complete and unconditional love he did, and there was no one else to whom I could so limitlessly give my love in return. He had diapered and bathed me while I was young, and it seemed right that, in turn, I would begin to do the same for him. In 2002, I'd begun to work as a director of photography and Pop was able to understand as he entered his late eighties that I'd attained an early goal. Now, I could imagine directing films one day and I confessed to him that I was sure that I would, in fact — and although he had little strength left, I remember him patting the back of my hand as if to say he agreed.

I continued to visit him as often as I could, sometimes making the 180-mile round trip from Los Angeles every day for a number of days in succession, particularly when he was ill as well as during those difficult days when I resolved to move him to an assisted-care facility in nearby Ojai. My mother, still very close to him as well, was often out of the country, of

286

course, but I spoke with her regularly to update her on Poppy's condition and to seek her advice. She and I agreed that Pop no longer could live at home—and he very reluctantly accepted our decision. As I got him ready to go, I remember asking him if we should take one of his violins with him to Ojai, and I still can hear the tone of his voice when he said no, he wouldn't be needing it.

Chapter 11

Dragons & Violins

EVERY ONE OF us was eager to get back home to America—even the several guys who planned to marry girls from Britain, France, and Holland—and the idea that we might have to clean up the mess that, as we saw it, was entirely the Germans' fault just plain didn't sit well. We got a taste of what might be in store for us when the 989th was ordered to travel on May 8 from Osterburg, where we'd been stationed since mid-April, to Bremen, to help return that city to basic operation.

I had seen terrible violence and destruction throughout my life, and I knew that people who had suffered great losses in war were never inclined to blame themselves—whether they rightly should or not. And I'm not sure why, but I personally responded to the massive destruction that lay around me by photographing it. In the few days we were there, I took dozens of photographs—far more than I had anywhere else since I'd arrived in Europe. It may have been because something in me wanted a permanent reminder of the realities of war—evidence that perhaps I would later share with my children to help rid them of any wrongheaded ideas about war's nobility—but instead, I think I was simply caught up by the utter folly of it all. No one was ever required to invade other nations and enslave their people; none of us ever *had* to starve people to death or burn them alive; we didn't need to destroy the cities and societies we had struggled so mightily to create. We didn't have to, but we did, and I think I hoped my photographs would help me never forget.

*

The Japanese surrender in early September had brought the whole of the war to a close and had dramatically changed the army's perspective on how many soldiers it continued to want to house and feed. Redeployments back to the States began to increase dramatically as the weather cooled, and the ranks of the 989th began to shrink. I said farewell to men like Herman, Thompson, Balzerski, and the others with whom I'd developed a strong bond—simply shaking their hands, slapping their shoulders, and telling them it had been an honor to serve alongside them, occasionally one of us promising to write or to get together back home someday, but each of us guessing, I suspect, that we might well be saying so long forever.

Then, the officers in our company began to get their shipping out orders as well. Captain Maeker headed for a ship docked in the harbor at Le Havre, then on to New York and then finally home to Texas, on a morning after we'd had a final dinner together. We made small talk about what we most looked forward to back home; we reminded ourselves how fortunate we'd been to lose as few men as we did, given the fact that the Germans' had constantly done their best to stop us, and I wanted him to know that I'd always appreciated his leadership. It was Maeker's style not to say much in return, but I remember that he called me George—something he'd never done before—as we said goodbye, and I wanted to think that his using my first name was something to which I could attach some meaning.

Conyers's ship docked at Le Havre and he left camp and headed for Georgia, and it seemed like a part of me was strangely missing. A few weeks later, I said a final farewell to Bill Baker, the two of us offering each other broad smiles and a warm handshake, and, with that, I said goodbye to the 989th. I boarded a British ship called the *HMS Mackay* that was bound for New York. Five months after the war had ended in Europe, the 989th Engineer Treadway

Bridge Company very soon would no longer exist. All the company's enlisted men had traveled home by now, as had every officer except one—Bill Baker. Because he was the unit's youngest officer and had been overseas less time than the rest of us, it fell to him to sign out his fellow officers, turn in all our final reports and last bits of equipment, and spend a final night alone in the squad tent—the 989th reduced to a single man, and then, at last, to none.

*

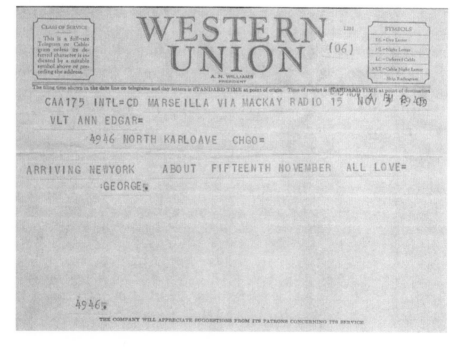

"Coming Home!"

When the *Mackay* passed through the Verrazano Narrows on November 13 and steamed into New York Harbor, every soldier on the ship seemed like a kid on Christmas morning. We crowded the ship's rails and craned our necks to see the city come into view, then grow large on the northern horizon. And near the New Jersey shore stood the Statue of Liberty, just as she had twenty-four years before when I saw the grand copper lady for the first time—back when I was one of the immigrants she welcomed to a new world. This time, however, I was returning *home*; I was as American as any other soldier on that ship and I doubted I'd ever leave the U.S. again. Even if my beautiful wife and daughter were with me, where would we want to travel? I'd seen enough of Europe to last me for decades; Russia, now part of the Soviet Union, was simply a faraway place from my distant past. I barely remembered Urmia and our ancestral home in northwestern Persia, and even Constantinople, now known as Istanbul, a city in which I'd delighted, no longer lured me the way New York did.

But my time in New York was brief, and during the eleven days I was there, I did little more than eat my mother's delicious bushala, help her with chores, and catch up on the hundreds of hours of sleep I'd missed in the nearly two years I'd been away. At meals, my mother and my sisters peppered me with questions about what I'd seen and experienced during the war, and I answered them all, as best I could. My mother nodded knowingly as I described the worst of what I'd encountered, remembering, I was sure, all the war into which she'd been thrown throughout her early life. And I hated the reminder that she, too, knew as much as I did about the needless slaughter of the many and unspeakable cruelty leveled against the few, about the mud, the daily misery, and the stomach-turning stench of death.

On Saturday morning, November 24, my mother and sisters were up early to see me off, and, as I departed, I assured them that yes, Ann and little Georgeanne and I would return to visit them soon, and when my mother began to cry I reminded her in Assyrian that I'd returned home from the war healthy and unhurt and that this was much more a cause for celebration than for tears. I was about to add that far too many guys like me hadn't come home at all, but I stopped myself before I did, realizing that she understood that fact better than most. And I began to see for the first time that it would be easy to drive yourself mad wondering why you'd survived when so many others had not.

Twenty-four hours later, following a long day and night spent traveling by train, I arrived at Chicago's Union Station, took a cab to Ann's parents' house, and waiting on the porch for me were the wife I'd missed every day for twenty-three months and the daughter to whom I was thrilled to be introduced. Held proudly in her mother's arms, Georgeanne had big, beautiful dark eyes, and in the morning chill her puffy little cheeks were bright red. She looked much more like her mother than she did me, I was happy to see, and although I'd steeled myself before arriving that she might be afraid of me at first, she was not. For a long time, I hugged the two of them as tightly as I could, Ann whispering her love for me in my ear and assuring Georgeanne that at last *this* was the daddy she'd heard about for so long, and when I took my daughter in my arms for the first time, her little hands reached out to touch my face and I was instantly in love with her in a way I couldn't have imagined before that moment.

Ann and I treated each other a bit like strangers as we got into bed that night. It had been so long since we had touched, or kissed, or made love. But soon our tentative attempts to reconnect gave way to our passion, and the years and continents and uncertainties that had separated us disappeared, and for that night at least, we weren't concerned in the slightest about whether we might be overheard.

*

During the two years I was in Europe, Ann had lived with her parents on Karlov Avenue on Chicago's north side, and so, for the time being, I moved in as well. Years before, we had argued about whether we would live in New York or Chicago and I'd vowed that I'd never move to the Midwest. But the world was a different place, and I had changed too, and I had an eighteen-month-old daughter now and no immediate way to support her. I remained in the army, but my reservist's pay was next to nothing, and until I found a good job, I knew I'd have to acquiesce to living with my in-laws, something Ann had found to be untenable when she moved to the Bronx in 1942, and a circumstance that proved to be a similarly challenge for me. Ann's parents and her brother Joel were extraordinarily sweet people—absolutely they were—but their Christian fundamentalism shaped every aspect of their lives, and it was a kind of zealous and rigid kind of religion—one in which arbitrary rules seemed important above all else—that I often found difficult to stomach, although I did my best not to show it.

What I didn't have a quarrel with was the grand celebration the family traditionally made of Christmas, and because my previous two holiday seasons had seen very little merrymaking, as well as the fact that this would be the first Christmas Georgeanne would be old enough to enjoy to some degree, I was excited to see it arrive. On a Sunday evening two weekends before the holiday, Ann's mother kept Georgeanne occupied in the kitchen while Ann, her father, and I worked feverishly in the living room to set up and trim the family's Christmas tree. It stood near the fireplace and looked perfect, the three of us agreed, laden with ornaments and tinsel and brightly colored lights.

We darkened the lights throughout the house, and then, on signal, Ann's mother opened the kitchen's swinging door and little Georgeanne—who ran wherever she went in those days—saw the strange but magical site the Christmas tree made from far down the hall. She raced toward the tree, squealing with delight, and I was as charmed as she was until I had to watch helplessly as she plowed right into the tree and it crashed down on top of her. I couldn't help but laugh as my first response, but Ann was terrified, and I think the horrified expression on her face frightened Georgeanne every bit as much as the accident itself. The little doll cried for a minute or two, but she was fine except for a small scratch on her forehead, and I remember her sitting safely on her mother's lap as the rest of us righted the tree, replaced broken ornaments, and made it perfect once more.

The 1945 holidays were a special time. I hadn't worried about what kind of father I'd be; I didn't think my father's relationship with me had made it impossible for me to be a different sort of parent, and, after all, I had experienced my mother's powerful love for me throughout my childhood. But what was surprising to me was the *depth* of my love for my daughter, as well as the suddenness with which it overtook me.

Over the course of the next few years, I had the good fortune to be able to try to make up for my absence during the first eighteen months of Georgeanne's life, spending as much time with her as I could—reading her bedtime stories and making up stories of my own, tales that often featured an adventurous Nile dragon reminiscent of my beloved pet in Constantinople, accompanying her on trips to the zoo, playgrounds, Riverview Park, and the amusement park at the Navy Pier—and trying my best to interest my beautiful, raven-haired little girl in music.

*

Captain George Edgar, home from the war, sees his daughter Georgeanne for the first time, November 1945

Following page, one year old Georgeanne, and below, August 1946

My own interest in music had never waned and now, as an army reservist trying to make his way in an American city I was increasingly at home in, I also found time to dive headlong into my violin studies after a four-year hiatus, in addition to my roles as a husband and father and our small family's sole breadwinner. In February 1946, I found a job as a liquid fuse inspector at Schweitzer & Conrad, then later moved to Crescent Industries, where I designed record changers and motors for phonographs. In 1953, I took a job I hoped I'd be comfortable in for a long time at Raytheon, where I initially worked on the development of the microwave oven and the color television—two products that seemed emblematic of the exciting new era the nation had entered after the war. My position at Raytheon allowed us to rent a tiny, one-bedroom apartment on Broadway, a few blocks north of Wrigley Field and finally it appeared that we could begin to make our way in the world and that I could forge a solid career with a bold and innovative company.

Ann and I had loved being in each other's daily company again in the first years after the war and I had been thrilled when my son Paul was born in September 1948. The Army had made me a captain in the reserves as I left active duty; and the Ohannes family, Assyrians who lived in the building, had become dear and very supportive friends. Yet it was the violin that still captured my heart, my passion, and my tenacity in ways that I found difficult to explain. And although little Paul remained too young to begin to evidence a similar zeal for classical music, Georgeanne did seem to love it in ways that delighted me, and in 1952 we were on solid enough financial footing that Ann warmly gave her blessing for both Georgeanne and I to begin taking weekly lessons at the Chicago Conservatory of Music.

Every Tuesday evening, I'd hurry home from work, then Georgeanne and I would take a short bus trip to the Sheridan Road El station, then travel by train to the Loop and the conservatory on

Michigan Avenue. We both loved the Buckingham Fountain in nearby Grant Park, and even in cold weather, little Georgeanne would laugh gleefully when the wind doused us with the fountain's spray. We would explore the downtown streets, taking in the many pleasures of the city, but I made sure we were always a few minutes early for our seven o'clock lessons.

Back when I was a boy, it would have been quite surprising for an immigrant family like ours to be able to afford a piano in the house, but in those first years after the war, I'd found an inexpensive upright that we somehow squeezed into our tiny apartment—a piano that early on had captured Georgeanne's attention. So, before I went off to my own lesson on those Tuesday nights, I'd escort Georgeanne into the practice room at the conservatory where Miss Peck, a rather starchy and no-nonsense instructor, awaited her, then go off to my violin lesson with Ann Crane Tischer, one of the best instructors I'd ever had, and a locally renowned violinist in her own right.

I'd been serious about the violin since I was a young man, of course, but it was Ann Tischer who really helped me begin to take my playing to an entirely new level, and it was Ann Tischer as well who helped me see that the violin might very well help me combat a psychological challenge I had begun to face. Who could explain why, but more than five years after I'd returned from the war, I began to be visited by terribly violent dreams—dreams in which I watched time after time as the soldier on the bridge had his face blown off by a piece of shrapnel. Every night, I'd awake in terror and drenched in sweat. I would always reach over to Ann and reassure her that I was fine and that I'd just had another one of my dreams, but as the weeks progressed, I began to dread going to bed and wound up exhausted, depressed, and very afraid of the future if the nightmares couldn't somehow be staunched.

To make matters worse, Ann, too, now was facing issues of her own. She had developed a chronic kidney disorder that her doctors had struggled to control and that regularly led to her hospitalization. Our friend and neighbor Nillie Ohannas helped out in innumerable ways, often simply sharing coffee and cigarettes with Ann and helping lift her out of her own depression, and also looking after our kids so often that we couldn't help but feel terribly guilty. Yet when Ann was hospitalized indefinitely, our only real option was to move the kids to Ann's parents' house. Georgeanne and little Paul loved their grandparents, but none of us was happy about the situation, and I remember with no nostalgia whatsoever the dozens of days when—still without a car—I'd attempt to put in a productive day's work, visit Ann at the Illinois Masonic Hospital, spend time with the kids before they went to sleep, eat a bite of dinner kindly provided by Ann's mother, then, ride the bus back home to our apartment and practice the violin late into the night in hopes that my utter exhaustion would keep my nightmares at bay.

It was a situation that showed no immediate signs of abating—Ann's doctors were frank in explaining to me that although her condition wasn't life-threatening, she might never return to full health, and nothing that the doctors I saw at the VA had tried limited my nightmares and their insidious hold on me. In retrospect, I understand that I might have simply given up, succumbing to alcohol or a leap from the Wrigley Building, but finally things began to change—for me at least, if not for Ann—in the winter of 1955 when Ann Tischer suggested that it was time for me to perform in a public concert.

Little by little, I had become a better violinist and I was proud of that fact. But I'd never imagined till then that I might become a performer. My first instinct was to guess that Ann, who had become a friend as well as instructor, was just attempting to lift my spirits at a complex time, but she continued to push me. She explained that it was performance, in fact, that drove musicians to reach their creative potentials, I understood that she was right, and so, apprehensively, I agreed to perform in a recital at the conservatory at the end of March, one that would include performances by several of her students.

In consultation with Ann, I decided to play the "Concerto No. 4 in D Minor" by Vieuxtemps, a violin concerto I loved and one that would allow me to be supported by the pianist who would accompany me—a fellow who was a colleague of Ann's and as solid and unflappable a pianist as I'd ever heard. As I practiced late into each night in the few weeks that preceded the recital, something quickly began to change. I wasn't staying awake long into the night simply to avoid my dreams, but rather because at last I had a new mission.

In the same way that commanding a platoon of engineer soldiers or laying a bridge under a hail of enemy fire had kept me focused and moving forward, so did the looming recital and my desire to perform impressively—for Ann, for my family, and for myself. And, in the end, I did a very respectable job. Following the recital, I was able to outline for Ann Tischer the several mistakes I'd made with the complex piece, but she was enormously congratulatory nonetheless—and I was hooked. I knew from the moment I offered a small bow in response to the audience's warm applause that this was something I very much wanted to do again. And if Ann still struggled with health problems that limited her quality of life, at least I could report that—almost miraculously, it seemed—my nightmares finally had retreated back to the dark place from which they'd come.

*

In the months that followed, Ann's health improved enough that she and the children were able to return home to our apartment, although she continued to have many difficult days. And the plain truth is that I became obsessed with improving my playing. The two kids slept in the sole bedroom; Ann and I slept on a Murphy bed in the living room, and with the help of a mute for my violin and earplugs for Ann, I was able to practice late into each night without disturbing anyone but the family canary—who had to be moved into the bedroom to keep him from singing along with me while I played, a bright and talented little bird we called Budgie who—when I would let him during daylight hours—loved to perch on my violin's scroll and improvise with me a bird and violin duet, always to the children's great delight.

One evening in January 1956, I noticed on a bulletin board that the conservatory was announcing a region-wide violin competition whose prize would be the opportunity to perform a solo at the conservatory's commencement concert with members of the Chicago Symphony Orchestra in the early summer. It was news that electrified me, not simply because of the long shot opportunity to do something extraordinary, but because it would be a *competition*. I'd been battling in one way or another to achieve my goals for thirty-five years—since the far distant days in Tiflis when I successfully scrounged for food to survive as well as in all the years I'd done gymnastics, swam competitively, played football, and run track. And what was combat, after all, but a very high stakes kind of competition?

It seemed to me from my own life experience that the secret to winning a violin contest would be to prepare for it as if everything in the world hung on its outcome, then, when the chips were down, to perform with such confidence and precision that nobody could surpass you. It was the kind of challenge I'd always dug into with both hands—and my ears and my hands were precisely what I'd employ to give this competition my all.

As soon as I'd gained Ann Tischer's wholehearted support for the undertaking, my first challenge was to select the best possible music to display my skills. Ann agreed that Mozart's "Concerto in A Major for Violin and Orchestra" would suit my talents and it was a concerto I loved. Its first movement opens with the orchestra establishing an allegro theme, with the solo violin adding a sweet adagio middle passage. The second movement is slow and haunting and features the violin, and the rondo finale is built around long passages of what, to Mozart's ear, was lively "Turkish" music—an irony I could thoroughly enjoy. The Turks had warred against my Assyrian ancestors for centuries, but it was in Turkey, too, where I first had come alive to the wonders of the creative world and to my own deep set desire to become someone of substance.

Throughout the winter and spring, I diligently practiced the concerto at my weekly lesson with Ann Tischer as well as at home in our apartment late into every night. It remained the only time of day when I could steal the opportunity to truly focus my attention on the piece and practice difficult passages repetitively—a metronome keeping time, my muted strings and Ann's earplugs my principal allies in ensuring that I didn't drive her crazy.

At my first audition for the competition, I was nervous, but I performed well, and I advanced to the second round. Next, I made it past the second round, and became a finalist. And when I was announced as the winner of the competition in early May, my exhilaration was muted by the fact that I had expected nothing less of myself. Each day since I'd set my sights on it, I'd imagined my debut solo with the Chicago Symphony—and now I could claim it. On Sunday evening, June 17, 1956, I would perform at Orchestra Hall with one of the most renowned orchestras in all the world. And although I didn't confess the truth to anyone—not even my dear Ann—I knew in a place deep inside that nothing I'd accomplished ever had mattered to me more than this.

*

George and daughter Georgeanne, 1946

Christmas Eve 1944 at Ann's dear friend Nillie Ohannas's home;
Ann is in back row left and Nillie is font row left

Christmas 1951, Georgeanne left and Son, Paul Edgar

Georgeanne practices the piano while Paul peeks around its far end, 1953

George and Ann, early 1950's

It was hard to imagine who was the most nervous of the three of us as we dressed for the concert—Ann, Georgeanne, or me. Paul, too young to attend the concert, was already at a cousin's house, and each of us was strangely quiet as we prepared to leave the apartment. Ann carefully brushed my newly purchased tuxedo trousers and white jacket; she adjusted my bowtie, then pronounced me ready, and with my freshly polished violin secure in its case, we made our way downstairs to a waiting taxi—it was an occasion of too much import, of course, for us to make the journey downtown by bus and train.

I left the two of them at a stage door at Orchestra Hall, and I promised to spot them in the mezzanine level seats where I knew they would be, then kissed them both and asked them to wish me luck. Throughout the first half of the program, I paced the green room where I waited like an animal trapped in a cage, then, during the intermission, Maestro George Lawner knocked on the small room's door to briefly buoy my confidence. I assured him I was ready, then followed him to the stage.

I stood in the wings as he walked to his podium and acknowledged the audience's applause. Then it was my turn and, on the stage manager's cue, I too walked onto the stage, and in the first instant that I felt the floodlights warm my face, whatever anxieties I may have still harbored simply vanished. I smiled broadly as I approached the maestro with my violin and bow in my left hand, confidently shook his hand with my right, then moved to my position near the first violins. I quickly checked the tuning of my violin with the concertmaster, then Maestro Lawner raised his baton, then turned to me. I lifted my violin and tucked it under my chin, gave Ann and Georgeanne up in the mezzanine a subtle salute with my bow, then nodded to tell the maestro that I was ready.

The three movements of Mozart's "Concerto in A Major for Violin and Orchestra" are just under thirty minutes in combined length, and the half hour of my performance was perhaps the most sublime time of my life. I played boldly and beautifully and the orchestra and I were in perfect communication; Maestro Lawner clearly was moved by the music we were making, and I could feel the audience that filled the hall responding with delight. Never before had I played the concerto better; never had I played *any* music better than I played at Orchestra Hall on that sultry summer night.

The applause I received was thunderous and, to me at least, it seemed to go on forever. I bowed repeatedly, gratefully, and I'm sure my face expressed my great joy. I had done precisely what I had hoped to—what I *knew* I could accomplish. And as I stood in the spotlight in that celebrated hall and allowed myself to bask in the achievement, I curiously felt my father's low opinion of me and his conviction that I was a bum simply wash away from me, and I knew it never would trouble me again. For all my life till that moment, I had struggled and fought for the respect from others that I always had wanted from him, and to prove to myself and to everyone that my talents and determination outweighed my deficits and that I could achieve great things. I knew that no doubt I would face new and difficult challenges as my future unfolded and I would battle those dragons the best way I could.

For now, I was free at last from the yoke of the past, and I was deeply proud to be an Assyrian husband and father, an engineer who'd proved his mettle, and an American citizen who had done his small part to rid the world of evil. I looked up into the mezzanine and found Ann and Georgeanne once more. I waved at my girls, blew them a kiss, offered everyone in the hall a final bow, then walked off the stage, proudest of all that I had proved I was a *violinist*.

Orchestra Hall, June 17, 1956

Santa Barbara, 2004

I ONLY RECENTLY discovered from my mother and family members who still live in Chicago, how serious my grandfather's nervous breakdown had been five years after the end of the war. Pop had told me about that time, of course, and the suffering he described sounded awful enough, but then I learned that at one point in his struggle, he became so wracked with fear and anxiety that he couldn't even ride in a car. He couldn't work, couldn't look after his children, and he must have been very afraid for a time that he would end up in an institution. This man who had always been so supremely disciplined and so capable in myriad ways found his whole life coming undone and it seemed he could do nothing about it.

Dreams haunted him every night, but the dreams were far more brutal than he had ever described to me. Each night, he would relive the moment when his fellow soldier's face was blown off, but then he would helplessly watch as the face of Alexander, his childhood friend, was seared away, as the Russian soldier lost his face to an exploding bullet, as Colonel Spengler's face was torn away by Germans, and, most disturbingly, Pop himself was always the demon who sliced the face from the woman whom he had nearly attacked at the German hospital. He would awaken from the dreams shattered by a sense of the monster he was, and, for a time, he believed he now knew something elemental and awful about himself that only his father had understood. He was unlovable and beyond redemption, and his father had been right all along.

I suspect, in the end, that the solo violin competition literally saved his life. Without a new and difficult challenge that would mercifully take his mind away from the war and his early strife, he might have continued his downward spiral. But instead, he now had something tangible and terribly important to work toward—and this time it was simply the goal of playing music as beautifully as he could. Pop had always told me with great pride that he never played better in his life than he did on that single summer night in Chicago, and I now I hold the hope that I'll be fortunate enough to experience such a moment in my life.

My grandfather contracted aspiration pneumonia in December 2003, and his physicians warned me that the infection would kill him. Yet I somehow knew he had one more dragon to battle before his days were finished, and sure enough, he recovered completely by the middle of January. The illness had taken a lot out of him; he grew very weak, and, for the first time in his elderly years, his mental acuity was gone. In a coma-like condition, he often conversed in Assyrian with his dead sister Maria now, and, if I could let myself believe such things, I hoped Maria's spirit had returned to escort her beloved brother to the other side. He began to refuse food, stubbornly clenching his teeth and turning his mouth away when I or anyone tried to feed him. Soon, he was sleeping almost constantly, and it was clear to me that he had decided to die, and I knew it fell to me to give him support in letting go.

In consultation with his doctors, I made the hardest and loneliest decision I've ever made, agreeing to terminate his IV feeding tube and help him surrender this life. But even without any nourishment, he continued to live on. In late January, his oxygen level remained high, but his breathing was raspy now, his skin was translucent, and he hadn't spoken in several days when I walked into his hospital room and I was surprised to see his eyes open. He recognized me and somehow announced with great pride to the nurse who was attending to him, "That's my grandson, David." Those were the last words I heard him speak.

As I'd been doing for four weeks, I drove up from Los Angeles on the morning of February 9, 2004 and found him unchanged from the day before. My commitment to him was to be sure that he did not die alone and I intended to keep it. I'd been with him for about ten hours, when, shortly after midnight, I somehow realized that his love for me and his desire not to leave me alone without him was playing a part in his inability, as yet, to make the transition into the death that he now clearly sought. The hospital *had grown very quiet in the early morning hours and his room was only dimly lit.*

I went to the head of his bed and whispered in his ear, "Pop, you can leave now. It's time for you to go. I love you and I will miss you terribly, but I'll be fine, and you have to be on your way." I spoke with as little emotion in my voice as I could, hoping he'd sense that it truly was okay to leave me. As I moved to the opposite side of his bed, a nurse entered and asked how he was doing. I told her I thought he was ready to go now. She knew what I meant but I'm sure she doubted that she was literally witnessing his departure. Yet I knew him better than anyone and I was certain that he would let go.

I caressed his forehead and watched him breathe with the same rhythm he had for the past month—haltingly, slowly, hardly at all. Then, he suddenly sat upright, opened his eyes wide and looked deeply, profoundly into my eyes for a second or more and took a huge gasping breath—as if he was going on an underwater journey from which he knew he would not return. He fell back against his pillows, closed his eyes and let his breath out in a long and serene sigh that endured for half a minute, one that seemed to surrender all the experience and challenge and triumph and deep emotion of his life. I watched a small vein in his neck pulse slowly, then ever slower, and after a minute or so, the vein was still, and the man who had entered a world of violence as Sargis Georges Yadgar departed peacefully as George Edgar. "Goodbye, Poppy. I love you," I whispered, then kissed him two times on his forehead, just as he had always kissed me goodbye.

Acknowledgements

FOR ADDITIONAL INFORMATION about the life and times of George Edgar, please visit www.dragonsandviolins.com.

Also, www.989thengineertreadway.com is a wonderful source of information about the remarkable combat engineer company in which he proudly served.

All photographs are from the George Edgar and Ann Edgar estate, unless credited otherwise. Any use of them requires the written permission of the author.

*

Dragons & Violins has been ten years in the making and I'm grateful to many people for their vital help to me in bringing this story to the page. George Edgar, my grandfather, kindly sat for more than thirty hours of videotaped interviews and recounted his early life for me in extraordinary detail. I also interviewed many surviving members of our family, and I'm particularly indebted to my mother, Georgeanne (Edgar) Melvin, cousins Robert "Bobby" Marshall, Florence (John) Johnson, Clara John, David Alan John, Natasha (Edgar) Pavia, Albert Sargis, Jeanne Noghli Youkhana, Pierre Noghli, Atoorina Noghli, Nancy "Pera" Shaw and longtime family friends Elliot Ohannes and Don Ohannes.

*

I was privileged to interview a number of surviving soldiers of the 989th Engineer Treadway Bridge Company: Arnold Maeker, Arnold Okeson, Leo Goeckel, Harold Schiltz, Joseph Chiafolo, Lawrence "Ted" Ferguson, August Leopold, Leo Chance, Orson Holt, Ralph Kuhn, Theodore "Ted" Serrurier, Raymond Johnson, and William

"Bill" Baker. I'm particularly grateful to Bill Baker for allowing me to use as research his memoir of his long and illustrious military career, and for carefully vetting the manuscript for errors and omissions concerning the nearly two years the 989th fought and served in Europe. I owe a special thanks as well to Dorothy Okeson, who helped locate these veterans for me and who supplied me with valuable information about the 989th. Without her, these interviews would never have taken place.

*

Dr. Larry D. Roberts, U.S. Army Engineer School Historian at Fort Leonard Wood, Missouri, served as the project's technical military advisor and offered critical assistance on numerous occasions. My thanks to Britt Menendez for her assistance in website design and additional copy editing of this book. Steve Costanza for his design of the 989th website. My thanks as well to Brad Peters and Jan Ross, researchers for the 300th Engineer Combat Battalion, for copy editing and photo restoration of this book.

And I'm grateful for the help offered by the staffs of numerous libraries, institutions, and research organizations, including the Military Research Associates, College, Maryland; the Ellis Island Foundation, New York, New York; *Stars and Stripes*, Washington, D.C.; Redbird Research, St. Charles, Missouri; Pike Military Research, Washington, D.C.; U.S. Army Heritage & Education Center, Carlisle, Pennsylvania; National Personnel Records Center, St. Louis, Missouri; the National Archives & Records Administration, College, Maryland; the United States Military Academy Archives, West Point, New York; Juniata College Archives, Research Center; Mighty Eighth Air Force Museum; Savannah, GA; Huntingdon, Pennsylvania; New York University, New York, New York; the United States Embassy, Istanbul, Turkey; the United States

Library of Congress, Washington, D.C., and the Chicago Conservatory of Music.

*

I'm deeply indebted to many friends and colleagues for their wonderful encouragement and support throughout the research and writing of *Dragons & Violins*, foremost among them, Nikki Carbonetta for her love & support, and my dearest friends, George Cathcart, Greg Sanders. I'm grateful to my brother in spirit, Brent Roach, who was always there for my grandfather when he needed help and friendship, and to our family physician, Robert D. Byers, for always caring for my grandfather with love.

Breck Costin and Sarah La Saulle are teachers who have helped guide my spirit and soul, and I owe them more than I can say. And finally, thanks to Russell Martin and Lydia Nibley for their guidance and expertise in helping me make a dream come true. Their friendship, support, and love made this book possible.

CPSIA information can be obtained at www.ICGtesting.com
Printed in the USA
LVOW130748070713

341708LV00002B/425/P